AOL's PictureThis!

Fun & Easy Photo Projects

Dear... Grandma,
This is our vacation postcard!
Love,

Summer fun!

JULY

S M T W T F S

Slide Show

By Edward Willett

AOL's Picture This! Fun & Easy Photo Projects

Printed in the United States of America.

Library of Congress Cataloging-in-Publication Data

Willet, Edward, 1959–
AOL's Picture This! : fun & easy photo projects/ by Edward Willett.
p. cm.
ISBN 1-891556-56-8 (alk. paper)
1. Computer graphics. 2. Image processing—Digital techniques.
3. Photography—Digital techniques. I. Title
T385.W5477 1999
00.6—dc21 99-38967
CIP

Table of Contents

Contents

Contents

Introduction

The world has become a digital place. We listen to digital music, drive cars full of digital devices designed to keep them running smoother, call each other on digital cell phones, watch digital recordings of movies featuring digital special effects, and send and receive messages from all of the world that are sent—how else?—digitally.

Driving this deluge of digitization is the computer. Digital is the only language its speaks, and it speaks it very well. And most intriguing of all, computers can not only transmit and receive information digitally, they can manipulate it in a multitude of interesting ways. They're particularly adept at manipulating digital images. Combine that capability with the fact that humans love pictures—"a picture is worth a thousand words," remember—and it's not surprising that hardware like digital cameras, scanners, and printers are among the most popular peripherals for computers. The growth of e-mail and World Wide Web has also fuelled the interest in digital images, as people realize they can send pictures electronically for a fraction of the time and effort required to mail them, or just as easily post them to the Web for friends, family, or even total strangers to enjoy.

Maybe you've recently purchased a scanner, color printer, or digital camera and are wondering what to do with it. Maybe you've even been really lucky and received one as a gift. Maybe you just discovered your local photo-processing lab will put your pictures in digital form onto a CD for you for just a few dollars, and you're wondering what you could do with your pictures once they're digitized. Or maybe you just enjoy collecting pictures you've found on-line, and you're wondering what else you can do with them. Whichever, *AOL's Picture This!* is for you.

What's in This Book?

AOL's Picture This! is divided into three main parts:

- In Part I, "Getting Started," you'll plunge right into the world of digital images with a series of projects you can complete with nothing more than your computer and your AOL account. After that, you'll learn how to use the featured program on the accompanying CD, PhotoSuite II SE, to edit photos.
- Part II, "Projects for the Whole Family," is the heart of *AOL's Picture This!* Here you'll find easy, step-by-step instructions for using digital images and the software included on the CD to make a digital photo album and create personalized calendars, greeting cards, invitations, announcements, and more. You'll see how you can create a digital family scrapbook and history. You'll learn how to turn the pictures from your latest vacation into a digital slide show you can share electronically with friends and family anywhere in the world and how to use AOL's Personal Publisher 3 to build a family Web site. You'll discover how to create a digital baby book, and if your kids aren't babies any more, they can learn how to create their own animated cartoons and digital storybooks and how to spruce up school reports with digital images. You'll also learn how you can use digital images to create a computerized inventory of your valuable possessions and how to use digital images to promote your small business.
- In Part III, "Choosing Hardware," you'll learn how digital cameras, scanners, and printers work, and what you should look for when you decide to buy them. You'll also learn more about the various data storage options available and more about the various kinds of digital imaging software available.
- Appendices containing more sources of information and a complete glossary of terms round out *AOL's Picture This!*

I hope you enjoy reading *AOL's Picture This!* as much as I enjoyed writing it, and I hope you enjoy trying out the various projects, but most of all, I hope that *AOL's Picture This!* will serve as a springboard for your own imagination. I'm sure you can and will come up with even more exciting projects of your own as you plunge deeper into the exciting world of digital images.

Now, what are you waiting for? Let's get started.

SECTION I:
Getting *Started*

Introduction

If you're like me, and most computer users I know, you hate reading manuals. You only open them when you have a question you need an answer for. Otherwise, you much prefer fiddling with your computer rather than a book. You especially don't like long-winded introductions, because you want to get right to the fun stuff.

Well, you're in luck! You presumably bought this book because you want to get started right away on some digital projects. So enough introduction—let's get started right now with five digital projects you can carry out without any special equipment beyond your current computer and your AOL software.

Project 1: Download Digital Pictures from the Web

The World Wide Web is full of wonderful things to read, but it wouldn't be nearly as interesting if it wasn't also full of pictures—everything from fancy buttons and text dividers to digitized versions of photographs, paintings, baseball cards, and cartoons. You'll see how to put your own computer pictures on the Web in Chapter 9. In the meantime, maybe you'd like to save some of the pictures you discover while roaming online to your computer.

Here's how to save pictures to your computer.

1. Sign on to AOL.
2. Enter the address of the Web page that contains the picture you want to download.

Figure 1-1 Interested in having your own copy of this picture of the International Space Station under construction? Just right-click on it!

3. Once the page has loaded, right-click on the picture you're interested in. This opens the pop-up menu you see in Figure 1-1.
4. Click Save Picture As. This opens the standard Windows dialog box, shown in Figure 1-2.
5. Choose a folder on your hard drive in which to store the picture, assign a name to it, and choose what format you want to save it in. You can choose between the format it's currently in—in this case, JPG—or bitmap (BMP) format.
6. Click Save.

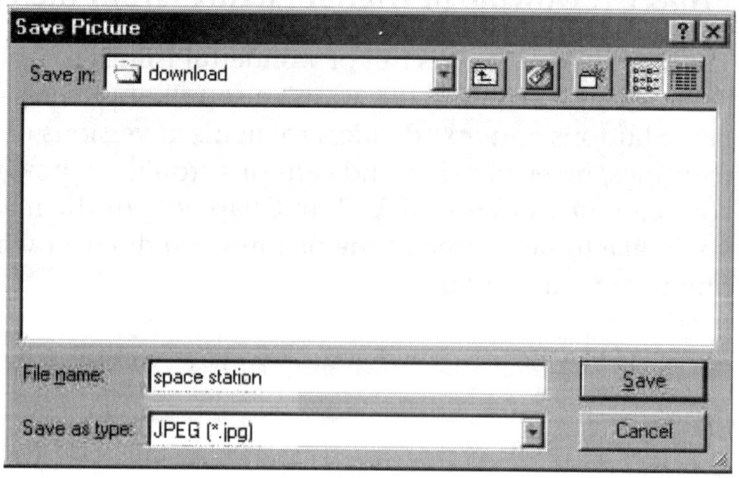

Figure 1-2 Using this dialog box, assign a location and a name to the picture you've downloaded from the Web.

See Chapter 19, "More About Graphics Software," for a complete explanation of the various graphics formats.

You can view your saved picture any time by double-clicking on it. Windows will open whatever program is assigned for viewing pictures in that format. That could be your browser Internet Explorer or a graphics program you've installed. If you've installed PhotoSuite II SE, which comes with this book, it will probably open to show you your picture.

If you don't currently have a program associated with that type of graphic file, you can view the file in AOL 4.0 by choosing File, Open. Then locate the file, highlight it, and click Open.

Some Web Sites Featuring Great Pictures

Here are a few Web sites where you can find interesting pictures to download:

- Hubble Space Telescope Public Pictures, at `http://oposite.stsci.edu/pubinfo/pictures.html`, features a gallery of spectacular shots of the heavens taken by the orbiting telescope.
- In a similar vein, NASA Image eXchange at `http://nix.nasa.gov/` lets you search more than 300,000 NASA images.
- If you're more interested in this planet, try NatureWorld at `http://www.natureworld.com/`, which is a great source of free on-line nature photographs.
- It hasn't been updated in a while, but the WebMuseum at `http://metalab.unc.edu/wm/` is still a wonderful place to find images of fine art from museums around the world.

Project 2: Make a Web Picture Your Wallpaper

In Windows, *wallpaper* is an image that covers the desktop, rather like a large blotter (or, in the case of my office, stacks of paper, CD cases, and the occasional soda pop can) might cover an ordinary desk.

Changing your wallpaper is a great way to personalize your computer. It's a particularly good idea if, like me, you spend pretty much the whole day staring at the screen; you might as well have something interesting to look at while you daydream—um, think deep creative thoughts.

Turning a picture you find on the Web into your wallpaper is as easy as downloading it to your computer—not surprising because it's essentially the same procedure!

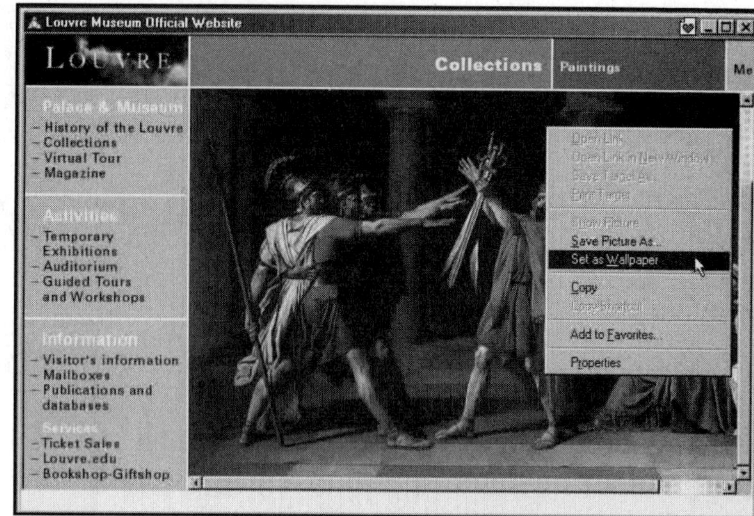

Figure 1-3 Clicking Set As Wallpaper instantly turns a picture from the Web into decoration for your Windows desktop.

Once again, go to the Web site that contains the picture you want to use as your wallpaper. In Figure 1-3, I've gone to the Louvre's Web site at `http://www.louvre.fr` in search of a heroic image to inspire me first thing in the morning. I found a painting, Louis David's *The Oath of the Horatti*, that I think should do the trick. To turn this into my wallpaper, I right-click on it as before, only this time I choose Set As Wallpaper.

Nothing appears to happen, but if I minimize AOL and any other programs I have running, I find that my desktop now displays Louis David's famous work (see Figure 1-4).

Figure 1-4 This is much classier than that Garfield wallpaper I used to have.

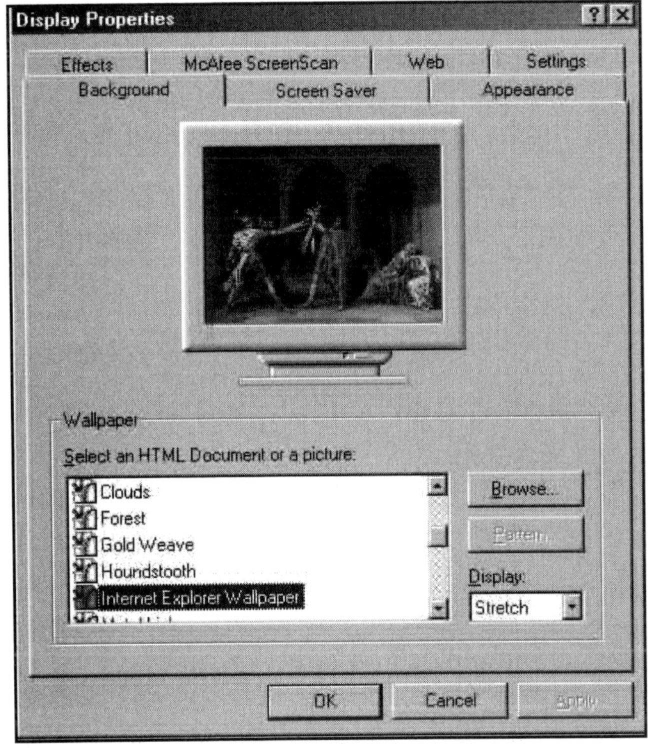

Figure 1-5
Modify the way your picture is displayed using these controls.

Exactly how the picture you chose is displayed on your desktop depends on your display settings.

To change the way your wallpaper is displayed, follow these steps:

1. Right-click anywhere on your desktop and choose Properties, or choose Start, Settings, Control Panel, Display. Either method opens the Display Properties dialog box, shown in Figure 1-5.
2. Make sure the Background tab is selected. This shows you a miniature version of the picture you're currently using as wallpaper. Click Browse to search your computer for any other picture you would like to use as your wallpaper.
3. Choose how you want the picture displayed from the Display list box. Stretch stretches the picture to the edges of the desktop, distorting the picture if necessary to make it fit. Center simply places the picture in the middle of the desktop and doesn't worry about the empty space around it. Tile places the picture in the upper left-hand corner and then displays multiple copies of it across the rest of the screen.

Wallpapering Tips

Changing your wallpaper can be a lot of fun, but here are two things you should consider before deciding that a picture is the perfect desktop decoration for your personal PC:

- **Resolution.** In the example in Figure 1-4, my display is 800x600 pixels. (All computer pictures are made up of thousands of tiny dots, called pixels, or "picture elements.") The original picture is smaller than that. From a distance the painting doesn't look too bad stretched to fill the desktop. A closer examination, however, reveals a certain amount of *pixellation,* jagged edges caused by picture elements being so enlarged that they're no longer seamless to the eye. Blowing up a very small picture to wallpaper size usually has disappointing results; that's when you should consider using the Tile display instead of the Stretch display.
- **Proportions.** I chose the picture in Figure 1-4 precisely because it looked like it had approximately the same proportions as my monitor. That meant if I stretched it out to fill the desktop, the people in the painting would still look like people and not appear to be either 12 feet tall and extremely skinny or 12 feet wide and extremely short. Pictures whose proportions are very different from those of the screen look best when centered or, sometimes, tiled.

Once you've experimented a bit, you'll be able to quickly tell if a particular picture would work well as wallpaper. Not that anything's stopping you from blowing up a tiny, tall, skinny image into a bloated, pixellated, illegible mess and using it as your wallpaper . . . if that's what you want.

4. Click Apply to see what your wallpaper looks like without closing the Display Properties dialog box. When you're satisfied with its appearance, click OK.

Project 3: E-mail a Picture to a Friend

Suppose your college roommate shares your intense interest in space exploration. You know he'd love to see that picture of the space station you discovered on the Web and downloaded to your computer, but there's just one problem: He lives in Rio de Janeiro now, and you live in Saskatchewan. How can you possibly share your breathtaking discovery with him?

Easy. You can e-mail it or any other digital picture. Here's how:

1. In AOL 4.0, click Mail Center, then choose Write Mail from the menu (or simply press Ctrl+M) to open the Write Mail dialog box, shown in Figure 1-6.
2. Write your e-mail as usual.
3. Click Attachments. This opens the dialog box in Figure 1-7.
4. Click Attach, and in the browsing box that opens, locate the file you want to send and click Open.
5. The name of the file now appears in the list of attachments. If you've changed your mind, highlight it and click Detach; if you're ready to proceed, click OK.
6. The Write Mail dialog box now shows. You can now see the name of the picture you've attached next to the Attachments button. Click Send to send your e-mail and the attached picture to the recipient you've specified.

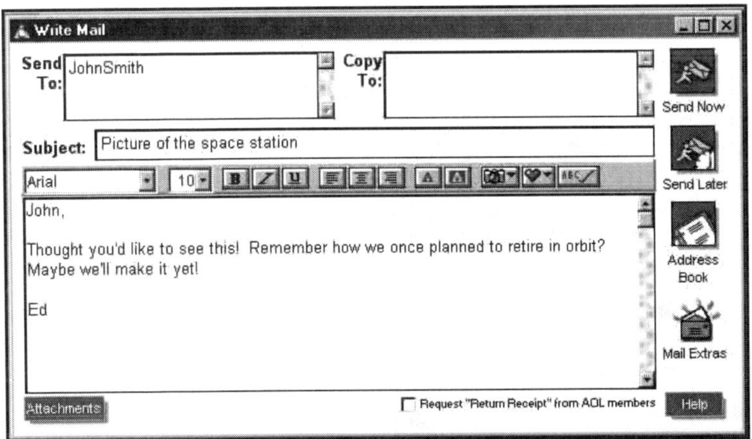

Figure 1-6
To e-mail a picture to a friend, first write the e-mail as usual . . .

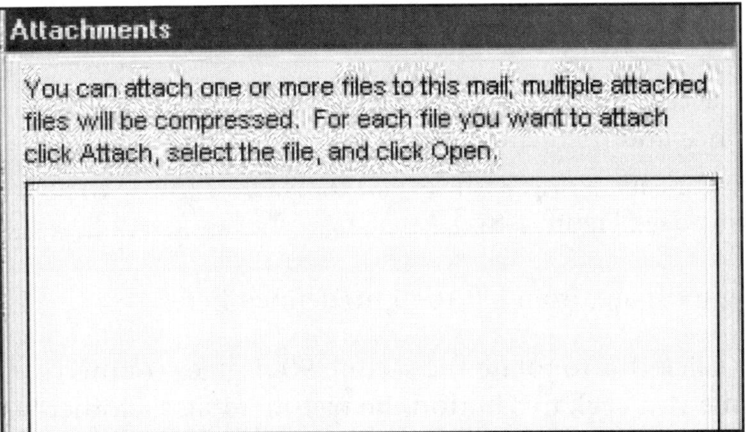

Figure 1-7
. . . then attach the picture to it using these controls.

When the e-mail with the attachment arrives, the recipient will see an active download button, which he can click to download the picture to his own hard drive. Once it is on his hard drive, he can look at it at his leisure.

Digital picture files come in all sizes, from quite small to very, very large—many megabytes, in some cases. Your friend may not appreciate it if you send him something that takes an hour or so to download! Most people prefer fairly small attachments—under 200K or so is ideal—so keep that in mind before e-mailing pictures.

Project 4: Edit a Picture

This book includes a very complete photo-editing program called PhotoSuite II SE, which you'll take a closer look at in the next chapter. AOL 4.0, however, includes basic photo-editing tools that you can use to make your photos look better before you e-mail them or turn them into wallpaper.

The first thing you have to do is open the picture. Here's how:

1. Choose File, Open.

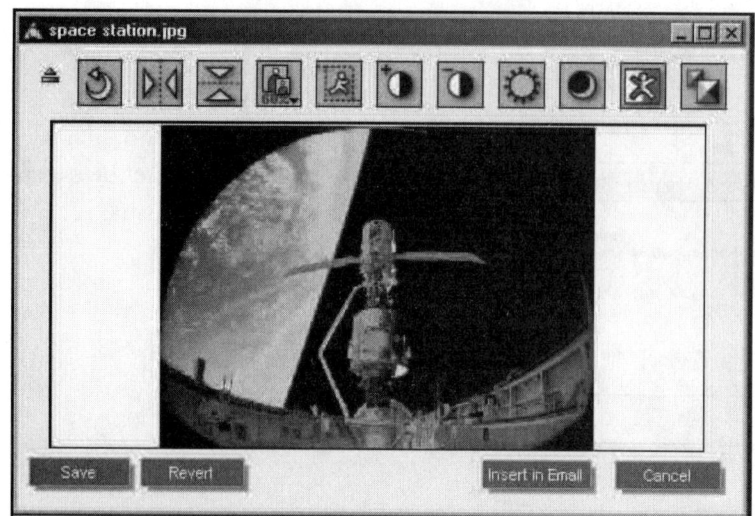

Figure 1-8
AOL 4.0 provides several tools for editing digital pictures.

2. Locate the picture file you want to edit; either double-click on it, or click it once and then click Open.
3. The picture appears, along with several tools you can use to alter its appearance (see Figure 1-8).

The picture-editing tools are, from left to right, defined here:

Rotate Picture. Click this to rotate the picture 90 degrees counter-clockwise. Each time you click this button the picture rotates another 90 degrees, so you can use it to turn a picture completely upside down with two clicks and bring it all the way back to where it was to start with four clicks.

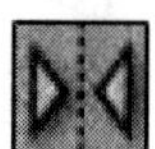

Flip Picture Horizontally. This reverses the picture right to left. The best way to visualize what that means is to think of the picture as a regular photographic slide. Flip Picture Horizontally has the same effect as turning the slide over lengthwise. Be careful using this button if there's any text showing in your picture because it will end up reversed!

Flip Picture Vertically. This works the same as Flip Picture Horizontally, except it has the same effect as flipping a slide height-wise.

Zoom In/Out. This lets you change the size of the picture. Clicking it opens a small menu from which you choose the percentage of the original you want the modified picture to be. If you don't see the percentage you want, click Other and specify it.

Select and Crop Picture. Clicking this changes the shape of your mouse pointer. Use the new pointer to draw a box around the section of the picture you'd like to keep. Anything outside that box will be discarded. Note that the box displays its own dimensions in pixels. Once you release the mouse button, the Select and Crop Picture button changes appearance, displaying a pair of scissors. Click it again to complete the crop.

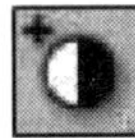 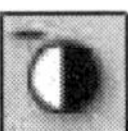

Increase Picture Contrast/Decrease Picture Contrast. These two buttons control the amount of visible difference between light areas and dark areas in the picture, just like the contrast control on your computer monitor or TV.

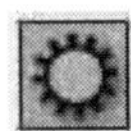 

Brighten Picture/Dim Picture. These buttons work exactly as you would expect: One makes the picture brighter, and one makes it darker. You can turn up the brightness until the picture is completely white or dim it until it's completely black, if you're the sort of person who tends to go to extremes.

Invert Picture. This turns the picture into a negative image of itself, like a photographic negative.

Convert Picture to Grey Scale. This turns a color picture into a black-and-white picture.

Once you're happy with the changes you've made to your picture, click Save.

> **NOTE**
> Clicking Save automatically saves the picture over any previously saved version, so never click it until you're absolutely sure you won't want to revert to the original version of the picture. If you want to keep the original version and save the new version, choose File, Save As instead and assign a new name to the edited version of the picture.

Project 5: Add Text to a Photo (or Vice Versa)

When you e-mailed a photo to a friend a little earlier in this chapter, you sent it as an attachment. But there's another way to e-mail a photo to a friend, one that allows you to integrate it directly into the text of the message. It also provides a way to print a copy of your picture with a caption attached.

To insert a picture directly into e-mail, follow all the steps in Project 4, then complete these steps:

1. Click Insert in Email.
2. A dialog box asks you if you want to resize the image to fit in the document or insert it as is. Which one you choose depends on

how big the picture is. If it's very large, it's probably a good idea to resize it; if it's not, you can leave it alone.

3. The standard Write Mail dialog box appears, but now your picture is visible in the message area (see Figure 1-9). You can use the alignment buttons to center it or move it to the right edge of the message space, if you wish.
4. Write and edit the message text as you normally would. If there's room, the text will appear immediately to the right of the picture near the bottom—as if the picture were just another, very large and ungainly, text character. If you'd prefer to begin text under the picture, just press Return.

You can use the Write Mail dialog box to print your picture with a caption under it. Press Return to place the cursor under the picture and type your caption (see Figure 1-10). Then choose File, Print. Choose a printer and other options as usual, and click Print.

Now What?

Now that you have your feet wet in the world of digital projects, it's time to move on to bigger and better things. After all, while tweaking existing digital pictures is fun and opens up lots of possibilities, what you're really interested in is creating your own digital images and doing exciting things with them, right?

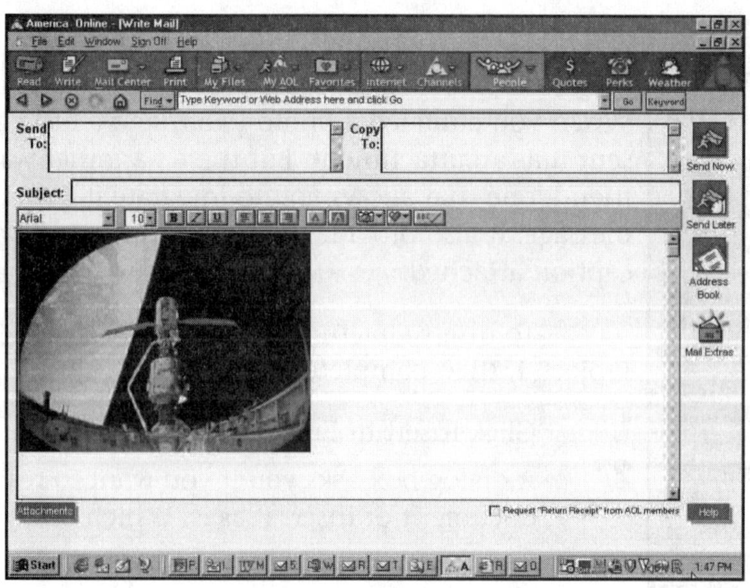

Figure 1-9
Here's my space station photo inserted at the beginning of a new e-mail message.

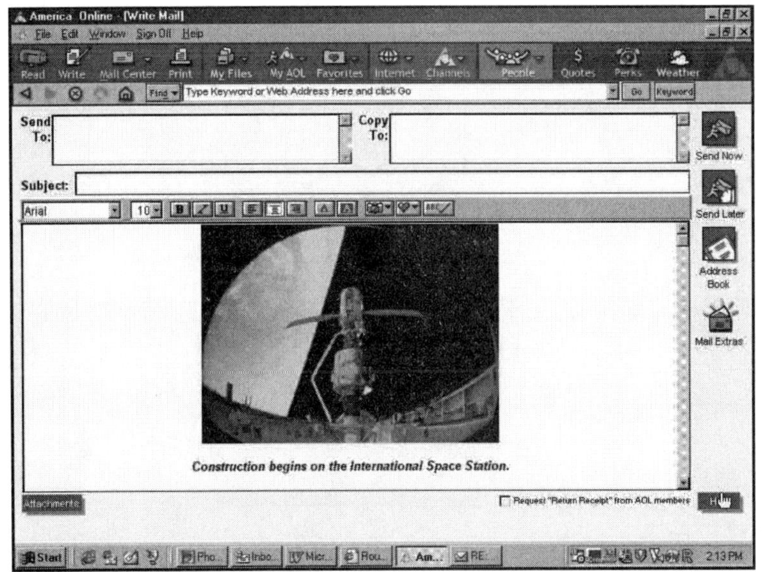

Figure 1-10
You can use the Write Mail dialog box to print pictures with captions attached.

Maybe you've just bought or (if you're really lucky) been given a scanner, or a new color printer, or a shiny digital camera, and you're wondering what to do with it. Well, everything you did with pictures in this initial chapter—save them, turn them into wallpaper, send them to a friend, edit them, and add text to them—can be done with the pictures you scan or photograph yourself. But I've only scratched the surface.

Digital projects are really limited only by your imagination. In this book, I'll do my best to get that imagination going by suggesting some things I think you might enjoy trying. But for every project outlined in this book, there are dozens of other possibilities. Let this book serve as a springboard to your flights of creative digitizing.

All set? Then let's jump!

CHAPTER 2

PROJECT: Digital Projects 101: What You Need to Use This Book

What You Need:

- Scanner (optional)
- Printer (optional)
- CD that comes with this book
- PhotoSuite II SE (on the CD)

Introduction

Although, as you saw in the first chapter, you can create digital projects with nothing more than your computer and an AOL account, to do some of the advanced projects you may want to look into a few more hardware and software options.

In particular, you may want to consider buying a scanner and/or a digital camera. A good color inkjet printer would be an asset, too. Finally, you may need some good imaging software, but that part is easy; I've included it on the CD that comes with this book!

If you're strapped for cash or don't think you'd ever get your money's worth out of all that hardware, I'll present some cheaper alternatives throughout this chapter.

In this chapter I briefly present some hardware and software options. In particular, at the end of the chapter, I'll introduce you to one of the most powerful pieces of imaging software on the CD, PhotoSuite II SE. You can use it, along with the other software, to create the digital projects discussed in the following chapters.

Scanners

A *scanner* is a device that turns an image (text, pictures, or anything else) on a printed page into a digital image that a computer can read and manipulate. It does that by turning what's on the page into a series of dots. The number of dots per inch (dpi) the scanner is able to convert the page into is known as its *resolution*.

Higher resolution isn't necessarily better or even necessary. It just depends on what you're going to use the finished product for. Pictures scanned for display online—on Web pages, for instance—look just fine at a mere 72 dots per inch. Higher resolutions are helpful if you have a high-quality color printer you're planning to send the picture to, but even then many scanners can scan at higher resolutions than printers can take advantage of.

You can choose from three main types of scanners:

- **Flatbed scanner.** This is the most common type of scanner. The page being scanned is placed face down on the scanner screen, just as you would place it on a photocopier.
- **Sheet-fed scanner.** Pages being scanned in sheet-fed scanners are fed into a slot, and then pulled in by rollers—much like feeding pages into a fax machine. This makes it easier to scan several pages one after the other. Unfortunately, it makes it impossible to scan anything with more bulk than a single sheet of paper, such as a book (unless you're willing to rip individual pages out of the book, which most of us aren't).
- **Hand-held scanner.** Hand-held scanners are the cheapest type of scanner, but they require extreme precision on the part of the person doing the scanning to produce the best results.

For general home use, I recommend a flatbed scanner.

You can also visit your local mailing store, such as Mailboxes Etc., or copying shop, such as Kinko's, for access to a scanner. You will have to pay a small fee for the use, but it could save you hundreds of dollars if you aren't planning on doing a lot of scanning.

For more detailed information on how scanners work and what to look for when buying them, see Chapter 15, "Choosing a Scanner."

For more detailed information on digital cameras, see Chapter 16, "Choosing a Digital Camera."

Digital Cameras

A *digital camera* is a video or still camera that records images in digital form. Analog cameras, what you may think as "regular" cameras, can record an almost infinite number of colors, but digital cameras can only record a fixed number of colors at a fixed resolution.

Digital cameras make it easy to upload pictures to a computer. They also eliminate the need for scanning. Once you take a digital picture, it's stored to a diskette or to your camera's memory. (When pictures are stored to your camera's memory, you must transfer the images to your computer through a cable.) After the pictures are on your computer, they can be manipulated, edited, copied, and e-mailed, just like any other image file.

Digital cameras range from inexpensive units that record pictures at a 640x480 resolution only to very expensive megapixel units. These have a much higher resolution and additional features, such as zoom lenses and microphones for attaching recorded notes to images.

If you're going to use your digital camera primarily to take pictures for on-line viewing, a lower-resolution model will serve you fine. If you're interested in making high-quality prints, however, a higher resolution may serve you better.

If you aren't ready to buy a digital camera, see about having your analog film saved onto a CD. More and more film processing stores are providing this service for just a few dollars more per roll.

Printers

Even if your main interest is creating digital projects for viewing on the Web or on your own computer, chances are that eventually you'll want something you can hold in your hand or post on your wall instead of just look at on the screen. That's where printers come in.

For detailed information on printers, see Chapter 17, "Choosing a Printer."

The two most common types of printers are laser printers and inkjet printers. *Laser printers* use a laser to draw the image of a page on a charged drum to which toner is applied and then heated so that it fuses onto the paper (except for the laser, it's much the same technology as a photocopier). *Inkjet printers* propel droplets of ink directly onto paper.

Both types of printers come in black-and-white and color versions. The vast majority of home users looking for a color printer will buy an inkjet printer simply because color laser printers are still very expensive. If you want to be able to print photographs and other digital images in full color without breaking your bank account, then an inkjet printer is definitely the way to go.

You can also use the printers at a business mailing store, such as Mailboxes Etc., or a copying store, such as Kinko's, for a nominal fee.

Imaging Software

The great thing about digital images is that you can use a computer to manipulate them. To do that, you need a special computer program called *imaging software*.

You can choose from hundreds, maybe even thousands, of software packages that let you edit, touch up, and enhance digital images. If you have a scanner, digital camera, or color printer, you probably have at least one such package because imaging software is usually bundled with those products. If you get your analog film pictures put on a CD at a film processing store, the CD will most likely include imaging software, too.

You can also download shareware versions of imaging software from many places on the Web, or you can purchase a commercial package (which will often, but not always, have more options). But because you've bought this book, you already have the software you need. The accompanying CD has it all! The CD contains a powerful piece of imaging software called PhotoSuite II SE and other exciting software programs.

For more information on imaging software, see Chapter 19, "More About Graphics Software." For more information about using PhotoSuite II SE, see the sections "Introducing PhotoSuite II" and "Editing Photos with PhotoSuite II" at the end of this chapter.

What's on the CD

Included with this book is a CD that contains several other programs in addition to MGI PhotoSuite II SE.

Barking Cards

Barking Cards from Blaze Technologies, Inc. lets you create animated e-mail greeting cards, ranging from the warm and fuzzy to the downright zany. You can choose from one of several highly stylized animated templates, complete with professional soundtracks, then personalize it by adding your own text, music, sound, photographs, or voice recordings. Once the greeting is complete, it's compressed and turned into a self-playing file. You can then e-mail it to someone else, who simply runs it to view the card.

You can choose Barking Cards for everything from birthdays and holiday greetings to thank-yous, romance, and congratulations.

The Home Gene-Splicing Kit

Have you ever wanted to be a mad scientist? The Home Gene-Splicing Kit from You-Betcha Interactive, Inc., is the perfect way to scratch that itch. It lets you mix and match facial features—eyes, head, mouth, nose—from real photos of people and animals to create strange hybrid creatures of your very own, using a fun interface like a chemistry laboratory. You can save the images you create on your computer and use them in all sorts of fun ways.

ShowOff

ShowOff from Vorton Technologies is a personal digital slide-show program that makes creating and sending multimedia slide shows amazingly easy by providing detailed wizards for most tasks. It also lets you organize your digital images into a virtual photo album.

The slide shows in ShowOff can include images, text, and/or sound, all saved as a single, compressed executable file that you can send via e-mail. No special viewing software is required by the recipient. More than 100 special transition effects add dazzle to your show, which can include images drawn from your computer, scanner, or digital camera.

Whether you want to send a virtual slide show of your recent skiing trip to your parents or a presentation about a proposed new product to your boss half a continent away, you can do it with ShowOff.

Photo-Objects Sampler Image Collection

The Photo-Objects Sampler Image Collection from Hemera Technologies is a collection of special digital images called Photo-Objects, which you can use on Web pages and in other digital projects.

A *Photo-Object* is a photographic image of an object without its surrounding background. That allows the object to be placed on any background, for maximum visual impact. Photo-Objects use very little disk space, and their high quality and resolution allow you to use them at virtually any size.

NetGraphics Studio2 SE

NetGraphics Studio2 SE, also from Hemera Technologies, contains two programs to help you make the most of all your digital images, including Photo-Objects:

- The NetGraphics Optimizer allows you to transform most images currently in a format that isn't compatible with Web browsers into one that is. You can resize images, see them combined with your background color or image tile, compress them in GIF or JPEG format while monitoring image quality, file size, and download time, and apply interlacing. Then you can insert them into your Web page by simply dragging and dropping.
- The NetGraphics Gallery allows you to easily search for a Photo-Object image. It simultaneously displays Photo-Object image thumbnails and their associated name and description. Type in keywords that describe the images you're looking for, or simply select image categories, and NetGraphics Gallery will instantly find the corresponding Photo-Objects.

Introducing PhotoSuite II SE

For details on installing PhotoSuite II SE (or any of the other programs) on your computer, refer to the instruction booklet included with the CD.

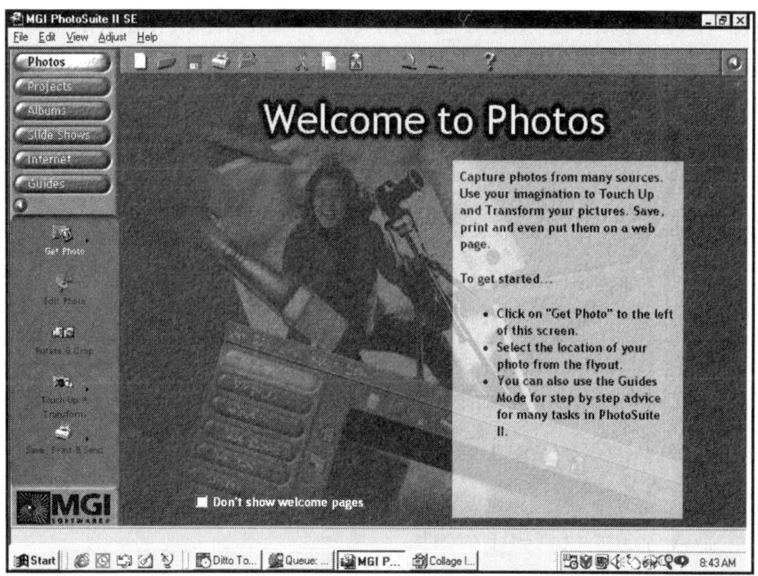

Figure 2-1
When you first start PhotoSuite II SE, you'll see this screen.

When PhotoSuite II SE opens, it will look as it does in Figure 2-1.

Before you learn to use PhotoSuite II SE to edit pictures, let's take a quick look at the how the program is laid out.

Across the top is the usual menu bar. Below that, in the upper-left corner, is a stack of buttons that activate PhotoSuite II SE's various functions. From top to bottom, those functions are

- **Photos.** Click this to open and edit digital images. You can import images from your computer, a scanner, a digital camera, a CD or disk, or the Internet.
- **Projects.** Click this to create a digital project using PhotoSuite II SE—a calendar, for instance, or a collage. You'll see several of the projects included in PhotoSuite II SE later in this book, but be sure to explore them all!
- **Albums.** Click this button to create digital photo albums that let you store, organize, and label your digital pictures. See Chapter 3, "The Digital Photo Album," for detailed information on using this function.
- **Slide Shows.** Click this button to create a slide show with your digital images, complete with interesting transitions and a soundtrack.
- **Internet.** Click this to electronically share your pictures with family and friends and find photos and digital-imaging information on the World Wide Web. You can surf the net without leaving PhotoSuite!

- **Guides.** Refer to these built-in tutorials for complete information on how to do various tasks in PhotoSuite II SE. I just cover the highlights in this book, so these guides should prove a valuable resource when you need more information.

Under the menu bar and to the right of the stack of buttons is a toolbar containing icons that activate many of the most commonly used commands in PhotoSuite. From left to right, these commands are

New. This opens a new photo, album, project, or slide show, depending on which of the function buttons you've activated.

Open. This lets you find and open an existing photo, album, project, or slide show.

Save. Click this to save your current work.

Print. This sends the photo you're currently editing to the printer.

Close. This closes the currently active photo, album, project, or slide show.

Cut. Click this to remove whatever you've currently got selected—either an entire photo or a section of one—from the work area and copy it temporarily to the Clipboard.

Copy. Click this to simply copy whatever you've currently selected to the Clipboard, without deleting it from the work area.

Paste. Click this to paste the object you've copied or cut into whatever you're currently working on in the work area. You could use this command along with Copy, for instance, to copy a photo from a calendar you've created and paste it into a greeting card.

Undo. Click this to cancel the last edit you made to a photo, album, project, or slide show. Click again to cancel the one before that and so on. You can undo all the edits that you've made since the file was last saved.

Redo. Click this to restore any edits you've removed with the Undo button.

Each feature of PhotoSuite II SE has its own specialized commands. These appear to the left of the large work area in which whatever you're currently working on is displayed. Also notice the button all by itself on the far-right end of the toolbar. It opens or closes the Photo Library, an area where thumbnails of all the photos you currently have open are displayed for easy access.

Editing Photos with PhotoSuite II SE

The heart of PhotoSuite II SE is its photo-editing tools, which are what the rest of the chapter focuses on.

Before you can edit a photo, you have to open a photo. To do so, click the Get Photo button. This opens the box in Figure 2-2.

As you can see, you have several options when it comes to finding pictures. You can

- Open a picture file that's already on your computer.
- Scan in a picture.
- Download a picture from a digital camera.
- Get a picture from a PhotoSuite II SE picture album.

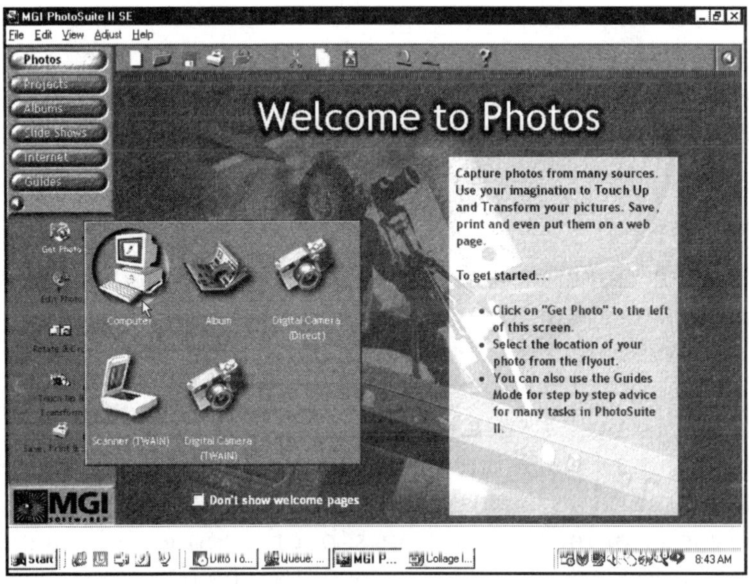

Figure 2-2
You can open a picture drawn from any one of a number of sources.

For more information on scanning, downloading from a digital camera, and working with photo albums, see Chapter 3, "The Digital Photo Album."

Figure 2-3
When you open a photo for editing in PhotoSuite II SE, this is what you see.

Wherever you get the photo from, once you open it your screen will look like the one in Figure 2-3.

Notice that below Get Photo there are four other buttons. Each of these buttons opens a new set of tools that you can use to manipulate your photo. Let's look at each of these.

Edit Photo

By default, the Edit Photo function is active. This opens the toolbar you see running down the left side of the workspace in Figure 2-3. From top to bottom, these new tools are

- **Zoom.** Sometimes you want to get a much closer look at the picture you're editing. Sometimes you'd rather look at it from farther away. You could press your nose up against the monitor for close looks and stand across the room for more distant ones, but the former is hard on the eyes and the latter puts you too far away to use the mouse. Instead, click on the Zoom tool to turn your mouse pointer into a magnifying glass. Click the magnifying glass on the spot on the picture you want to zoom in on, and then hold the mouse button down while you move the pointer up or down on the screen. Moving up zooms you in on the point indicated by your initial click; moving down zooms you out (see Figure 2-4).

  You can zoom in other ways, as well. Notice that a new little toolbar has opened below the workspace. The two tools on the left of this toolbar let you zoom in twice as close or zoom out twice as far. The third button fits the picture to the workspace so you can see all of it. The fourth button displays it actual size. Use the scroll box at the far right of the toolbar to specify what percentage of full size you want the picture to be displayed. For instance, if you wanted to see it at one quarter of full size, you'd use the scroll box to set the zoom factor at 25 percent.

- **Select.** What do you do if you only want to edit part of a picture? With a regular photograph, you'd have to get out the scissors and try to carefully cut out the bit you wanted. You can "cut out" parts of a digital photograph much more easily. Click on the little triangle just beside this button to open the subtoolbar, shown in Figure 2-5. Each of these tools lets you select part of the photo, but each works a little differently.

The default Elliptical Selection tool lets you select an elliptical area of the photo; just click and drag, and an ellipse will appear. Everything inside that ellipse will be selected. The Rectangular Selection tool works exactly the same way, except it draws a rectangle.

The Freehand Selection tool lets you draw any shape you want with the mouse and selects everything inside that shape. To close off the shape, double-click it. A final straight line will be drawn between your mouse location and the start of the freehand selection line.

The Magic Wand lets you select areas of the same color. In Figure 2-6, for instance, I used it to select the large dark area on the right edge

Figure 2-4
Move the mouse up and down to zoom in or out in Zoom mode.

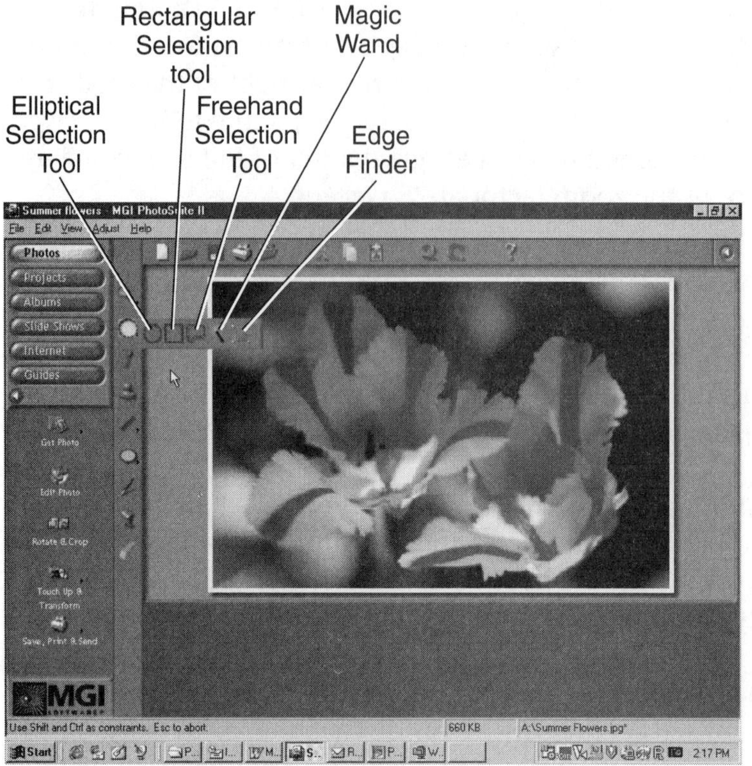

Figure 2-5
These selection tools let you select a specific area of a photo to work on.

Figure 2-6
With the Magic Wand you can easily select areas of the same color.

Figure 2-7
Here I'm using the Edge Finder to select the flower from its background.

of my picture of flowers. This is a great way to remove objects of fairly uniform color from a picture—clouds from a picture of the sky, for instance. Just click the Magic Wand, and then scribble over the area you want to define. (Use the Tolerance Control slider under the work area to specify how closely colors have to match to be selected by the Magic Wand.) Suppose your picture includes a lawn with many different shades of green in it. If you set the tolerance very low, only sections of the lawn of exactly the same shade of green will be selected by the Magic Wand. If you set the tolerance high, all the green areas in the lawn will be selected.

Finally, the Edge Finder does just that: finds edges. Pull the Edge Finder box (see Figure 2-7) across the picture; encompass the edge of an object you want to define. The Edge Finder looks for contrasting colors and makes its selection on that basis. The slider at the bottom of the workspace controls the width of the Edge Finder box.

- **Color Selector.** Click this and your mouse pointer takes on the shape of an eyedropper. Hold down the left mouse button and move the eyedropper onto an area of your picture displaying the color you want to use with your paint tools. Let off the left mouse button and the color appears in the leftmost of the two overlapping boxes at the bottom of the work area (see Figure 2-8). Repeat holding down the right mouse button to set the color that will be used with the commands that fill objects with color. You can also select any of the

Figure 2-8
The Color Selector tool lets you use any color from any photo for painting and filling.

colors in the displayed color palette or double-click on the Paint Fill Color box to open a dialog box that lets you access any color your computer can display.

- **Clone.** Cloning isn't just something done to unsuspecting sheep in Scotland—it's also a technique you can use to change the appearance of your photo, by letting you duplicate one area over another area. Click this button, and then click once on the area you want to copy. Crosshairs will appear at that point. Move your mouse pointer and click again where you want the first area to be copied to. An area equal in size to whatever brush size you choose from the scroll box at the bottom of the work area is covered with a copy of whatever is in the target area. If you click and drag, both the target crosshairs and your current mouse pointer move together, and whatever is under the target crosshairs is copied to your mouse pointer's current position (see Figure 2-9). This is a great way to, for example, paint grass over a bare spot in the lawn in your photo.
- **Unfilled Shape.** Use the Unfilled Shape tool to draw a variety of shapes, including a line, an ellipse, a rectangle, a rectangle with rounded corners, and a freehand shape. The line used to draw the shape is determined by what brush shape and size you're using (more on that soon), and it's drawn in whatever color you've chosen for painting (see the section on the Color Selector a bit earlier).

Figure 2-9
You can use the Clone tool for many useful purposes beyond simply putting yourself in two places at the same time!

- **Filled Shape.** This lets you draw the same shapes as the Unfilled Shape tool, but these shapes are filled with whichever color you've chosen to use for filling (again, see the section on the Color Selector).
- **Brush.** This lets you draw right on your picture with your mouse. The size of the line you create and whether it has fuzzy edges or hard edges depends on the brush shape and size you select. To select a brush shape, double-click on the scroll box at the bottom that also lets you select the size of brush. Brush shapes range from simple circles and squares to more complicated shapes (see Figure 2-10).

  You can use your brush to paint a variety of effects and enhancements onto your picture. You'll explore that later in this chapter.
- **Flood Fill.** This fills large areas of your photo with the paint color. Click this button, and your mouse pointer changes into a small bucket that leaves a thin trail of the selected color behind as you drag it. Drag it over any areas you want to fill. PhotoSuite remembers the color of every pixel the pointer passes over. When you release the mouse button, all contiguous areas of the picture containing any of those colors fill with the paint color instead (see Figure 2-12).

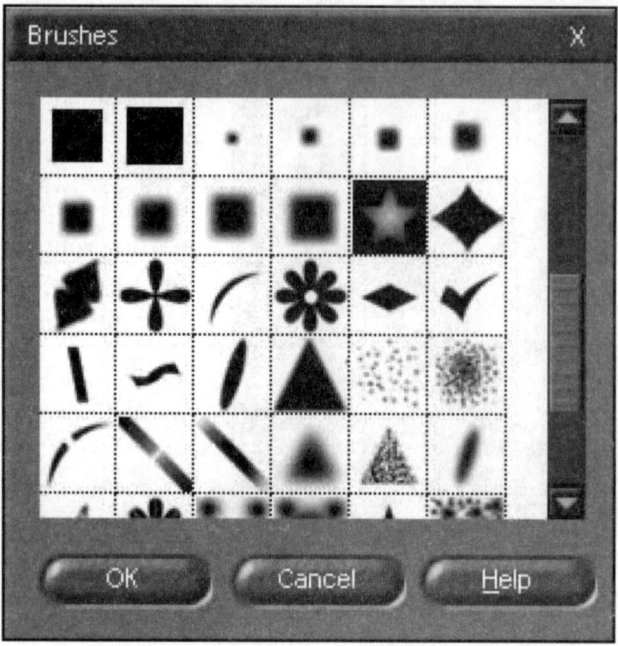

Figure 2-10 Choose from one of these brush shapes . . .

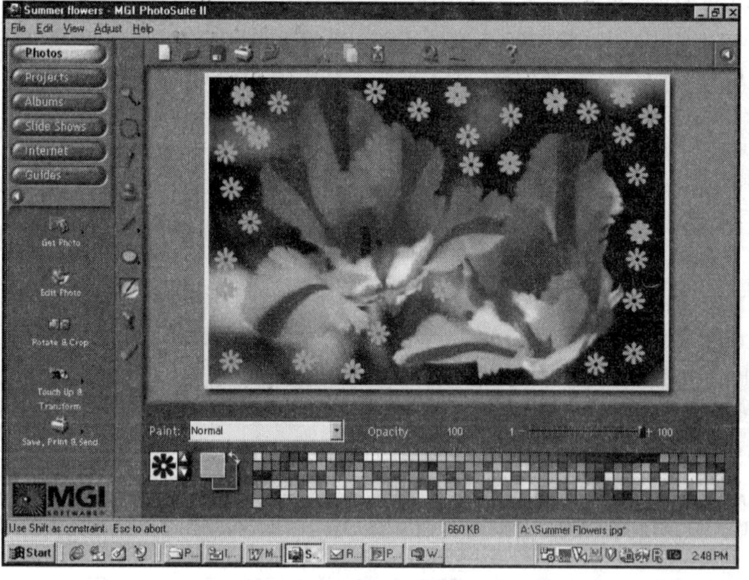

Figure 2-11 . . . to create effects like this, (You can never have too many flowers, can you? Well, maybe you can . . .)

Figure 2-12
Using the Flood Fill tool, I turned one of my yellow flowers blue!

- **Erase.** If you've never made a mistake, you're obviously some kind of superhuman and probably don't need to be reading this book. If, instead, you're like me and you make lots of them, mixed in with a fair helping of second thoughts, then you'll find the eraser a particularly useful tool. This doesn't erase sections of your photo, as you might expect; instead, it erases any changes you've made to your photo, removing any edits you've done and returning the photo to the way it looked the last time it was saved. The intensity slider determines how effective the eraser is. Normally you'll want to set it at 100 so that the edit is completely removed. If you set it lower, the edit is only partially removed. That would mean that if, for example, you had covered up a boat on a lake by using the Clone button, once you ran the eraser over the picture the boat would still be partially covered by the clone, resulting in a ghostly effect. The Erase effect uses the same brush shapes as Paint.

Rotate and Crop

Click the Rotate and Crop button to bring up the next set of tools, which let you change the orientation of your picture or remove part of it.

Another toolbar appears to the left of the work area. The four buttons here include

- **Rotate/Mirror.** Click this to rotate your picture left or right or flip it to create a horizontal or vertical mirror image. The controls at the

Figure 2-13
I've flipped this picture horizontally to create a mirror image of the original.

bottom of the workspace are, from left to right, rotate the picture 90 degrees to the left, rotate the picture 180 degrees, rotate the picture 90 degrees to the right, flip it vertically, or flip it horizontally (see Figure 2-13).

- **Free Rotate.** Click this to rotate the picture however many degrees left or right you want, either by using the controls at the bottom of the workspace or by clicking on the rotation handle that appears in the middle of the picture (see Figure 2-14) and moving it left or right.
- **Crop.** This places a frame around the picture. Adjust the frame's size with the handles or move it around by clicking on its edge until only the part of the picture you want to keep remains inside the frame. Then click the Crop button at the bottom of the workspace. Everything outside the frame is removed (see Figure 2-15).
- **Straighten.** It's happened to all of us: While you were closing the lid to your scanner, you inadvertently knocked the photo you were scanning off-kilter, so that it scans slightly crooked. This tool lets you correct this without having to rescan the picture. Just click on it, then click on a spot near one edge of the picture. Click on another spot near the edge so that the line that appears between them corresponds to the angle the edge should have been at if you'd scanned the picture straight the first time. Click Straighten, and your little scanner miscue is corrected.

Figure 2-14
You can enter a specific number of degrees to rotate your picture or you can do it by hand.

Figure 2-15
Here I've already cropped my picture once, and I'm adjusting the frame prior to cropping it again.

Figure 2-16 PhotoSuite II SE offers you several tools for touching up and transforming your photo's appearance.

Touch Up and Transform

The really fun parts of PhotoSuite II SE and imaging software in general are the tools that let you apply all sorts of funky effects to your digital pictures.

When you click Touch Up and Transform, you'll first see the box in Figure 2-16 that offers you four more choices: Remove Red Eye, Touch Up, Special Effects, and Warp.

Remove Red Eye is a specialized painting effect that can be used to remove that red, devilish gleam that sometimes shows up in people's eyes when they were photographed using a flash in a dark room. Choose this, and then zoom in on your picture until you can see the red pupils in the picture clearly. Adjust the size of your brush and the intensity of the effect, and paint over the pupils. The red is removed.

Choose Touch Up to fix problems with your photo. To apply touch ups, you first have to either select the entire photo (choose Edit, Select All) or select a specific area you want to touch up (using the selection tools described earlier).

Then, choose the touch up you want to use from the list. Each touch up is automatically previewed when you click on it; if you decide you like the results, click Apply.

Possible touchups include

- **Auto Enhance.** PhotoSuite automatically adjusts and enhances the photo's colors.
- **Brightness and Contrast.** These controls work just like brightness and contrast controls on a TV: The Brightness slider adjusts the overall brightness of the photo, while the Contrast slider makes dark areas darker and light areas lighter.
- **Fix Colors.** This lets you adjust the hue, saturation, and grayscale values of a photo with sliders. All the colors in the photo are adjusted simultaneously.
- **Scratch Removal.** This automatically removes scratches from a photo (by filling them in with the surrounding colors). You can adjust the intensity of the effect by using the Radius slider.
- **Sharpen.** This enhances details in a photo. You can choose between a moderate sharpening effect and one that is more pronounced.
- **Soften.** This is just the opposite of sharpen; it blurs your photo. The Intensity slider controls the intensity of the effect.
- **Invert.** This essentially turns your picture into a photographic negative, replacing black with white, red with green, and so on. (See Figure 2-17.)

Figure 2-17
This picture has been inverted.

Figure 2-18
Eeek! I've become a cartoon!

Special Effects are a lot of fun to play with. The various effects are divided into categories, each of which contains several effects, such as the Cartoon effect in Figure 2-18. There are too many to describe here; play with them yourself to see what you can do. Many of them include secondary controls that let you fine-tune the effect.

Warp is even more fun to play with (see Figure 2-19). You can choose from four Warp effects (they appear as buttons at the bottom of the work area). To use them, click on a Warp button, and then click on the picture where you want the warp to take effect. The size of the warp effect can be controlled with the slider.

From left to right, the Warp buttons are

- **Grow.** Click this and then on the picture; the area immediately surrounding the mouse pointer is pushed outward.
- **Shrink.** Click this and then the picture; the area immediately surrounding the mouse pointer is sucked inward.
- **Drag.** Click this and then click and drag on the picture. The area immediately surrounding the mouse pointer is pushed outward and can be dragged and stretched.

Figure 2-19
I've used all the Warp effects on this picture. I used Grow on my head, Shrink on my stomach (don't I wish!), Drag on the Calgary skyline, and Melt on the edges of the photo.

- **Melt.** Click this and then click and drag on the picture. The area immediately surrounding the mouse pointer is sucked inward and, again, can be dragged and stretched.
- **Restore.** Click this and then click and drag on the picture. The areas you drag your mouse pointer over will be gradually restored to their prewarp appearance.

Save, Print, and Send

The Save, Print & Send button opens the box in Figure 2-20, where you have several options for saving your photo to disk, printing it out, or sending it to someone else electronically.

You'll see some of these options in more detail as they come up in the digital projects in this book.

Ready to Go?

Now you have excellent imaging software that you can use to edit your digital images. Sounds like you're ready to go.

So what are you waiting for? In the next section of this book, more than a dozen exciting digital projects await.

Let's get cracking!

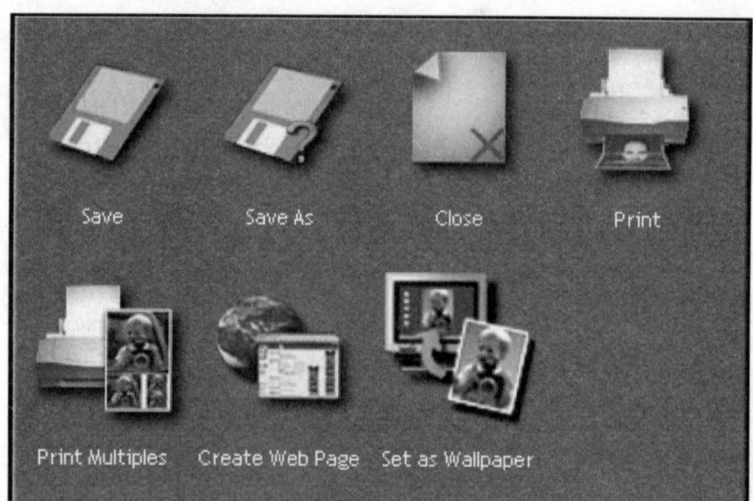

Figure 2-20
Save, Print & Send provides you with these options.

SECTION II: Projects for the *Whole Family*

Chapter 3

Project: The Digital Photo Album

What You Need:

- A scanner or digital camera (optional)
- FlipAlbum (on the CD)
- AOL 4.0

Introduction

My mother has dozens of photo albums—and they're wonderful! A few years ago she made a special album for me and my two brothers, full of pictures from when each of us was growing up. I've had a great time sharing it with my wife. (Even the embarrassing pictures aren't *too* embarrassing—20 or 30 years later.)

I wouldn't trade those albums for anything, but they do have some downsides. First off, they're bulky. And in some cases, the photos are starting to fade or have gotten scratched or dirty over the years.

With a digital photo album, you can avoid or solve all of those problems. Not only that, but you can send as many copies of your photos as you like to friends and relatives without ever having to get them reprinted. (That savings alone could eventually pay for a digital camera!)

In this chapter, I'll take you step by step through the process of creating a digital photo album using FlipAlbum and a scanner (or scanning service) or digital camera.

Creating an Album with FlipAlbum

No matter what program you use to create your digital photo album, it will lack the tactile element you get with a real album: the feel of the pages, the weight of the book, and the smooth leather of the binding.

FlipAlbum is an exciting software program that can add visual interest to your digital album by at least giving it the appearance of a "real" album, right down to the coil binding and the flipping pages.

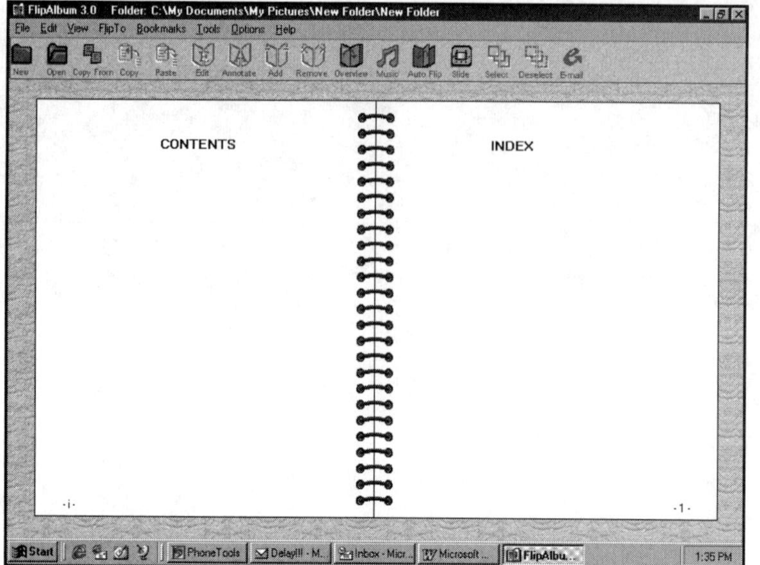

Figure 3-1 A new FlipAlbum looks like this.

Here's how to create a FlipAlbum album:

1. Start FlipAlbum. This automatically opens the last album you were working on or, if you haven't created one yet, creates a blank album. The album has two pages to start with: a contents page on the left and an index page on the right (see Figure 3-1).
2. Click the Copy From button on the toolbar. This opens the dialog box in Figure 3-2.
3. Locate the file folder containing the images you want at left and highlight it.
4. Choose the type of files you want to display from the File Type list box in the bottom-right corner.
5. In the resulting list, highlight the picture you want to add to the album. A preview of it appears at right, complete with information about its dimensions and the file size.
6. Click Copy From. A thumbnail of the picture you selected appears on the left page, while the contents page moves to the right and contains the name of the file and its position in the album (for example, number 1, 2, 3, and so on). See Figure 3-3.
7. Repeat Steps 2 to 6 until you've added all the images you want from your computer.

In addition to images, you can add WAV (sound), MIDI (music), and AVI (video) files to your album. Each appears as a special icon. For example, entry number 9 in Figure 3-3 is a WAV file; it appears as a tiny image of a speaker.

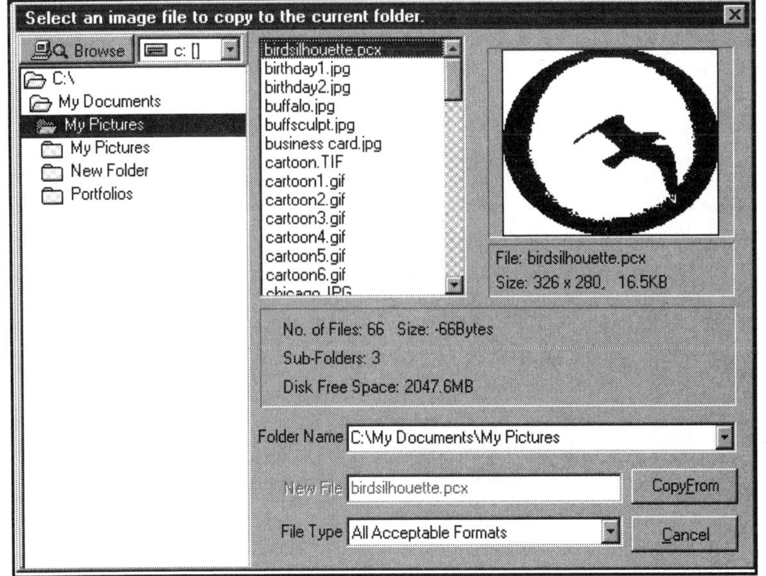

Figure 3-2
Choose the existing files you want to add to your album using this dialog box.

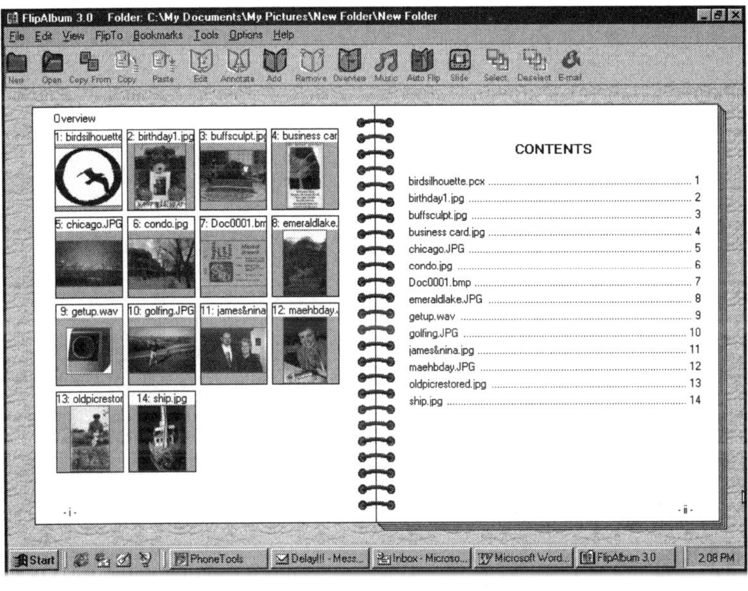

Figure 3-3
Here's how FlipAlbum organizes your images.

You can also add pictures directly from a TWAIN device, such as a scanner or digital camera. To do so, choose File, Get Image. Select the TWAIN source you want to get the image from, and then click Acquire. The software for that device opens, and you can scan or download a picture in the usual manner.

Viewing a FlipAlbum Album

Once you've created your album, you can view the images, sounds, music, and movies in a number of ways.

Figure 3-4
If you click on one of the thumbnails in your FlipAlbum scrapbook, your image appears all by itself on the screen.

Editing Pictures in FlipAlbum

Although it's not primarily an image editor, FlipAlbum does include its own set of powerful image-editing tools, which are similar to but different from those in PhotoSuite II SE that I described in Chapter 2.

To edit a picture in your album, click on it to preview it, as in Figure 3-4, and then right-click on it and choose Edit from the pop-up menu. This opens the Editing tools shown in Figure 3-5.

Aim your mouse pointer at each button to see what it does, and then experiment.

You'll find some tools here, such as Shear (which makes the picture slant to the right) and Gamma Correction (which brightens the mid-tones of a picture without affecting the brightest or darkest areas), which are not available in PhotoSuite II SE. By combining the tools in FlipAlbum with the tools in PhotoSuite, you should be able to make any picture look its best before or after you place it in your scrapbook.

To view a single entry, click on its image on the Overview page. If it's an image, it will appear on the screen all by itself (see Figure 3-4); if it's a sound, music, or video file, it will play.

The whole point of FlipAlbum, however, is that it allows you to view images as though they were pasted into a conventional photo album or scrapbook. To flip the pages, simply click anywhere on the page (except on images or text on the overview, contents, or index pages). Each image is automatically resized to fit the FlipAlbum pages (see Figure 3-6).

You can move directly to any part of your album by clicking on the entry you want on the contents page.

If you flip all the way to the back of your album, you'll see that in addition to a contents page you have an index page where your images are arranged alphabetically by filename (see Figure 3-7). Again, clicking on any entry in the index will take you directly to that item.

Figure 3-5
Edit your images in FlipAlbum using these powerful tools.

Figure 3-6
FlipAlbum resizes pictures so that they fit neatly onto the FlipAlbum pages, which look just like the pages of a real album.

NOTE

Besides using the index or the contents pages, you can locate a particular image quickly by bookmarking it. To do so, flip to the page where the image is located; choose Bookmarks, Add; and choose the page you want the bookmark to appear in. The bookmark shows up as a little tab sticking out of the FlipAlbum; click on the tab, and you'll go directly to the bookmarked page.

Yet another way to view your images is as a slide show, which displays four images at once (see Figure 3-8). Just click the Slide button in the toolbar to start the slide show; you can pause it during its display by pressing the space bar. To exit, press Esc.

Finally, to get a quick overview of the contents of your FlipAlbum, click the Auto Flip button. This flips back and forth from the beginning to end of your album automatically. You can change the speed at which Auto Flip runs, as well as the speed at which the Slide Show runs, and set other options by choosing Options.

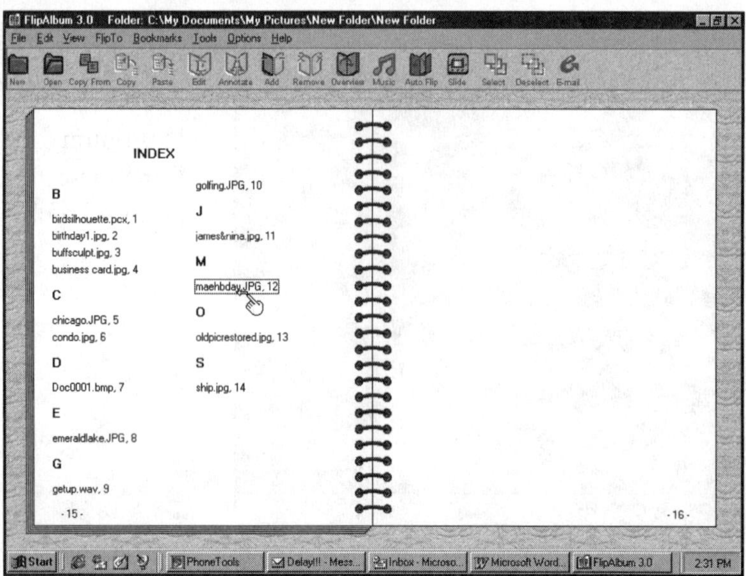

Figure 3-7
Here's how FlipAlbum organizes your images.

Figure 3-8
The FlipAlbum slide show displays four items from your scrapbook at once.

Labeling the Items in Your FlipAlbum Album

To get the most out of a photo album, you need to label the pictures you put in it; otherwise, in a few years' time, you won't have a clue what you're looking at. In some types of real photo albums, you can write that information right on the page. You can do that in FlipAlbum, too!

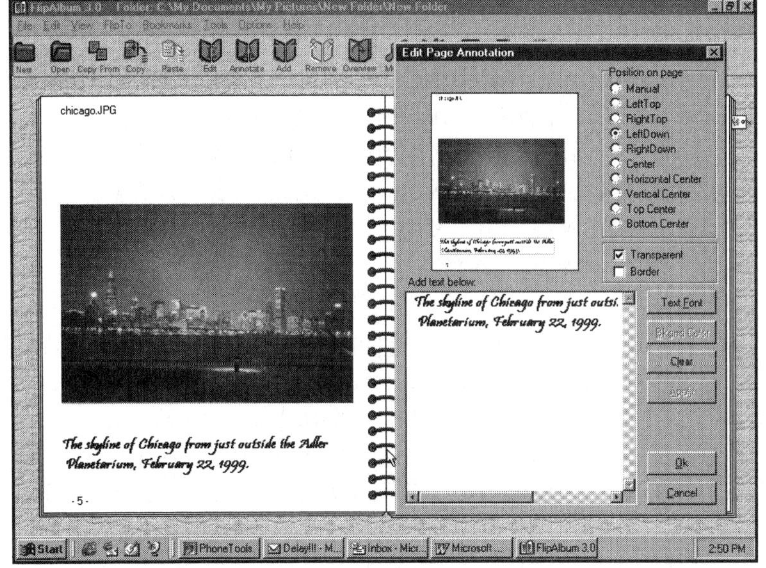

Figure 3-9
This dialog box lets you add text to the pages on which your scrapbook items appear.

To label any item in the album, follow these steps:

1. Flip to the page on which the item appears.
2. Click the Annotate button. (Notice that this button, like several of the others, has two sides—one for each visible page of the scrapbook. Make sure you click the correct side.)
3. The dialog box in Figure 3-9 opens. Enter the text you want to appear on the scrapbook page in the box labeled Add Text Below.
4. Choose the font, style, and size you want by clicking Text Font.
5. Position the text using the radio buttons in the upper-right corner. The preview area shows you the effect of each button as you click it.
6. When you're satisfied with your text and its positioning, click Apply.

Ten Tips for Taking Better Photographs

Whether you're using a regular film camera or a digital camera, the basics of taking good photographs are the same. Here are 10 tips for better photography recommended by Kodak on its Web site at `http://www.kodak.com`:

- **Carry your camera around.** It's happened to everyone. You see something that would make a great photograph, a once-in-a-lifetime photograph, even— and you don't have a camera with you. Many cameras now are small enough to carry easily in a pocket, so why not have one with you at all times?
- **Get the close shot.** In general, the closer you get to your subject, the better the photograph because distracting backgrounds are eliminated and the subject is clearer. Be careful not to get too close, however; check your camera manual to see how close your camera can focus.
- **Try action shots.** Extremely formal poses had their place when photographic plates

Ten Tips for Taking Better Photographs (Continued)

capture action clearly. Pictures of people doing something are always more interesting than pictures of people standing in straight lines. You'll also get much more relaxed, natural-looking facial expressions.

- **Keep the background simple.** If the background is too busy, it distracts from the main subject. If you can, reposition your subject or yourself until you find a clear, simple background.
- **Target off the center.** There's nothing wrong with having your subject in the center of the picture—sometimes that's exactly what you want—but sometimes placing the subject slightly off-center makes for a more interesting composition.
- **Add a foreground for depth.** If you're taking a picture of the scenery, you'll find that including some people or objects in the foreground gives the picture a greater sense of scale and depth and helps draw in the viewer.
- **Look for good lighting.** Good lighting isn't just lighting that's bright enough for a proper exposure; it's also lighting that's dramatic or colorful and enhances the scene. It's interesting that cloudy days are actually better for photographing people outside than sunny days; the sun makes people squint and creates extreme contrasts between light and dark areas that can be hard to deal with.
- **Capture with a steady hand.** The shutter isn't open very long, but if the camera is moving during the tiny interval when it is open, the resulting picture will be blurred. Press the button gently rather than jabbing it, and, especially in low light, brace your arm or use a tripod.

Sharing Your Digital Album

In order to share the photos in a regular photo album with someone else, you have to physically give them the pictures. Digital pictures, however, can be shared with dozens of people at a time without you ever having to part with them.

The digital photo you've created with FlipAlbum isn't a single file you can e-mail, unfortunately; it's a visual index of a number of pictures you may have scattered all over your computer. The only way to share it with someone else would be to make sure that all the photos in the album are gathered into a single directory, copy that directory to exactly the same location on the other person's computer, and then copy the photo album file to the other computer as well. They'd also have to have the FlipAlbum software.

However, as described in Chapter 1, you can easily e-mail the photos from your digital album to a friend. Here's how, by way of reminder:

1. In AOL 4.0, click Mail Center, then choose Write Mail from the menu to open a Write Mail box.
2. Write your e-mail as usual.

3. Click Attach, navigate to the first picture file you want to send, and click Open.
4. Repeat Step 3 to attach additional photo files.

When your e-mail arrives, your friend will see a Download button on the screen which he or she can click to download the picture.

Ten Tips for Taking Better Photographs (Continued)

- **Use a flash to your advantage.** Flashes aren't just for taking pictures in low light; they're also great for filling in detail and softening contrasts in outdoor pictures. Check your camera manual, though, to see how far your flash can reach. Taking a flash picture of the stage during a rock concert won't do you much good if you're in the top row of a football stadium and your flash only has a range of 12 feet—not that it stops people from trying.
- **Choose the right film or the right resolution.** For a regular camera, the choice of the right film depends on lighting conditions and subject matter. Try 100 ASA film for ordinary outdoor photography, but if you're going to be shooting indoors and can't necessarily use a flash you may want 400 ASA or even 800 or 1600 ASA film. The trade-off in regular films is that the more sensitive to light they are, the more grainy the final print will appear. In a digital camera, the choice of resolution depends on the final use you'll be putting the images to. If you're taking pictures destined for the Web, you can safely use the lowest resolution. Pictures you're planning to print need higher resolution, however. Of course, you have to balance the need for resolution with how many pictures you have to take. High resolution images eat up your camera's data storage in a hurry!

CHAPTER 4

PROJECT: Creating a Calendar

What You Need:

- A digital photograph
- PhotoSuite SE
- Access to a color printer

Introduction

I've always been a sucker for beautiful calendars. Oh, sure, I know that if you buy them in, say, January they're marked down to 50 percent of what they were in December, but I still find myself buying them in December. I just can't help it; I'm attracted to their big, beautiful photographs and their infinite variety of designs.

Apparently I'm not the only one because recently I saw an entire store devoted to selling nothing but calendars.

There's only one thing that's better than buying a really great calendar, and that's creating your own. In this chapter, you're going to do exactly that. In the process, you'll learn more about using PhotoSuite II SE's Projects feature.

Creating a Calendar

The first step in creating a calendar is to open a calendar template. To do so:

1. Open MGI PhotoSuite II SE.
2. Click the Projects button in the navigation bar in the upper-left corner.
3. Choose the Cards & Calendars button. This opens the dialog box in Figure 4-1.
4. Here you can choose to make either a yearly calendar (one on which all 12 months are displayed at once), a three-month calendar, or a monthly calendar. Click the one you want. Each of

Figure 4-1 Pick the type of calendar you want from this list.

these is only a single-page calendar, so if you want to make, for example, a full yearly calendar with a different picture for each month, you'll have to make each page of the calendar a new project.

5. Next you'll see some templates for that type of calendar (see Figure 4-2). Choose the one you'd like to work with. In addition, set the year and month you want the calendar to begin with from the list boxes below the workspace. Once you're happy with your choices, click Select.

Figure 4-2 Choose the calendar layout you'd like to work with.

Figure 4-3
When you open a calendar template, it looks something like this.

The template you chose opens in PhotoSuite's Project workspace (see Figure 4-3). You'll see all the tools in this workspace a little later in the chapter, but for now, you just want to add a photograph to the template as it stands.

To add a photograph to your calendar:

1. Click the Photos button in the upper-left corner of the PhotoSuite screen. (See Chapter 2 for more information on the Photos function of PhotoSuite II SE.)
2. Click Get Photo and get a photo as usual, either from a photo album (see Chapter 3 for more information on creating digital photo albums in PhotoSuite II SE), your computer's hard drive (or floppy or CD drive), a scanner, or a digital camera.
3. The photo you open is automatically placed in the Photo Library. If you return to your calendar by clicking Projects and then open the Photo Library by clicking the button at the far right of the main toolbar, you'll see a small thumbnail image of the picture you opened in the Photo Library (see Figure 4-4).

Figure 4-4
You can use any of the photos in the Photo Library in your calendar.

Figure 4-5
Here's what my calendar looks like with my photo added to it.

NOTE

Because your photo may not have exactly the same proportions as the gray box in the template, part of it may be cut off. Check carefully to make sure it's all there. You may want to return to the Photos workspace and crop the photo yourself so that it fits better into the template.

4. To add a photo from the Photo Library to your calendar, just click on it and drag it into place. The template indicates where the photograph should go with a gray box. When you drag the photo into that box, the photo is automatically resized to fit. See Figure 4-5.

If you're happy with the template you've chosen and the final look of your calendar, then that's it: You're done, except for printing (more on that at the end of this chapter)! But if you'd like to make a few changes to your calendar (or any project created with PhotoSuite), then read on. You have lots of editing tools at your command.

Editing Your Calendar (and Other Projects) in PhotoSuite II SE

No doubt you've already noticed that a whole lot of new tools popped up when you opened up the Projects workspace. These tools make PhotoSuite II SE a pretty powerful mini-desktop publishing program, allowing you to modify templates to your heart's desire.

One new section of the workspace you'll notice right away is the *Object Manager*, which is directly to the right of whatever you're working on. Each of the boxes with an *A* inside represents a text box. You'll also see icons representing other items on the page, such as photos, backgrounds, and props (more on those later).

If you were creating your calendar by hand, you'd end up with several pieces of paper. You might have a piece of paper on which you'd drawn the boxes for the calendar, a whole series of numbers you'd cut out of a magazine because you liked the type style, a photograph or two, and maybe another piece of paper with the day of the month on it. As you worked, some of these pieces of paper would get hidden under other pieces. You'd have to carefully rearrange them to be sure that what you wanted visible in the final calendar didn't end up hidden under something else.

The same thing can happen in a digital project involving many different items. The Object Manager lets you set which items are on top and which are partially (or even completely)

Five Practical Ideas for Calendars

Wondering just what you need a calendar for? Here are five practical uses for the kinds of calendars you can create with PhotoSuite II SE. (For five not-so-practical calendars, see the next sidebar!)

- **Organize your family's time.** Create a calendar for each month with everything that you already know is scheduled for that month indicated on the appropriate days. (Talk to each member of your family to be sure everyone's activities are included!) Family birthdays, visits to Grandma's, doctor's appointments, and more can be placed right on the calendar in PhotoSuite before it's printed. That way everyone can arrange their schedules during the month so there are fewer conflicts.
- **Stick to your diet.** Plan out a healthy diet a month in advance, and list the meals on a calendar. It will help you maintain good eating habits and make shopping easier, too. You could even feature a picture and details of your favorite recipe!
- **Remember your vacation.** Create a calendar that features photos from your last vacation. It will bring back pleasant memories every time you look at it and make the time go faster until your next vacation!
- **Show off your family.** Almost everyone has a calendar at work and almost everyone has a picture of his or her family, too. Why not kill two birds with one stone: Create your own calendar, featuring pictures of your family. It will help remind you why you're working so hard!
- **Honor someone on a special occasion.** Are your parents celebrating their 50th anniversary? Is Grandma celebrating her 90th birthday? Is George celebrating 25 years with the company? Give copies of a special calendar full of important dates and pictures from the individual's life to everyone who attends the celebration. It will make the occasion memorable for honoree and guests alike.

hidden underneath, just by clicking and dragging the various icons. Those at the top of the Object Manager are, in turn, on top in the project itself. In Figure 4-6, for example, I've dragged my photo to the top of the stack. As a result, part of the calendar text is half-hidden.

You can also use the Object Manager to select the item you want to edit, by clicking on its icon in the stack. (Of course, you can also select an object by clicking on the object itself.) Once an object is selected, you have many tools for changing its appearance.

For example, suppose you want to place text over top of your photograph, but still let the photograph show through a little. You could do that by choosing the text, and then adjusting the Opacity slider in the Settings area underneath the workspace. As you reduce the Opacity setting, the object becomes more transparent.

The other slider, Edge Fading, has a similar effect but only on the edges of the object. The result is edges that seem to blend into whatever is behind them.

In Figure 4-7 I've applied Edge Fading to the photograph, and used the Opacity slider to reduce the opacity of the letters indicating the days of the week.

Figure 4-6
Use the Object Manager to stack items the way you want them.

Figure 4-7
Changing the opacity of entire objects or just their edges are two ways you can alter their appearance.

It doesn't matter how good your objects look if they're not where you want them to be. The controls just above the Opacity and Edge Fading sliders control the placement and alignment of objects. From left to right, they are

To Front. This moves the selected object to the top layer.

To Back. This moves the selected object to the bottom layer.

Forward. This moves the selected object one layer closer to the top.

Backward. This moves the selected object one layer closer to the bottom.

Rotate Left. This rotates the selected object 90 degrees to the left.

Rotate 180 Degrees. This rotates the selected object 180 degrees.

Rotate Right. This rotates the selected object 90 degrees to the right.

Flip. This flips the selected object vertically. (To understand this effect, think of the object as a transparent slide that can be turned over.)

Mirror. This flips the selected object horizontally, creating a mirror image of it.

Delete. This deletes the selected object.

Restore Aspect Ratio. Whenever you resize an object by clicking and dragging on its handles, it's easy to stretch it out of shape. Sometimes this can be fun, if you're looking for a funhouse mirror sort of effect. However, sometimes it happens by accident. That's when you click this button, which restores the object to its original proportions.

The other tools you have to work with appear in the toolbar to the left of the workspace. The first tool at the top, Zoom, you're already familiar with. Below that is the Object Selector tool; this restores your standard mouse pointer so you can select objects by clicking on them, and it opens the Object Selection tools mentioned above.

Below that are several additional tools you can use to personalize your calendar or any other project. From top to bottom, they are

- **Text.** A picture may be worth a thousand words, but all the same, sometimes you need a few words. In a calendar, it could be a humorous saying, a pithy quote, a bit of poetry about the season, or details about someone's birthday. Whatever the text, you add it to your project by clicking the Text tool and then clicking where you want the text to appear. This creates a text box (see Figure 4-8). Adjusting the size of the text box automatically adjusts the size of the text. Type your text into the window that has opened in the Settings area, replacing the phrase "Put your text here!" You can format the text using the buttons to the right: Choose a font from the list box; click the text effects buttons to bold, italicize, or underline the text; and click the alignment buttons to align text with the left or right edge of the text box or center it.
- **Props.** As an actor as well as a writer, I can testify to the importance of props. The proper prop makes the task of creating a believable character and telling a believable story much easier. The same holds true in your calendar: A good prop can make the difference between a real crowd-pleaser and a bit of a dog. In PhotoSuite, props are self-contained pictures supplied with the software that you can easily add to your project. To use a prop, click the Prop button. From the Category listbox that appears in the Settings area, choose the type of prop you want: business, sports, or toys and games. Then choose the specific prop you want from the ones displayed. Drag it into the workspace, and presto! In Figure 4-9, I've added a toy lion to my flower. (Why not? Hey, maybe it's a dandelion!).
- **Word Balloons.** One of the great unheralded inventions of the Twentieth Century, if you ask me, is the word balloon. Before it came on

Figure 4-8
You can easily add additional text to your calendar.

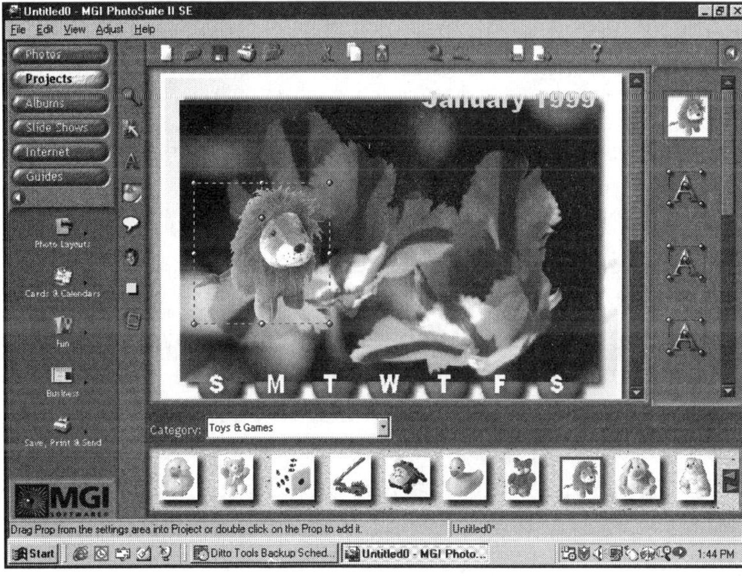

Figure 4-9
Props are small images you can add to any project.

the scene, it was very hard to tell who was speaking in a crowded cartoon scene. Now it's as clear as crystal. And the shape of the word balloon can even convey inflection and emotion—better than we can with our own voices, if you ask me. Don't you wish, when you made a coldly cutting remark, that your words would hang above you in a little balloon dangling icicles like they do in comic books? Well, you can have your wish, in a way, in PhotoSuite, which lets you add word balloons to projects so you can attribute text to specific people (or anything else)

Figure 4-10 Word balloons are another fun PhotoSuite feature.

within a picture. You add word balloons just like you add props, by choosing the specific style you want, and dragging it into your project. In Figure 4-10, I've added a rather emphatic one. To add text to your word balloon, simply place a text box inside it, as described earlier.

- **Body Switches.** Indulge that hidden urge everyone has to don a lab coat, wring your hands, and cackle like a madman. This fun mad-scientist accessory lets you put the head of someone in a photo onto a new body. (You can also use it to add wigs and hats.) You choose the body you want just as you choose a prop or a word balloon. If it happens to be the right shape, you can simply plop the body down in front of the actual body in the photo, as I did in Figure 4-11. Otherwise, you'll need to go back to the Photos section to cut the head out of the photo so you can paste it onto the new body. (See Chapter 2 for more information on editing photos in PhotoSuite.)
- **Drop Shadow.** Finally, the Drop Shadow tool lets you add a drop shadow—and along with it, a nice sense of three-dimensionality—to any object. Select the object you want to add the shadow to, and then adjust the settings. The Shadow Direction control at left selects the direction the shadow will be cast. The Movement slider determines the distance of the shadow from the object—and hence its width. The Opacity slider sets the transparency off the shadow, and the Fading slider determines how hard-edged the shadow will appear, by controlling the transparency of the shadow's edge. Finally, you can set

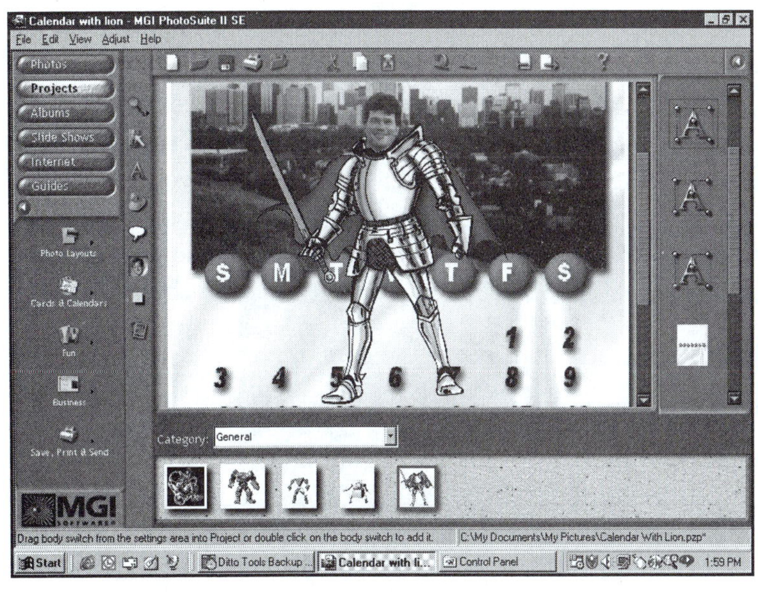

Figure 4-11
I think I like this body better than my own!

Figure 4-12
A drop shadow can make an object seem more real in a photo.

the color of the shadow by clicking the Color button. In Figure 4-12, I've added a drop shadow to the lion I added to my flower earlier.

Printing Your Calendar

The final step in creating a calendar using PhotoSuite II SE is to print it. Click the Print button on the top toolbar to open the Print Preview screen and call up the printer settings controls (see Figure 4-13).

Figure 4-13
Print Preview lets you see exactly how your project will be printed and make changes as necessary.

Print Preview offers several new tools in the top toolbar:

Previous Page. If your project has more than one page (your calendar won't, but some projects do), this takes you to the page before the one you're currently viewing.

Next Page. This takes you to the next page in a multipage project.

Zoom In. This increases the magnification of the page you're previewing.

Zoom Out. This decreases the magnification of the page you're previewing.

Center On Page. This centers your work both horizontally and vertically within the printable area on the page.

Center Vertically. This centers your work vertically within the page's printable area.

Center Horizontally. This centers your work horizontally within the page's printable area.

You can resize the image that will be printed by dragging its handles, and then reposition it on the page by clicking and dragging it.

In the Settings area, you can make the usual kinds of choices you make in any Windows program for printing. Choose a printer, set its properties, choose a print size (click Maintain Aspect Ratio to ensure that your project doesn't get distorted by a change in print size), enter the number of copies you want, and choose an orientation. Click Print Current Page Only if you only want to print the current page of a multipage project. Finally, click Print.

CHAPTER 5

PROJECT: Greeting Cards, Invitations, Announcements, and More

What You Need:

- Access to a scanner or digital camera
- PhotoSuite II SE
- Barking Cards (optional)
- Sound card (optional)
- Microphone (optional)
- Access to a color printer

Introduction

Card shops are wonderful places because they are full of cards for almost every occasion: birthdays, Mother's Day, and Valentine's Day. But sometimes you search the shelves in vain for the card that says exactly what you want to say, for something that perfectly fits your personality and that of your recipient, or for something, in other words, that doesn't feel like it's been mass-produced.

Well, there's one way to ensure that your card won't feel mass-produced, and that's to produce it yourself!

In this chapter you're going to use PhotoSuite II SE to create a greeting card, complete with a photo on the front and a humorous phrase in the middle. You can use exactly the same technique to create invitations, announcements, and many other kinds of cards.

You'll also look at using an entirely different program, Barking Cards, to create an animated card that you can send electronically.

Figure 5-1
You can choose from many different types of cards.

Creating Cards with PhotoSuite II SE

You've already had some experience working with PhotoSuite's projects in Chapter 3, where you created a calendar. Creating a card is very similar. To begin:

1. Open MGI PhotoSuite II.
2. Click the Projects button in the navigation bar in the upper-left corner.
3. Click the Cards & Calendars button.
4. Choose Greeting Cards.
5. From the selection provided, choose the type of card you want to create (see Figure 5-1).
6. Click on the template you want to use, and then click Select. The template opens in the workspace (see Figure 5-2).

If you're looking specifically for wedding-related cards, choose The Wedding Collection instead of Greeting Cards after you click Cards & Calendars.

The first thing you'll want to do is add a photograph. To reiterate, here's how you do that:

1. Click the Photos button. (See Chapter 2 for more information on PhotoSuite II SE's Photos function.)

Figure 5-2
This is just one of the many card templates PhotoSuite supplies.

2. Click Get Photo and select a photo from a photo album (see Chapter 3); your computer's hard drive, floppy drive, or CD drive; a scanner; or a digital camera. This places the photo in the Photo Library. Open all the photos you'd like to add to the library for possible use in this card or others you may create in this session.
3. Return to your card by clicking Projects, and then open the Photo Library by clicking the button at the far right of the main toolbar.
4. Click on any photo in the library you'd like to add to your card, and then drag it into the gray box on the card. The photo is automatically resized to fit that space (see Figure 5 3).

Now you can edit your card just as you did your calendar. Refer to Chapter 4 for a

Types of Cards You Can Create with PhotoSuite

PhotoSuite has many card templates to choose from, which you can adapt for many different purposes, including:

- **Announcements.** These are cards designed to let people know about upcoming events, such as store openings, art shows, plays, and auctions.
- **Apology.** Sometimes you hurt people without meaning too. An apology card can go a long way toward healing the rift.
- **Celebrations.** Special occasions, such as anniversaries, call for special cards.
- **Christmas.** Tired of buying Christmas cards? Create your own!
- **Congratulations.** Graduations, promotions, births, anniversaries—

Figure 5-3
Here's what my birthday card looks like with a photo added to it.

> **Types of Cards You Can Create with PhotoSuite (Continued)**
>
> here are dozens of reasons each year to congratulate the people around you. A special card is a good way to do it.
>
> - **Encouragement.** When friends or family are going through tough times, a kind word from you can make a big difference. That's what encouragement cards provide.
> - **Friendship.** Sometimes you just want to remind someone that you're their friend, and thank them for being yours. A card is a great way to do that.
> - **Invitations.** Planning a party? Send out your own custom-designed invitations.
> - **Love.** Create a card that tells someone how deeply you care.
> - **Thank You.** When someone helps you out, the least you can do is give them a unique thank you card—one you created yourself!

complete discussion of all the tools PhotoSuite makes available for changing your card template's appearance, from adding props to adding text.

One big difference between most greeting card templates and the calendar is that greeting cards have more than one page. Just like commercial greeting cards, there's a message inside as well as on the front. You'll look at editing the inside of the card in a moment; for now, let's finish changing the front.

You'll probably want to add your own text to your card. For this birthday card for my wife, for instance, I want to add the phrase, "I want to be your teddy bear!" (Thank you, Elvis. Thank you very much.)

Here's how I'd do that:

1. Click the Text button (third from the top in the left-hand toolbar).

Figure 5-4
To add text, I first have to create a text frame with the text tool.

2. Click my mouse pointer on the spot on the card where I want the text to appear (see Figure 5-4). This creates a text frame into which I'll type my text.
3. Now I highlight the phrase "Put your text here" in the box in the Settings area and type in "I want to be your teddy bear!" Because I want it on two lines instead of one, I add a return after the word "be."
4. Because the text box is much smaller than I want the phrase to be, I resize it by clicking and dragging its handles. I could also rotate it by clicking and dragging the central handle, which extends down inside the text frame, but I decide to leave it straight. (See Figure 5-5).
5. The text is hard to read and it's in a very boring font. There are three things I want to do to format it. First, I click the Center button, which is second from the right in the row of buttons under the font list in the Settings area. This centers the text inside the text box.
6. Next, I change the color by clicking the Color button. This first pops up a selection of 16 colors, but I don't see exactly what I'm looking for there, so I click More. This allows me to create exactly the color I want, using the controls in Figure 5-6. The slider at left

lets me choose a hue I want, and I can set the intensity of it by dragging my mouse pointer over the box in the middle. The two smaller boxes at the bottom show me what the color I've selected looks like compared to the current color of the text. When I'm satisfied with my color, I click OK.

Figure 5-5 I've added my text; now I have to format it.

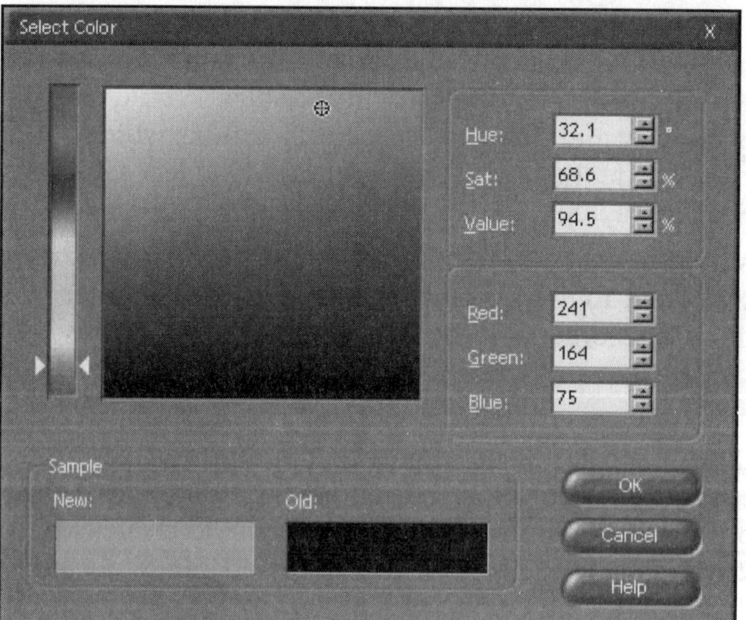

Figure 5-6 Change the text color using these controls.

7. Finally, I change the font used for my added text to the same font PhotoSuite used for the "Happy Birthday." To find out what that font is, I simply click on "Happy Birthday." It's in a text box, too, so as soon as I do so, the font it uses appears in the font list (KidTYPEPaint). Now I just click on my new text box and select the same font from the font list.
8. That's it! The finished card front appears in Figure 5-7.

So much for the front. As I noted, however, these cards also include inside messages. To see what's inside the card, click the Next Page button at the right of the top toolbar a couple of times. (The first time it brings up a blank page, which is the inside of the front cover.) The inside message appears on the third page; the final page, which corresponds to the back of the card, is also blank. Of course, you can add pictures, text, or whatever you want to the blank pages, as well. On the back page, for instance, you might want to add text that says, "This card made by . . ." and your name, if you're particularly proud of it. If you're creating greeting cards to sell to other people, this would be a good place to put the price and the logo and name of your greeting card company—even an address or contact name. That way every greeting card you create also becomes an advertisement for your business.

The message PhotoSuite put in the card by default, "It's your birthday and I couldn't bear to forget," appears in Figure 5-8.

Figure 5-7
Here's the finished front of the card with new text added.

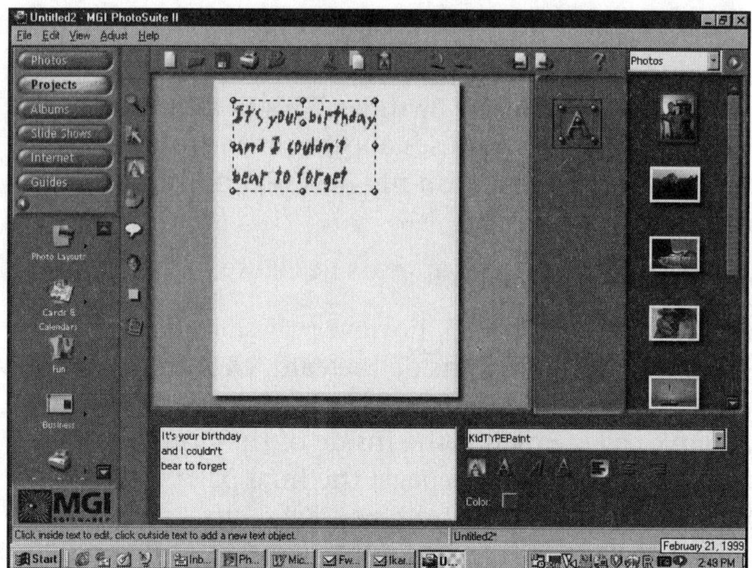

Figure 5-8 PhotoSuite provides a default phrase, but you can probably come up with something better.

I suppose that's not bad, but it's not what I have in mind. I'm going to use PhotoSuite's editing tools to make this birthday card much more interesting.

I'll leave the text box where it is for now because I'll need it later. First, though, I want to add a prop and a word balloon. To do so, I

1. Click the Prop button on the toolbar to the left of the workspace.
2. Choose the Toys & Games category from the listbox in the Settings area.
3. From the props provided, I choose a teddy bear and drag it onto my card (see Figure 5-9).
4. The bear is a little smaller than I'd like it to be, so I resize it by clicking and dragging on the corner handles.
5. To add a word balloon, I click the word balloon button on the left-hand toolbar, choose the balloon I want from those displayed, drag it onto my card, and resize it (see Figure 5-10).
6. The word balloon is pointing the wrong way, so I need to flip it. To do that, I leave it selected and then click the Object Selector button (the second one from the top in the left-hand toolbar). This opens the various positioning tools in the Settings area. Clicking the Mirror button (the fourth from the right) flips the word balloon along its horizontal axis, pointing it the other way (see Figure 5-11).

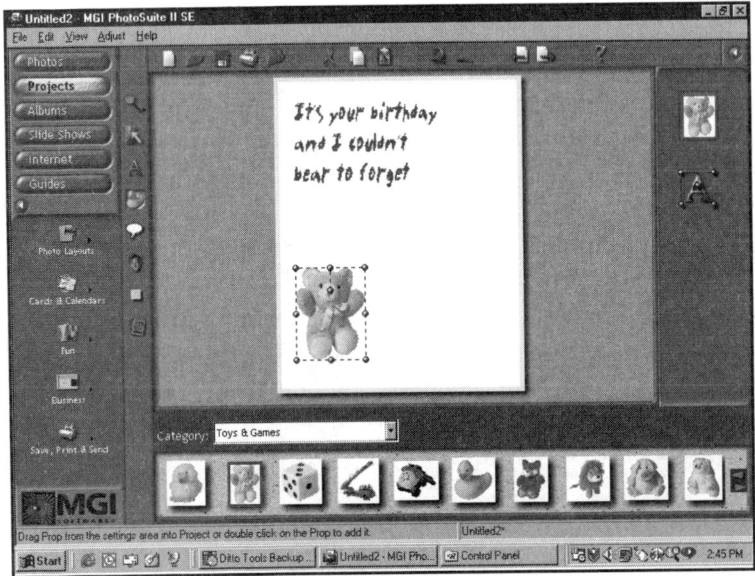

Figure 5-9
You can never have too many teddy bears.

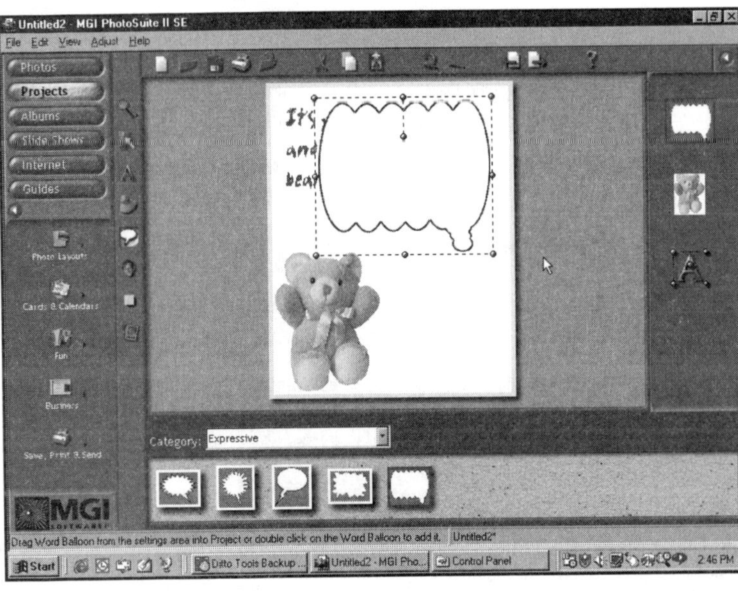

Figure 5-10
Here's my card with a word balloon added. Unfortunately, it's pointing the wrong way!

7. After a little resizing and moving of objects so it looks like the word balloon is coming from the bear, I decide to add a drop shadow to the balloon to add some visual interest. To do that, I keep the balloon selected and then click the Drop Shadow button (second from the bottom in the left-hand toolbar). I click the bottom-right button in the Shadow controls that appear in the Settings area so that the shadow will appear below and to the right of the balloon. I then make the shadow wider by increasing the setting of the Movement slider (see Figure 5-12).

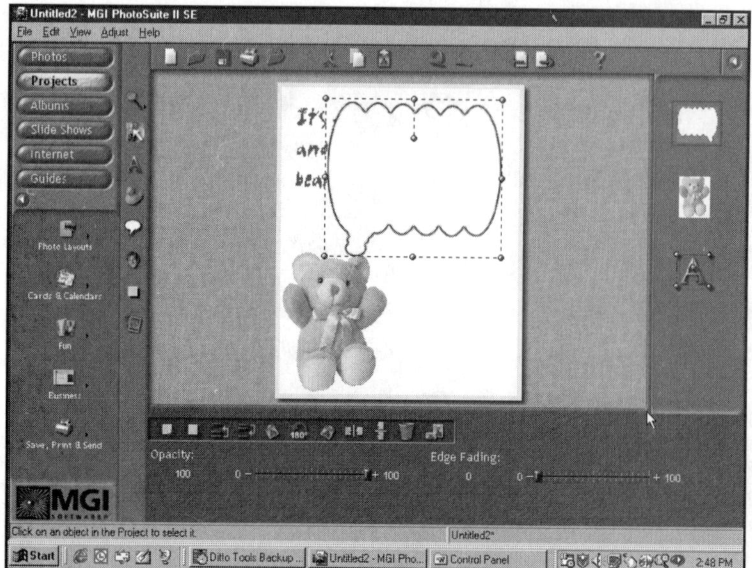

Figure 5-11 With the Mirror button I'm able to easily point the word balloon in the proper direction.

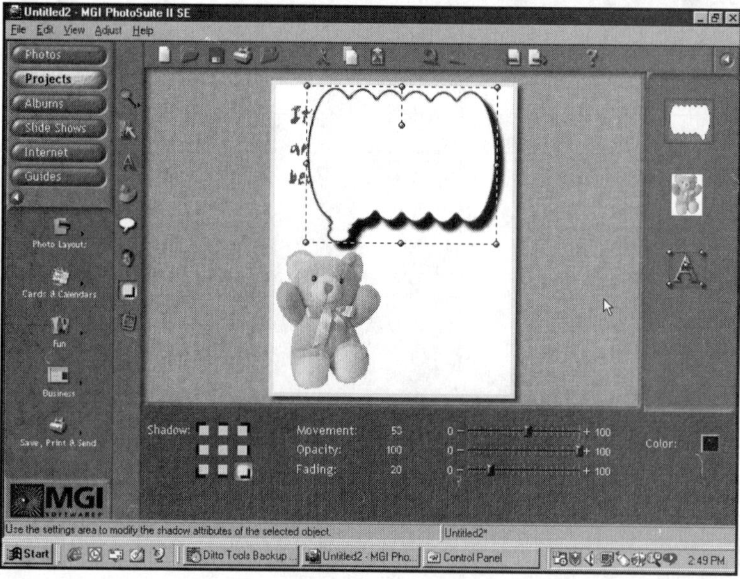

Figure 5-12 A drop shadow makes my word balloon stand out more and gives the card a nice 3-D feel.

8. Now I'm ready to revise the text. First I move the text box on top of the word balloon by clicking on the text box icon in the Object Manager, just to the right of the workspace, and dragging it to the top of the objects listed there.
9. Next, I click the Text button on the left-hand toolbar. This opens the text window with the current text inside it. I select the current text, and type my new text in its place.

Figure 5-13
Here's the completed interior of my card.

10. Finally, I reposition the text box so that all the text falls inside the Word balloon, and I'm done! (See Figure 5-13).

Printing Your Card

Printing a greeting card from a PhotoSuite template is a little different from printing from some other templates because you have to print both the inside and outside of the card.

To print your greeting card:

1. Click the Print button (fourth from the left) in the top toolbar. This opens the preview in Figure 5-14. Notice that although, in the workspace, each page of the greeting card appeared separately, they'll actually all be printed on the same sheet of paper.
2. Choose a printer from the Printer listbox and change any of its properties if you wish by clicking the Properties box.

Five Tips for Creating Great Greeting Cards

Five tips for creating great greeting cards:

- Keep your message short and sweet! A brief message carries more impact than a long-winded one and will be remembered more easily and longer.
- The best way to create a card someone else will want to receive is to create one that you'd love to receive!
- Be original! If you're just going to use something you've seen in a thousand greeting cards before, why not just buy one? Try to come up with something you've never seen or read before—something with special meaning for the person you're sending the card to.
- If it's at all appropriate, be funny! Obviously a sympathy card isn't a place for humor (unless it's a sympathy card for someone's 40th birthday), but most cards will be appreciated and cherished more if they're

Five Tips for Creating Great Greeting Cards (Continued)

light-hearted and amusing. Most humorous greeting cards have an attention-getting one-sentence lead-in on the front of the card, followed by a brief, effective punch line inside. It's like a one-two punch of humor! And if you've read any commercial cards recently, you know that it also tends to be off-the-wall humor: irreverent, outrageous, and sometimes even risqué. Again, it's important to know your audience. Risqué is probably not the route to go when sending a birthday card to your new church minister, for example!

- Create cards for events commercial card companies don't cover. A few examples are "Congratulations on your New Puppy," "Happy Housepainting," "Thanks for the Hot Stock Tip," "Our Profoundest Sympathy on the Sad Occasion of the First Ding in Your New Car," or even "Happy Arbor Day." They'll make more impact than just one birthday card among dozens, no matter how cleverly designed it might be.

3. Click the Print Size you want; if you change the print size, remember to check the Maintain Aspect Ratio button to ensure that the images on your card don't get distorted.
4. Choose the number of copies you want to print.
5. Click Print.

Sending a PhotoSuite Card via E-mail

Using AOL, you can send your card as an image embedded right in your e-mail. To do so:

1. Go to the first page of your card in Projects.
2. Choose Edit, Save As, and Save to save the card under whatever name you like as a JPEG or GIF image.
3. Go to the inside page of your card, and save it under a different name. (You have to save it under a different name because each page of your card is saved as a separate image.)
4. In AOL, click Mail Center, and then choose Write Mail.
5. Address your e-mail as usual, and write any notes you want to accompany the card. Then click the Insert Picture button, the button with the image of a camera on it (it's third from the left in the row of buttons just above the message area).
6. Locate and select the image file you created from the first page of your card, and then click OK.
7. Click Insert Picture again and locate and select the image file you created from the second page of your card, and click OK. Both pictures will be inserted directly into your message (see Figure 5-15).
8. Click Send to send your card on its way!

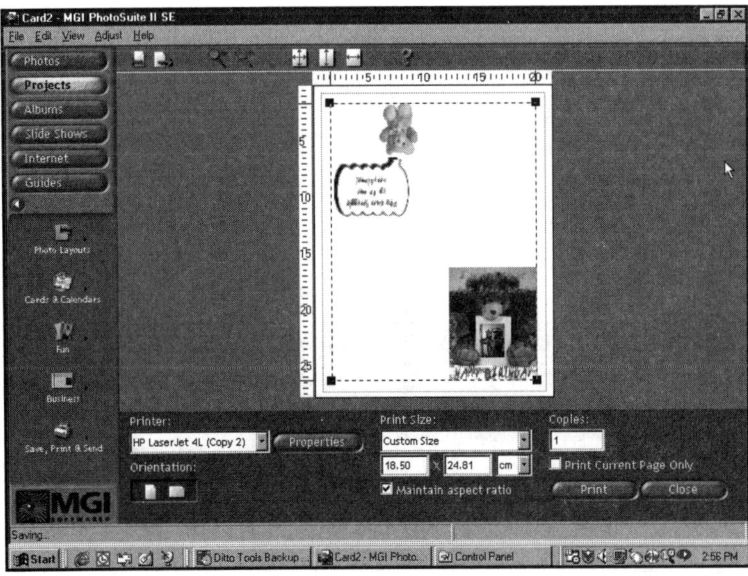

Figure 5-14 Greeting cards are printed on a single page that has to be folded to create the finished product.

Confused about how you should fold your printed card so the outside is out and the inside is in? PhotoSuite has the answer. Click Cards & Calendars, then Greeting Cards, just as if you were starting a new card. Now choose Folding Instructions from the Category listbox. There's only one template in that category; open it up and print it out. It tells you exactly how to fold your card once it's been printed.

Figure 5-15 Once you've created a card in PhotoSuite, you can e-mail it to its recipient using AOL.

Creating Animated Cards with Barking Cards

You can send even more elaborate greeting cards, complete with animation and sound effects, by using the Barking Cards program on the CD that came with this book. Here's how:

1. Start Barking Cards.
2. Click New Card.

For more information about graphic file formats, see Chapter 19, "Understanding More About Graphics Software."

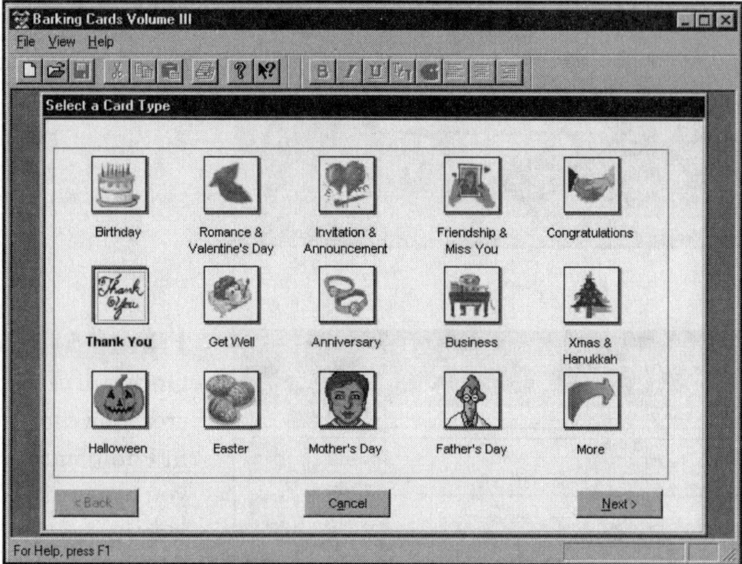

Figure 5-16 Barking Cards offers you many different types of cards to choose from.

3. From the screen in Figure 5-16, choose a card type. (I chose Thank You.)
4. From the next screen (see Figure 5-17), choose the card you want from Cards menu on the left and the phrase you want to use in it from the Verses menu on the right. Click Play to preview the card. Click Next when you're happy with your choice.
5. Now personalize your card. To change the text, click on it, and then replace it with your own words; to add new text, click Add Text, which creates a text box into which you can type. Format the text using the toolbar buttons, which include the usual options for changing font type, color, and style (bold, italic, or underlined).
6. To add a picture, click Add Picture. The resulting dialog box (see Figure 5-18) lets you browse your computer for a picture (starting with Barking Card's own extensive collection of clipart) or add an image from a scanner or digital camera. Barking Card attempts to

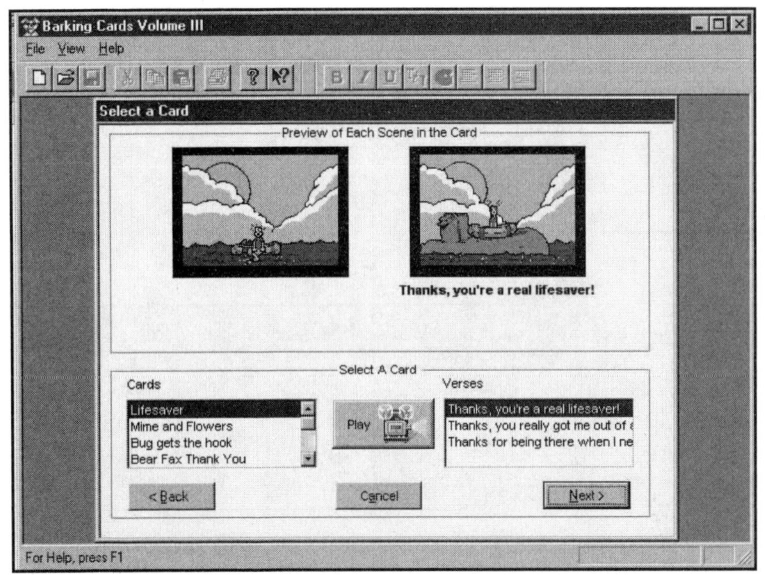

Figure 5-17
Choose the card and text you want, and preview your card, from this screen.

Figure 5-18
Browse your computer for a picture or get one from a scanner or digital camera.

determine if the background should be transparent (for clipart) or not (for a photo); if it makes the wrong choice, you can make the background transparent by clicking the Remove Background checkbox.

7. Finally, you can add a sound by clicking Add Sound. Get a sound that's already stored on your computer, or record one by clicking Record Now. While you're recording, you'll see the small dialog box in Figure 5-19.

When you're done, you're asked if you want to save your changes, and then you're given three choices:

- **Save without player.** This saves the card so you can edit it in the future. However, it doesn't include the animation player anyone wanting to view the card on a computer that doesn't have Barking

Figure 5-19
Add your own sound to your card.

Cards installed will need. You can always open it, edit it, and then save it with the player sometime in the future when you're ready to send it to someone else.

- **Save with player.** This saves the card with the animation player but doesn't save any changes you've made since the last save.
- **Save both ways.** This is the recommended option. It saves both the changes you've made to the card and the animation player.

Once the card is saved along with the player, you can send it to someone via e-mail as an attachment. The recipient just saves the card to his or her hard drive and runs it like any other program.

Between PhotoSuite II SE and Barking Cards, you may never have to visit a card shop again!

Chapter 6

PROJECT: The Family Scrapbook and History

What You Need:

- Access to a scanner or digital camera
- PhotoSuite II SE
- Net Graphics Optimizer (on the CD)
- Sound card (optional)
- Microphone (optional)

Introduction

If there's one thing better than a photo album for bringing back memories, it's a full-fledged scrapbook—a book in which photos mingle with newspaper clippings, pieces of cloth, pressed flowers, concert admission tickets and just a faint smell of patchouli from that night in 1967.

Alas, there is as yet no way to capture scent with your computer, but the other elements of a scrapbook can be preserved digitally (except maybe the pressed flowers and even that isn't out of the question if you don't mind making a mess of your scanner, but I wouldn't recommend it).

In addition, a computer scrapbook has another advantage: It can preserve sounds and even moving pictures, if you have the right equipment.

A good scrapbook can do more than just rekindle your memories of days gone by: It can help answer that question your children will all eventually ask, "Where did I come from?" No, not *that*—where their family came from, what you were like before they were born, what their grandparents did for a living, who their ancestors of a hundred years ago were. For a young person, even the days when they were babies seem an impossibly long time ago, in a fascinating, almost mythical past. If you've kept a scrapbook from the very beginning, you'll be able to offer them a window into that past. And if you also use your computer to create a complete family history, complete with old photographs, anecdotes and more, you can make it a very large window indeed—one offering a view you yourself will enjoy gazing at from time to time.

Figure 6-1
Here's where you begin your digital scrapbook.

In this chapter, you'll look at creating both a digital scrapbook and a digital family history.

Starting Your Scrapbook

The first step to creating a digital scrapbook in PhotoSuite II SE is to start a new PhotoSuite Photo Album. Here's how:

1. Open MGI PhotoSuite II SE.
2. Click the Albums button in the upper-left corner.
3. Choose File, New, or click the New button on the toolbar. This opens the dialog box shown in Figure 6-1.
4. Give your scrapbook a name and decide how big you want the *thumbnails*, small images of the items in the scrapbook, displayed. The three choices are 64x64 pixels, 96x96, and 128x128. For a scrapbook, I recommend using the largest size.
5. Click OK. PhotoSuite creates a blank album like the one in Figure 6-2.

Scanning Photographs into Your Scrapbook

You can add photographs to your digital scrapbook in two ways: You can scan them in or download them from a digital camera.

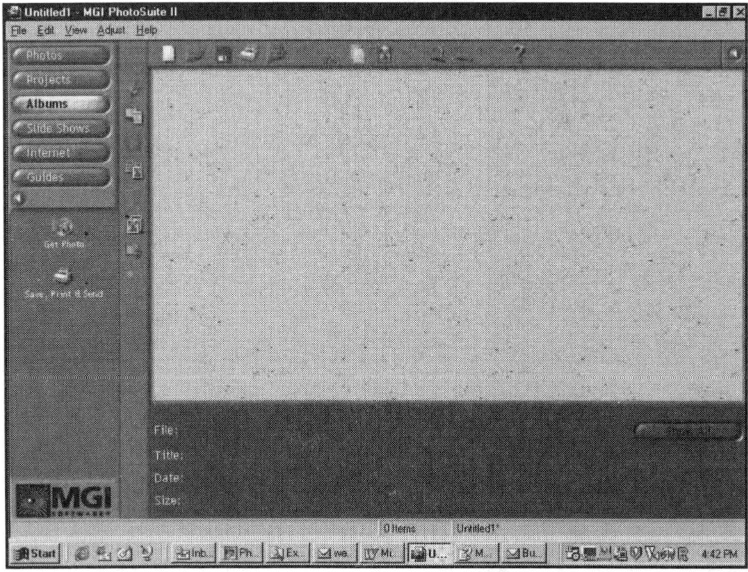

Figure 6-2
Your scrapbook isn't much to look at when you first start.

To scan a photo into your scrapbook:

1. Click Get Photo. This opens the box with your options, as shown in Figure 6-3.
2. Click the Scanner (TWAIN) button, and you'll see a screen like the one in Figure 6-4. Choose your scanner from the Twain Device list (it will probably be the only one listed, unless for some reason you have more than one scanner driver installed), and click the checkbox labeled Add to an Album. (If you've created more than one album or scrapbook, you can choose which one to add to from the listbox below that.)
3. Take the first photograph you want to add to your digital scrapbook, and place it into your scanner.
4. Click Get Photo. This will open your scanner's own software. Refer to your scanner's user manual if you have any questions about it, and carry out the scan. Once scanned, the picture will appear much like the one in Figure 6-5.
5. Repeat Steps 3 and 4 until you've scanned in as many items as you want to during this session.
6. When you're finished, click Close, and you'll see everything you've scanned as thumbnails within your album (see Figure 6-6).

Figure 6-3 PhotoSuite offers you several different ways to add items to your album/scrapbook.

Figure 6-4 These controls let you add the picture you're scanning to the album you've created.

Figure 6-5
My family scrapbook begins with a picture of my parents.

Figure 6-6
Your scrapbook is starting to take shape!

Adding Images from a Digital Camera to Your Album

To add images from a digital camera to your scrapbook:

1. Open MGI PhotoSuite II SE.
2. Click the Albums button. Either start a new album, as described earlier, or choose File, Open (or click the Open button) and open an existing album.

3. Click Get Photo. Depending on what kind of digital camera you have, either the Digital Camera (Direct) or the Digital Camera (TWAIN) button will be active.
4. If your camera is not one of those that PhotoSuite supports directly, you'll have to click the Digital Camera (TWAIN) button. In that case, the procedure for downloading pictures is essentially the same as getting pictures from a scanner. Refer to the first section on scanning pictures, but choose the digital camera from the list of TWAIN devices instead of your scanner.
5. If PhotoSuite directly supports your camera, you'll see a screen like the one in Figure 6-7. Choose your camera from the list, and click the checkbox labeled Add to an Album. If you've created more than one album, you can choose which one to add it to from the listbox below that.
6. Click Configure by the camera name to configure your camera for downloading (see Figure 6-8). You can set the connection type, port, and speed manually if necessary by choosing the appropriate entries from the listboxes. But if you let it, PhotoSuite tries to autodetect the camera. If that works, it's much simpler than changing settings yourself.
7. Click OK and, if the connection is working, you'll see thumbnails of all the pictures stored on the camera in the work area.
8. When you're done, click Close. All the pictures you've scanned as thumbnails will appear in your scrapbook/album.

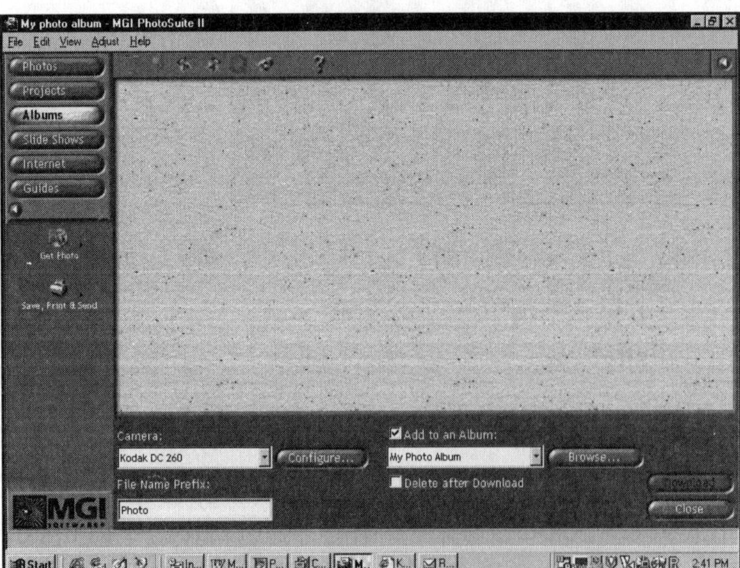

Figure 6-7
Add images from a digital camera with these controls.

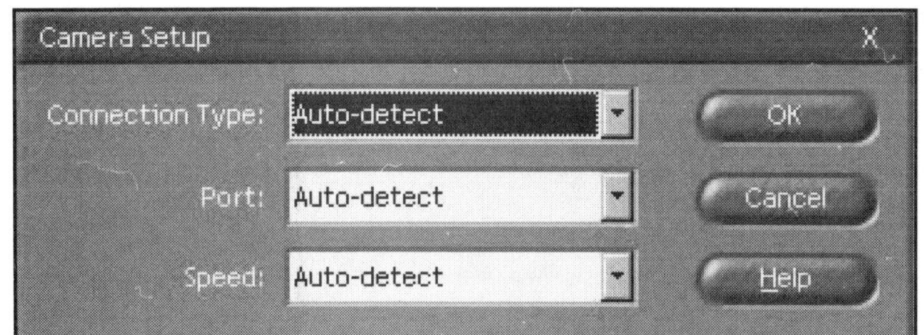

Figure 6-8
Configure your camera for downloading with the Camera Setup dialog box.

9. Click on the thumbnails you want to download into your scrapbook. To select more than one thumbnail at a time, hold down the Ctrl key while clicking.
10. If you want the pictures to be deleted from the camera's memory as soon as they're downloaded into your album, check the Delete after Download box.
11. Click Download. The pictures from your camera appear in your digital scrapbook.

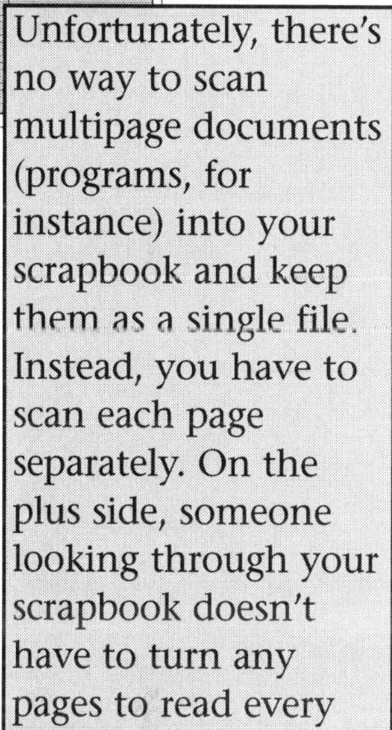

Unfortunately, there's no way to scan multipage documents (programs, for instance) into your scrapbook and keep them as a single file. Instead, you have to scan each page separately. On the plus side, someone looking through your scrapbook doesn't have to turn any pages to read every page of a multipage document!

Adding a Document to Your Scrapbook

To add a document to a digital scrapbook, you have to scan it in. Here's how:

1. Click Get Photo.
2. Click Scanner (TWAIN).
3. In the Settings area, choose your scanner from the TWAIN Device list.
4. By default, anything scanned into PhotoSuite is given the filename prefix Photo. Because this is a document, change the filename prefix to Doc in the File Name Prefix box. It may help you find the file on your computer later and in any event will make it easier to distinguish from scanned photos.
5. Make sure Add to Album is marked and that your scrapbook album is the one you're adding the document to.
6. Click Get Photo.
7. Your scanner's software will activate. Scan the document as usual.
8. The document is added to your scrapbook (see Figure 6-9).

Adding a Sound File to Your Scrapbook

Most of this book focuses on ways to make use of digital images, but pictures aren't the only thing that can be digitized: Sounds and video can, too—and you can add either to your scrapbook.

Figure 6-9
Now I've added a theater ticket to my scrapbook.

To add a sound file:

1. Click Get Photo (yes, I know, a sound file isn't a photo, but that's still what you click).
2. Choose Computer.
3. When the Add photo to Album dialog box opens, pull down the Files of type listbox and click on Audio files, which is second from the bottom (see Figure 6-10).
4. Locate the sound file you want to add to your album, highlight it, and click OK.
5. The sound file appears in your scrapbook with a special icon (see Figure 6-11).
6. Right-click and define properties for the sound file just as you did for the photo and the document.
7. To play the sound, double-click on the icon. The sound will be played by whatever program you've designated to play sounds on your computer.

If you have a sound card that permits auxiliary input, you can create your own sound files. Most sound cards come with software that allows you to record sound from other devices, such as CD and tape players (but be aware that the size of such files can grow astronomically

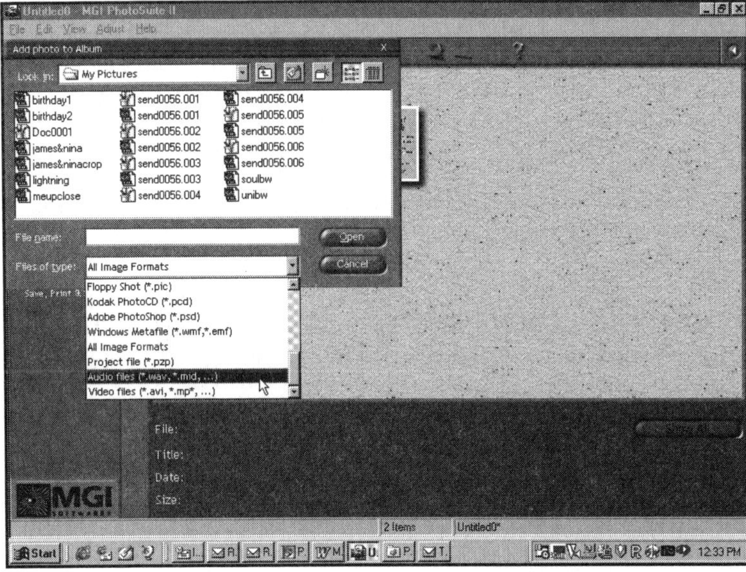

Figure 6-10
Tucked out of the way at the bottom of the Files of type list, when you add a "photo" from your computer, is the option to add a sound file, instead.

Figure 6-11
Here's what a sound file looks like when added to your scrapbook.

large in very short order). Thus, if you want to, and have the disk space available, you can add to your scrapbook a recording of, for example, your daughter singing a solo with her high school chorus.

On a more modest but extremely useful scale, you can create voice recordings right at your computer. These can be added to your scrapbook as stand-alone files—you could record, for instance, your baby saying Dada (if you can convince her to do so before your hard disk fills up)—or you can attach them to other files in the scrapbook. That means that if you wanted to, you could attach a recording of your voice to each item in your scrapbook that not only explains what that item is, but why you felt so strongly attached to it that you included it. Over the years, those recordings may well take on more and more significance for you and for your family.

Your sound card's software probably provides for microphone recording as well, but you don't have to use it; Windows itself lets you record a sound file at the drop of a hat.

To record, first make sure your microphone is plugged into your sound card and is in working condition. Then follow these steps:

1. Choose Start, Programs, Accessories, Entertainment, and finally Sound Recorder.
2. You'll see a set of controls very much like those on an ordinary tape recorder. The record button is the one on the far right; click it, say what you want to say into your microphone, and then click the stop button (second from the right). While you're recording, you'll see a visual representation of the sound waves your voice is creating in the oscilloscope window in the middle (see Figure 6-12).
3. Choose File, Save to save your recording as a .wav file.

Figure 6-12 Windows' built-in sound recorder lets you create a recording of your voice in seconds.

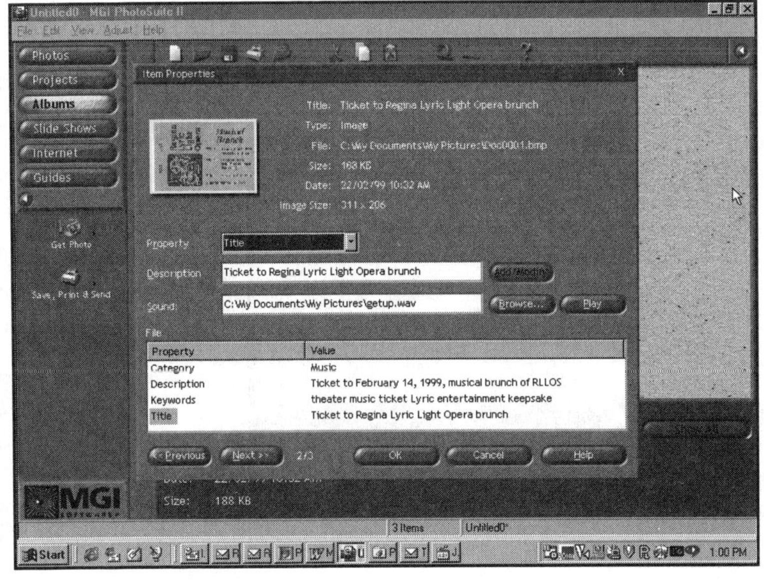

Figure 6-13
You can attach a sound file to an item in your scrapbook using the Properties dialog box.

Now you can add the file to your scrapbook as a stand-alone sound file (as described earlier) or attach it to another item in your scrapbook.

For instance, to attach the sound file I just created to the theater ticket I placed in my scrapbook earlier, I would

1. Right-click on the theater ticket and choose Properties.
2. In the Properties window, click the Browse button next to the Sound box, locate my sound file, highlight it, and then click OK.
3. Click Play to hear what it sounds like.
4. Click OK (see Figure 6-13).

To hear the sound file attached to any item in the scrapbook, just right-click on it, choose Properties, and then click Play in the Properties dialog box. (You'll look at the Properties dialog box in more detail a little later in this chapter.)

Adding a video file to your scrapbook

You can add a video file to your scrapbook in much the same way as an audio file:

1. Click Get Photo.
2. Choose Computer.

Figure 6-14 Here's what a video file looks like when added to your scrapbook.

3. When the Add photo to Album dialog box opens, pull down the Files of type listbox and click on Video files (the bottom category).
4. Locate the video file you want to add to your album, highlight it, and click OK.
5. The video file appears in your scrapbook with a special icon (see Figure 6-14).
6. To play the video, double-click on the icon. The video will be played by whatever program you've designated to play videos of that type on your computer.

Organizing Your Scrapbook

A scrapbook isn't very useful if it's not organized and if none of the items in it are labeled. It may all be clear now, but in 15 years, you'll be wondering who that strange little man is in that picture of you and what's-her-name, and exactly why you kept that piece of tissue paper with the lipstick stain on it.

The easiest way to rearrange items in your scrapbook is to simply click on each one and drag it to where you want it (see Figure 6-15).

You can organize items several other ways, but you need to provide more information about each item first. To do so, right-click on the item and choose Properties from the pop-up menu. This opens the Item Properties dialog box (see Figure 6-16).

Figure 6-15
To move items where you want them, just click and drag.

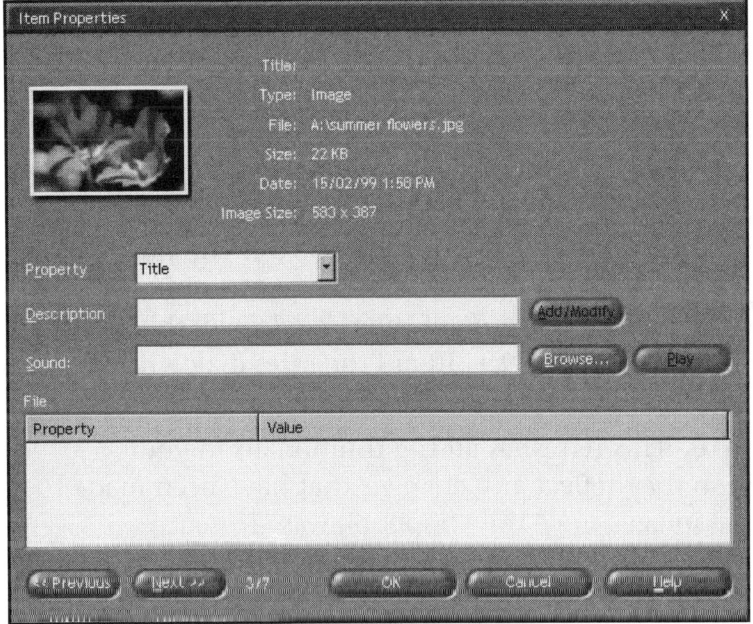

Figure 6-16
The Item Properties dialog box contains more information about each item.

The Property listbox contains several properties you can provide information about, ranging from aperture (for photographs) and author to subject and title. Choose the property you want to describe, and then type in a description. When you're happy with it, click Add/Modify. The property and its description will appear in the File box at the bottom.

Getting the Whole Family Involved

Scrapbooks can be very personal, but that doesn't mean they have to be the work of just one person. Digital scrapbooks are a great way to get the whole family involved in a digital project, by virtue of the fact that just about anything can go into them.

The key is to get people to think in terms of the scrapbook. Whenever anyone takes a roll of film (with a regular camera) or fills up the digital camera with images, make sure they designate certain pictures for the scrapbook. When the kids win ribbons at the science fair, scan the ribbons into the scrapbook. (Keep the real ribbons, too, of course; digital scrapbooks should complement the other kind, not replace them entirely!) When Granddad is interviewed by the local TV station for Veteran's Day, make a sound file and a video file if you can and put it in the scrapbook.

When you're recording sound files to attach to items in the scrapbook, don't just make them yourself; get everyone to say a word or two about the item. That way the scrapbook provides a record not only of events but of people's thoughts about those events.

A good scrapbook is an organic, growing thing; so is a good family. When you get everyone involved in creating and updating your digital family scrapbook, you'll soon find that you're also recording the growth and development of your own lives together.

You can move from item to item in your scrapbook without having to close the Item Properties dialog box by clicking the Previous and Next buttons. When you do want to close the Item Properties box, click OK. (Cancel closes the box without saving any of the information you've entered in it.)

Using Album Tools to Maintain Your Scrapbook

Down the left side of the Album screen is a toolbar with several useful tools you can use to maintain your scrapbook. From top to bottom, these tools are

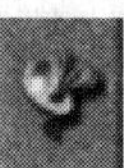

Open Photo. Click this button to open a photo for editing (see Chapter 2 for more information on using PhotoSuite's photo-editing tools).

Properties. If you have an empty scrapbook or haven't started one yet, this opens the Album Properties dialog box, where you can select the size of thumbnails and name your album/scrapbook. If you do have pictures in an open scrapbook, and one of them is selected, this opens the Item Properties dialog box described earlier.

Regenerate. This refreshes all the thumbnails in your scrapbook so they reflect any changes that have been made to the original images since the scrapbook was created.

Add. This lets you add a new photo (or sound, or video file) to your scrapbook.

Delete. Click this to delete a selected item from the scrapbook.

Sort. This opens the dialog box in Figure 6-17. You can sort the items in your album by any one of the many different properties you can describe in the Item Properties dialog box. Choose the property from the list provided, and then click Ascending or Descending to determine in which order items will be sorted.

Search. This opens the dialog box in Figure 6-18, where you can again select any one of the image properties and conduct a search for a particular word or words found in your description for that property. If you have a large album, this can help you find a particular image much more quickly.

With PhotoSuite II SE and a good scanner or digital camera, you may never need to buy a regular photo album again!

Sharing Your Scrapbook

You can't physically hand your digital scrapbook to someone to look at, but you can do something that in some ways is even better: You can turn it into a Web site, and post it to the Web in the space provided to you by AOL so that anyone can enjoy it.

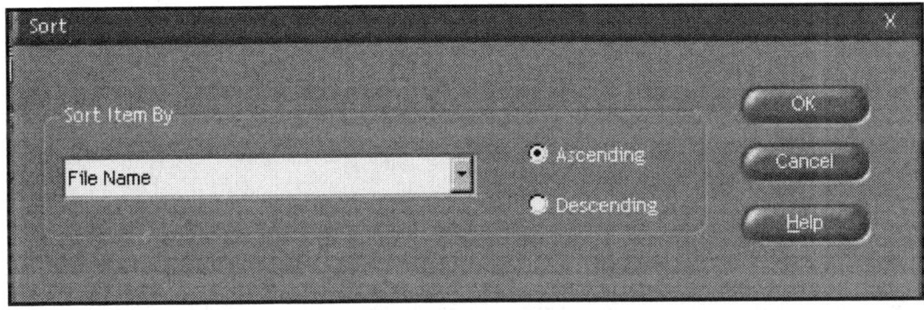

Figure 6-17 Sort your pictures by any one of the properties you've described.

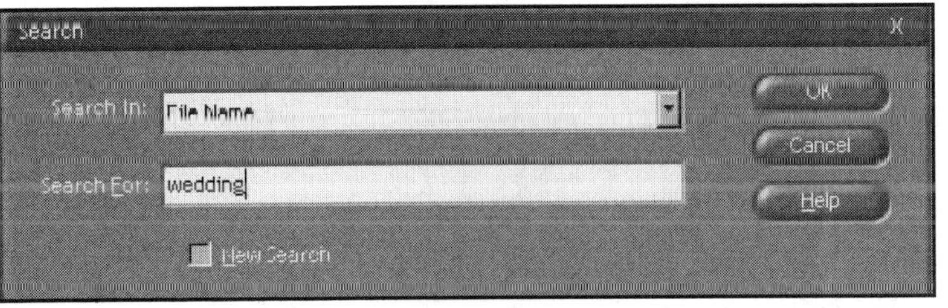

Figure 6-18 Use Search to quickly find specific images in a large album.

AOL does not allow spaces in the names of files uploaded to your Web space. To ensure that you'll be able to more easily post your album to your AOL Web space, do not include any spaces in its name.

Turning your scrapbook into a Web site is a one-click job:

1. Open your scrapbook.
2. Choose File, Create Web Page, or click Save, Print & Send, and then click Create Web Album.
3. A message appears telling you where the Web page is being saved. Note this for future reference.

That's all there is to it! To preview your Web page, enter the path PhotoSuite II SE indicated in Step 3 above into your browser. You'll see something like Figure 6-19.

Click on any one of the thumbnail images to open the full-sized image, as in Figure 6-20.

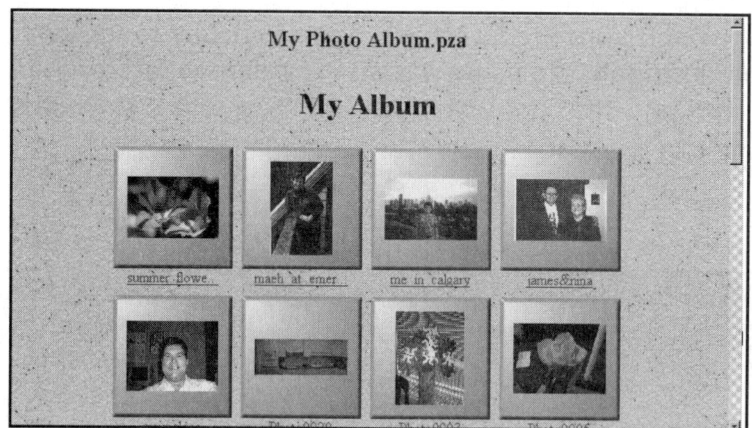

Figure 6-19 PhotoSuite can instantly turn your digital scrapbook into a Web site for sharing.

Figure 6-20 The full-sized images are only a click away.

The page containing the full-sized image includes the name of the image file, the title you gave it in the Item Properties box, and a link back to the scrapbook index page.

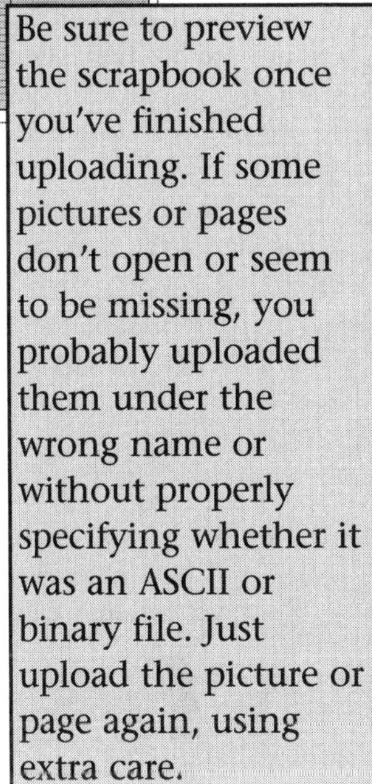

Be sure to preview the scrapbook once you've finished uploading. If some pictures or pages don't open or seem to be missing, you probably uploaded them under the wrong name or without properly specifying whether it was an ASCII or binary file. Just upload the picture or page again, using extra care.

The next step is to post the digital scrapbook to your AOL Web space. To do that, you'll have to use FTP. FTP stands for *File Transfer Protocol*, a tool for transferring files from your computer to the Internet, and vice versa.

To post your new Web album to your Web space:

1. Sign on to AOL.
2. Go keyword MYPLACE.
3. On the My Place welcome screen, click My FTP Space.
4. After a moment, the screen in Figure 6-21 will appear. It shows a list of everything that is currently stored in your FTP space. I recommend creating a new directory just for your scrapbook. To do so, click Create Directory, enter the name you want to assign the new directory (no spaces are allowed), and then click Continue. After you get a message telling you the new directory has been created, click Cancel to close the Create Directory dialog box.
5. Open the directory you want to upload your Web album into by double-clicking it.
6. Click Upload.
7. When prompted for Remote Filename, type in the name of your photo album, adding the file extension .htm. Click the ASCII (text documents) radio button, then click Continue.

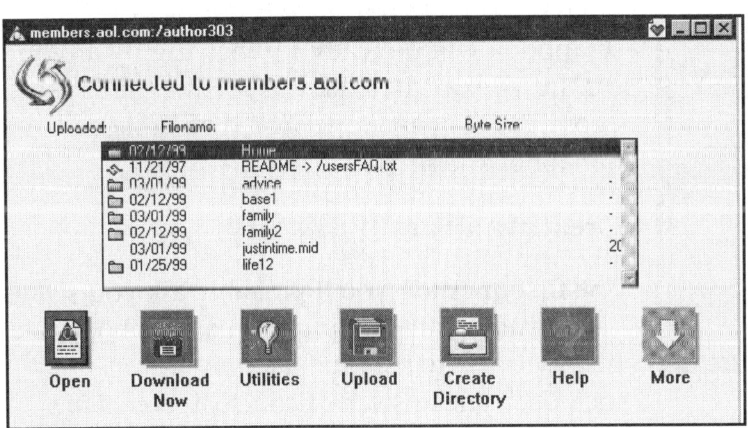

Figure 6-21
This dialog box shows you everything in your FTP space, which is also your Web space.

> **Optimizing Your Graphics with NetGraphics Studio 2 SE**
>
> If space is tight on your hard drive, a large digital scrapbook can fill it up in a hurry. One solution is to buy more storage space (see Chapter 18, "Make Room! Make Room!: Data Storage Options," for some suggestions); another is to reduce the size of the graphic files themselves.
>
> The NetGraphics Optimizer that's included on the CD as part of the NetGraphics Studio 2 program can do just that.
>
> For complete details on using this program, see Chapter 9, "The Family Web Site." Briefly, however, here's how you go about optimizing a graphic file:
>
> 1. Open the Optimizer.
> 2. Enter the location of the graphic you want to optimize, browse for it, or arrange your windows so you can click on it and drag it into the Optimizer. Click Next.
> 3. Specify the size of the graphic, and flip it horizontally or vertically, if you wish.
> 4. Click Next again, and the Optimizer analyzes the graphic and recommends either GIF or JPEG format (the two most common formats for graphics on the Web).
> 5. Click Next once more, and move the slider to choose between a small, lower-quality file or a larger, higher-quality file.
> 6. Click Next again, and choose whether you want the image to be interlaced or not. Interlaced images appear immediately as they are being downloaded, first at low resolution and then gradually sharpening until they reach full resolution. Noninterlaced images slowly take shape from the top down. This really only applies to images you're placing on the Web; if you're just trying to reduce the size of the pictures in a digital scrapbook, you don't really need to worry about this.
> 7. Finally, save your revised image. To save it over the original version, click Save; to keep the original file and the new version, click Save As. (Of course, that's not going to do a thing to free up disk space!)
> 8. To work with additional images, click Back to Beginning.

8. The Upload File dialog box opens; click Select File, and locate the index page of your Web album on your computer, highlight it, and click Open.
9. Click Send.
10. The first page is sent to your Web space.

Now you can send the rest of the files included in your Web scrapbook. The procedure is the same for each HTML file. The procedure for sending picture files is also the same, except that you must click the Binary (programs and graphics) radio button instead of the ASCII (text document) radio button after you've entered the Remote Filename.

Within the same directory as the index page, upload the picture files labeled cell_back and htmlbck. Then create a new directory called Pages inside your main directory, and upload all the files from the Pages directory of your Web scrapbook to the Pages directory inside your main directory. Finally, create a new directory called Thumbs inside your main directory, and upload all the files from the Thumbs directory for your Web scrapbook into the Thumbs directory inside your main directory.

This can take a long time if you have a large scrapbook, but once it's done your scrapbook will be ready for viewing by anyone on the Web at the URL `http://members.aol.com/YourScreenName/ScrapbookName/ScrapbookName.htm`.

Creating a Family History

The first question you'll probably ask yourself as you contemplate moving from a scrapbook to a history is, "What should a family history include?" The answer, of course, is *everything*.

Tips for beginning family historians

So you've just begun searching your family's past and you don't know where to start. Why not try these tips to get you going:

- **Relatives.** The greatest repository of knowledge about the family is the family, especially the oldest family members. Talk to them about their childhoods and the relatives they remember from when they were young. Tape record these conversations. Later, you can even make digital recordings of some of the anecdotes, and add those to your digital family history as sound files.
- **Your hometown library.** Your family may be widely scattered now, but chances are at one time many of the family members lived in the same town or district. A visit to the library there can unearth a treasure trove of historical material that mentions your relatives. The local librarian can help you research.
- **Your hometown courthouse.** Will, deed, and marriage books may contain some of those dates and details about who married whom when, as well as birth dates and death dates.
- **E-mail (and regular mail, too).** Not only should you correspond with other living family members to find out what details they may have about the family history, you should write and e-mail other organizations and societies members of your family have been involved with over the years. They may be able to provide details about a family member's cultural, political, or philanthropic activities.
- **AOL.** A good place to start is AOL's Family Life and Genealogy area (keyword Family Living). Here you'll find links to many other on-line sources of genealogical information and tips for researching your family tree.

All right, maybe *everything* is a bit broad but barely: No one who has developed an interest in their family's past has ever complained because too many photographs, letters, or other memorabilia were saved.

That said, future family researchers will be most interested in certain basic facts: who married whom, how many children they had, where they lived, when they were born, when they died, and what they did for a living. Once you have those basic facts, you can start filling in the details of lives lived.

Those details can include digital photos of keepsakes like "Grandma Spears' Wireless" or "Uncle Charles's Teddy Bear," as well as scanned images of old photographs, letters, invitations, dance cards, shipboard menus, or whatever else can bring the past alive.

Holding all these images together, however, will be text that explains what they are and how they fit into the context of the person whose life you're describing. To do the family history justice, someone has to sit down and write it: Write down the family stories that have been passed down about Great-Great-Aunt Samantha's hazardous passage to the New World aboard a leaking freighter or Great-Grandpa Alfred's heroics during the Great War.

The key to making a family history interesting, beyond the choice of images to include with it, is to bring the story alive through your text. As I said, genealogical researchers want all the facts included, so make sure they're there, but make sure the lives of the people involved don't get whittled down to nothing more than a dry recitation of dates, births, deaths, and addresses. You may not know much about some of your ancestors, but whatever stories have survived, preserve them. That's what a family history is for—keeping the family's collective memory alive.

Scanning Old Photographs

One basic task you'll probably find yourself doing often while you're working on your family history is scanning in an old photograph. Such photographs are often faded, yellowing, torn, cracked, scratched, stained, or dirty. But with PhotoSuite II SE you can go a long way toward restoring them to the way they looked when they were taken 70 or 80 years ago.

You scan in an old photo just like you scan in any other photo. (You should use a fairly high resolution—it will make fixing problems like cracks and scratches easier later. Generally, 300 DPI is a good choice.) In Figure 6-22, I've scanned an old black-and-white picture in PhotoSuite II SE. The picture has problems: it's yellow, cracked, and missing one corner.

Here's how I went about restoring this picture:

1. The first problem I noticed is that the picture is yellow. To restore it to pure black and white, I click Touch Up & Transform, Touch Up, and choose Fix Colors from the list of Touchups. Sliding the Hue and Saturation sliders to the far left removes all color from the image, making it look like a modern black and white photo (see Figure 6-23). I click Apply to apply the changes to the photo.
2. The picture looks rather dark. To lighten it up a bit, I choose Brightness and Contrast from the Touchups list and slide the

Figure 6-22
Old pictures, like this one of my grandfather holding my father, often aren't in very good shape.

Figure 6-23
By reducing hue and saturation to zero, I get rid of the picture's yellow tint.

Brightness slider a little further right. I don't touch the Contrast slider; the picture has plenty of that. Increasing contrast would make it look blocky and destroy detail. To get the brightness level just where I want it, I also choose View, Zoom In to get a closer look at the picture while I work (see Figure 6-24).

3. The picture has a number of cracks in it. To fix these, I click Edit Picture, and then click the Clone Tool button. The Clone Tool allows you to copy pixels from one area of a picture over another

Figure 6-24 Increasing brightness brings out a few more details from the shadows of the picture.

area. You click first where you want to copy the pixels from (the spot is marked with crosshairs), and then click again where you want the pixels to be copied to (where a second crosshairs appears). Holding down the mouse button allows you to paint the pixels under the first crosshairs into the place where the second crosshairs are. Using this carefully allows me to hide the cracks in the picture with unblemished pixels from other areas of the sky.

4. You can even use the Clone tool for more drastic repairs. This picture has one corner torn off. While I can't really replace that corner—who knows what was on it?—I can hide the damage. All I have to do is use the Clone tool to fill in the corner with dirt and rocks from another part of the picture, which is what I'm doing in Figure 6-25.

5. Finally, I save my restored picture under a new name. Figure 6-26 shows the differences between the original picture and the restored one.

Using Personal Publisher 3 to Create Your Family History

Once you've gathered together images, text, and maybe even sound files with which to create your family history, you'll want to assemble them into a coherent whole. And, since, presumably, everyone in the family will be interested in seeing the final project, you need to put it somewhere almost everyone has access to.

Figure 6-25
Careful use of the Clone tool can even fill in the missing areas of a picture.

Figure 6-26
My restored picture (on the right) may not be as good as new, but it's clearer, brighter, and no longer looks cracked or torn.

That somewhere is the World Wide Web, and the tool for putting it there is Personal Publisher 3, AOL's home-page creation tool. (For a more detailed discussion of using Personal Publisher 3 to create Web pages, see Chapter 9, "The Family Web Site.")

You can create your family history using any template, or even starting with a blank page, but you can save yourself a bit of work by using the Genealogy template AOL has already provided.

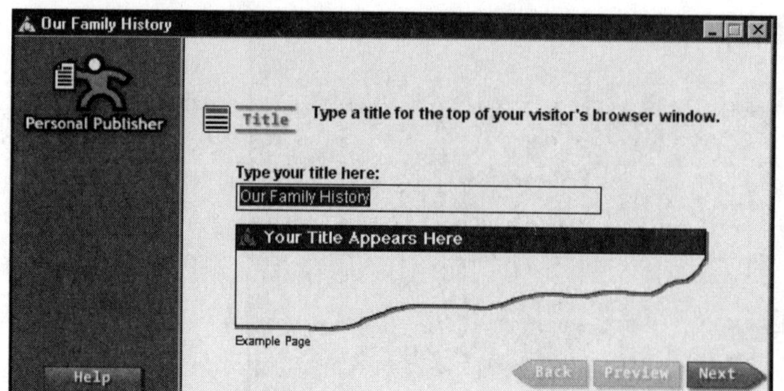

Figure 6-27 Your family history begins here.

> **NOTE**
> Make good use of the Link button while you're adding text. For example, suppose your text describes how your uncle came to Canada from Edinburgh; you could add a link to Edinburgh's city Web page. If he was a lifelong member of a professional organization, you could add a link to its Web page as well. Just highlight the text you want to add a link to, and then click Link. From the list of choices provided, choose Type Any URL, and type in the address of the Web page you'd like the text to link to.

To do so:

1. Sign on to AOL.
2. Go keyword PP3.
3. Click Create a Page.
4. Choose Genealogy from the list of templates.
5. Click Use This Template. Personal Publisher 3 will take a moment for the template to be downloaded to your computer, and then you'll see the screen in Figure 6-27.
6. Replace the sample text with your own title, and then click Next. (This title is what will appear at the top of your page in a browser and in the list of favorite places.) Now you have a choice of color schemes. Choose the one you like and click Next.
7. Now you get the opportunity to add a headline for the top of your page. I used "Our Family History." You can use the text-editing tools to make it bold or italic, change the size, or change the color. When you're done, click Next.
8. In the next window (see Figure 6-28), you can start entering the text of your family history. You can type it in directly if you wish, but an easier method is to open the text in a word processor, select it there, copy it, and then paste it into this window. Click Next when you're done.
9. Next, you're asked to add a picture. In my case, I'm going to add the picture I restored earlier in the chapter. To do so, I click Get My Picture, locate the file folder I stored the restored picture in, highlight it, and click Open Gallery. This shows me thumbnails of all the pictures in that folder; I find the one I want and double-click on it to add it to my page. A thumbnail of it replaces the "placeholder" picture in the template (see Figure 6-29).

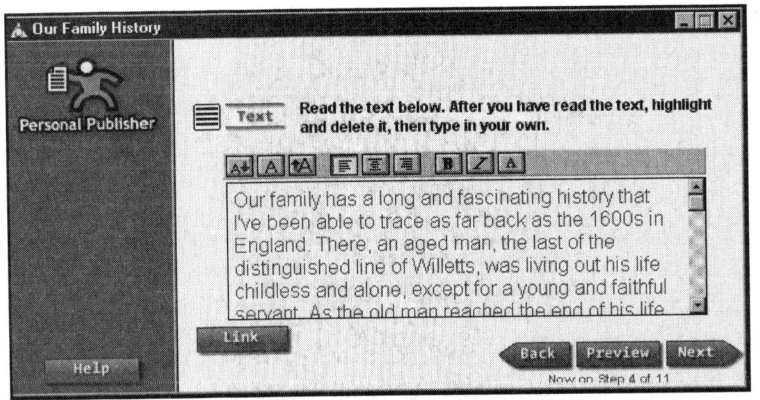

Figure 6-28
Here I've added the text for the first part of my family history.

Figure 6-29
I've added my restored picture to my Family History Web site.

10. Type a caption for the picture in the box labeled Enter Caption.
11. To change the size and orientation of the picture or add a border around it, click Format Picture. From the Format Picture window, you can click Edit Picture to do some additional editing of the photo (changing brightness and contrast, for instance); however, you'd be better off doing all that kind of editing in PhotoSuite II SE, which has more sophisticated controls.
12. Click Next, and continue to add text and pictures as the template prompts you. Eventually you'll be asked to add a list of Favorite Places. You can choose from your own list of favorite places or add a new link by clicking New and entering a description and the URL. When you're finished, click Next again.
13. The final option is to add an e-mail link that people can click on to drop you a line and a logo telling people you made this page with Personal Publisher 3. Make your choices, and click Done.
14. Personal Publisher will preview your page for you (see Figure 6-30). Click Edit if you'd like to make any changes. The Editor

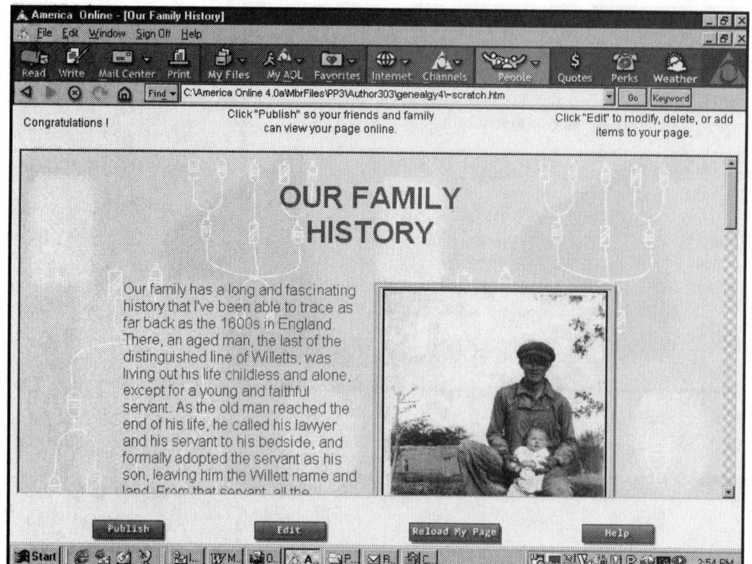

Figure 6-30 Here's the preview of my new Family History Web page.

provides a list of all items on the page. Click on an item in that list, and then click Edit Item to make changes.

15. When you're happy with your page, click Save. This saves the page on your computer. If you're ready to send it to your personal Web space on AOL, click Publish. AOL automatically saves the page in a directory within your Web space named after the template and, by default, names it index.htm. It tells you exactly where it's saving the page before it publishes it, so make a note.

Once the page is published, anyone can visit it by entering the correct URL into his or her browser.

Adding Additional Pages to Your Family History Site

Of course, it's quite likely that one page isn't enough to do your family history justice. To create a multipage site, create additional pages using the same template, but give them different names. Here's the easiest way to do this:

1. Open Personal Publisher 3 (keyword PP3).
2. Click Edit/View My Pages.
3. In the dialog box, as shown in Figure 6-31, find the first page of your family history in the list of files on your computer at right and highlight it.

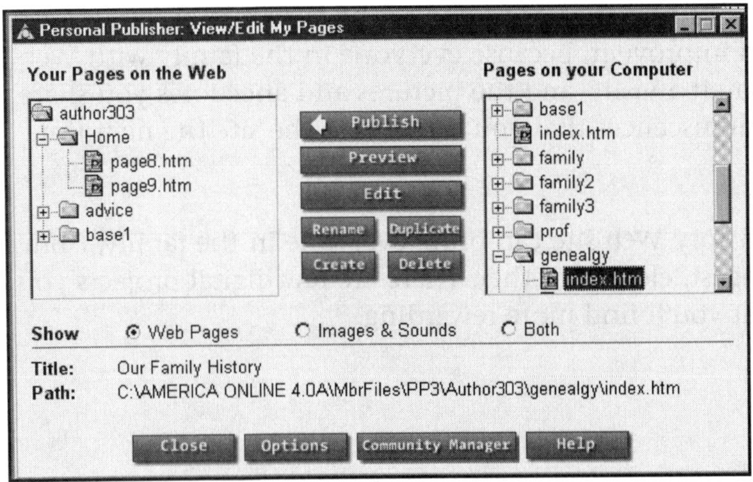

Figure 6-31
The easiest way to create new pages that look like your home page is to duplicate your home page here, and then edit the new pages.

4. Click Duplicate. This creates an exact duplicate of your index.htm page, with the name index2.htm. Click Duplicate several times to create as many additional pages as you need.
5. Highlight each duplicate page and click Rename to give it a name that makes organizing your site easier. For instance, if the second page of your site will focus on your grandparents, you could call it grandparents.htm.
6. Highlight each duplicate page in turn and click Edit to bring up the Editor; use it to change the pictures and text on the page as necessary.
7. Publish each page to your Web space.
8. Once the pages are published, click Options, and, in the window that opens, click Menu. You can choose which of your published pages you want to add to a menu that will appear at the bottom of all pages. The menu will become a built-in navigation system to help visitors get around your pages more easily.

Creating a Digital Family Tree

Here's a neat idea: Why not use Personal Publisher 3 to create an interactive family tree?

A traditional family tree begins with one couple, whose legacy branches off into offspring, who in turn branch off into more offspring, and on and on, just like a tree growing and spreading from a single trunk.

In a digital family tree, the initial couple has its own Web page, with links leading from it to Web pages for each of their offspring—whose pages, in turn, have links to pages devoted to their offspring.

Each page includes whatever information and pictures are available for that member of the family. By clicking from one page to the next, you can move smoothly through decades of family history.

Personal Publisher 3's built-in menu-creation function won't handle this very well. You need to manually create the links from each page to the offspring's page. Those links could be either text-based or activated by clicking on, for example, a baby picture.

It would take a lot of work to create even a small digital family tree, but the results would be spectacular and a remarkable portrait of that most remarkable of families: yours!

Once your family history is posted to the Web, you'll find it even easier to grow and improve it, because everyone in the family with Web access is sure to pay it a visit—and the pictures and anecdotes you share will spark new reminiscences that you can add to the site the next time you update it.

A family history Web site can bring everyone in the family, from the eldest to youngest, closer together. There are few digital projects you can undertake that you'll find more rewarding.

CHAPTER 7

PROJECT: The Vacation Slide Show

What You Need:

- Regular camera and access to a scanner or access to a digital camera
- ShowOff (on the CD)
- Microphone (optional)
- Sound card (optional)
- Vacation time
- A laptop computer (extremely optional)

Introduction

A few years ago I spent a month in Europe touring with my university chorus. I returned with 10 boxes of slides—almost 350 pictures in all. And I started showing them to people: just my family, at first, but soon those subjected to my travelogue grew to include friends, acquaintances, and eventually strangers I dragged off the street. It took a court order to finally bring the madness to an end!

Okay, so I exaggerate, but not much. Slide shows, along with home videos, have a bad rep, having been the butt of endless jokes in sitcoms for decades. There's a good reason for that: A bad slide show, full of uninteresting pictures of uninteresting people doing uninteresting things, is boredom city. The trick is to make it interesting.

When you create a digital slide show—as you will in this chapter—you've got ways to perk up your presentation that old uncle who used to bore you every summer with his slides never dreamed of, ranging from eye-catching transitions from slide to slide to a musical soundtrack, or even pre-recorded narration.

However, it all still starts with the pictures.

Planning Ahead

You have several options on how to get pictures for your digital slide show while you're on vacation. If you have a scanner, you can take regular photographs with your film camera—just be prepared for a long scanning session when you get back, and be sure you have lots of disk space!

Tips for Travel Photography: How to Photograph Anything

Here are some tips on how to photograph many of the subjects you're likely to come across in your travels:

- **Buildings.** Looking up at a building results in a distorted image, so try to find a high viewpoint, instead—up stairs, at the top of another building, or at the crest of a hill. If you can't get high, stand back. Try to include people for scale and human interest. Look for interesting details that you can zoom in on.
- **Interiors.** Stand back or shoot from outside through a window. Interiors are usually dim, so you'll need a long exposure—and that means you'll need a tripod, if they're allowed. (Flashes are rarely allowed in places like museums and churches, and the small flashes on most digital cameras can't fill a large room anyway.) If tripods aren't allowed, find some other kind of support (a wall or a railing, for instance). Using the self-timer can cut down on camera movement.
- **Landscapes.** Always have something in the foreground to give the image depth and scale. If that something is a person, you've added human interest, too! Look for a high vantage point such as a balcony, rooftop, or hill. Late afternoon is a good time for shots because the low sunlight casts longer shadows, highlighting more details.
- **Water.** If you're taking pictures of spraying water—a fountain, for instance—try to get the light to the side or behind the water so that it appears translucent (this works well with smoke, grass, and leaves, too). If you can control your shutter speed, try using a tripod and a slow shutter speed to give rushing water a soft, romantic blur.

You can also have your photos scanned to a CD at the same time as you're having them developed. Most photo stores offer this service now. It will save you time, and it means you don't have to buy a scanner!

An even easier method is to use a digital camera, but that comes with its own problems. You'll either need lots of extra storage capacity (usually flash memory cards), or you'll need to take a laptop computer with you so you can download pictures from the camera regularly, freeing it up for more.

The other option is to take both kinds of cameras. That way if the digital camera fills up and you don't have an opportunity to download it, you can take photos with your film camera, and you don't miss anything.

Also, be sure to take any camera accessories you might need. Both regular and digital cameras can benefit from the use of a tripod in low-light conditions. Tripods also let you take pictures of yourself, using the self-timer. Full-size tripods can be bulky, but a small table-top tripod can be very useful.

Additional lenses (if your camera lets you use them), a good camera bag that's comfortable enough to carry around all day, and a notebook to jot down notes about your pictures are also useful items.

Creating Your Slide Show

Once you have your photographs, you're ready to create your slide show.

On the accompanying CD, you've got a terrific piece of software for creating a personal slide show, called ShowOff.

The first step to creating your show, obviously, is to make sure that all your photos are in digital format. That means downloading them from your camera, either using the software that came with the camera or PhotoSuite II SE. Although it's not absolutely necessary, you'll find it a bit easier to create a slide show in ShowOff if you put all of the photo files into the same directory on your computer.

To turn your digital photographs into a slide show:

1. Open ShowOff.
2. By default, ShowOff immediately starts the ShowOff Wizard, which guides you step by step through the process of creating a slide show (see Figure 7-1). (If you don't want to see this wizard every time you start the program, uncheck the box in the lower-left corner labeled Show Wizard at startup.) Click Next.
3. The next screen of the wizard offers you four choices of actions. Click the top radio button, Create a Slide Show, and click Next.
4. The next screen (see Figure 7-2) lets you choose the location where ShowOff will initially look for pictures for the slide show. Click Change image location to browse your computer for the directory where you've stored the photos from your trip, locate it, highlight it, click OK, and then click Next.
5. When the next screen appears, click Finish to proceed with making your slide show. This opens the Slide Show dialog box in Figure 7-3.
6. By default, all the files in the directory you specified in Step 4 are shown in the top box at the right. If the directory is cluttered with non-image files, like the one in Figure 7-3 is, you can choose

Tips for Travel Photography: How to Photograph Anything (Continued)

- **Sunsets.** The best times to take pictures of sunsets are just as the sun is about to touch the horizon and about five minutes after it has set. Again, adding an object or person in the foreground adds depth (the object or person will appear as a silhouette). Keep the horizon low in the frame—the sky is what you're interested in. If you're taking a picture after the sun has set, you may need a tripod, because the shutter time may be slow.
- **In Bad Weather.** Bad weather can actually produce good photographs! For example, overcast skies reduce contrast, which makes trees and foliage show up better. If everything looks gray anyway, try shooting in black and white. Storms can result in very dramatic photographs, and as they arrive and clear, their clouds can create interesting patterns. Fog makes lakes, rivers, and valleys look ethereal and primordial. Rain or snow makes people wear colorful clothing, which can be an interesting contrast to the otherwise almost monochrome world.

Original version of these tips appears at http://www.photosecrets.com, *© 1999 Andrew Hudson, used with permission.*

to view only image files of a particular type with the Files of type listbox at left. SlideShow can use files in all the most popular image formats and a bunch more I've never even heard of. Once the box is displaying the files you want, add them to the slide show by highlighting them and then clicking Add. You can add one file at a time, select several at once by clicking on them one after the other while holding down Ctrl and then clicking Add, or add everything in the directory by clicking Add All. The order in which the slides are listed is the order in which they'll be displayed.

Figure 7-1 ShowOff is very helpful, immediately launching a wizard to help you create a slide show.

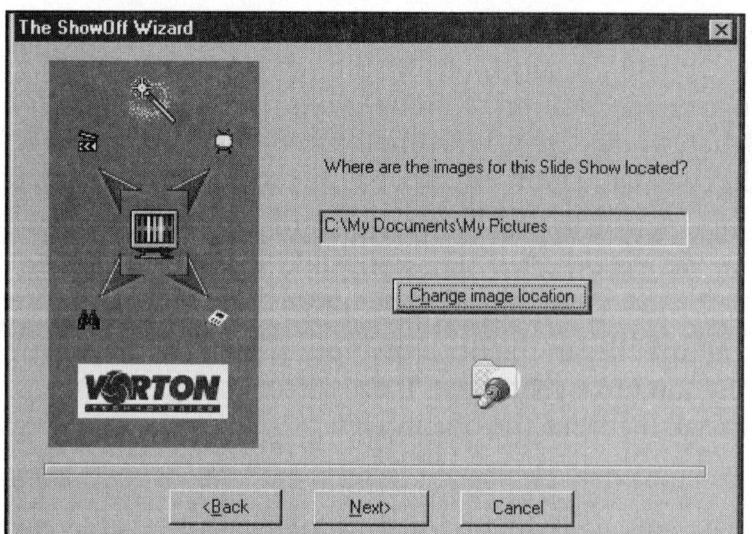

Figure 7-2 Specify the directory where you've stored your vacation pictures.

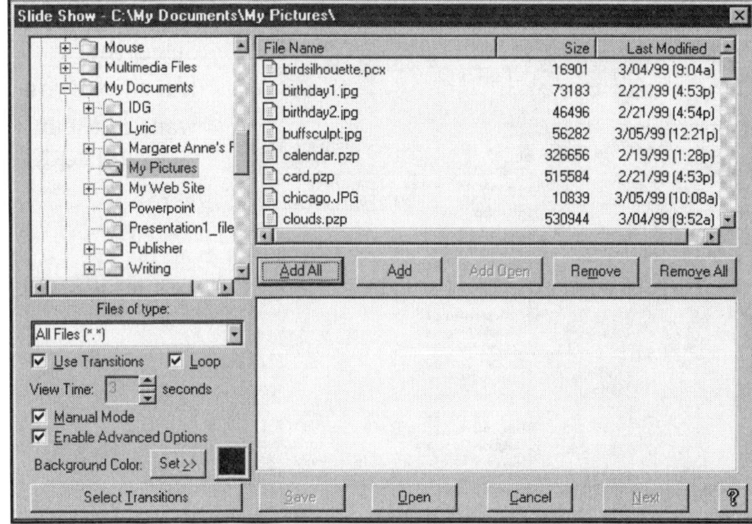

Figure 7-3 Use these controls to assemble the pictures for your slide show.

7. Once you've added the pictures you want to your slide show, check out the other options to set in the lower-left corner. By default, the Use Transitions checkbox is checked. Transitions are animations that make pictures slide on, fade in, pop up, and perform other interesting maneuvers as they appear. They add a lot to your slide show. To choose which transitions you want to use, click Select Transitions. This opens the dialog box in Figure 7-4.

8. As you can see, you can choose from a lot of transitions: They're listed in alphabetical order, and the ones in Figure 7-4 only go up to D! In this figure, all of the transitions are active and are applied to your slides randomly, so you never know how each slide will appear. To assign specific transitions to specific slides, click Remove All to deactivate any currently active transitions, moving them to the left side of this dialog box. Next, click the In Order radio button in the Mode area. Then highlight the first transition you want to use, and click Add. Repeat for each additional transition until you have one transition selected for each slide in your show. When you're satisfied with your transition settings, click OK.

9. Next to the Use Transitions checkbox is the Loop checkbox. Check this if you want the slide show to start over from the beginning when your reach the end.

10. Select the Manual Mode checkbox to advance slides manually by clicking a mouse button (clicking the left mouse button advances the slow to the next slide, while clicking the right calls up the

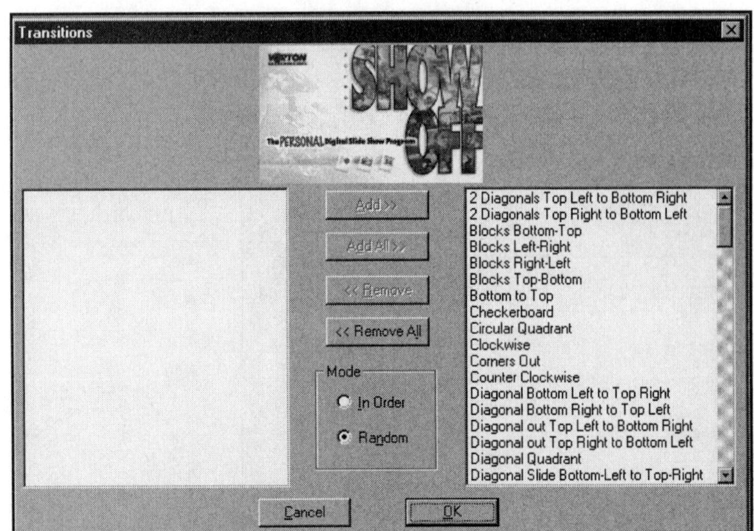

Figure 7-4
Select the transitions you want to use in your slide show here.

previous slide). You can program your slide show to run automatically by deactivating Manual Mode and then using the View Time scrollbox to set the number of seconds you want each slide to be displayed before the next one comes up.

11. Very few pictures take up the entire computer screen. To set the color that appears behind pictures in the slide show, click the Set button and choose the color you want from the palette provided.

If all you want to create is a simple slide show, then you're finished at this point. Deactivate the Enable Advanced Options checkbox, and the Save option becomes active so you can save your slide show now.

Generally, you'll want to do some additional tweaking. In that case, click Next. Now you can see the images you've added to your slide show in the Slide Show Images window at right (see Figure 7-5). You can also set many new options in the Advanced Slide Show Options dialog box. Suppose you left out a picture you meant to include: You can add it now by clicking Add New Image(s) and browsing for it. You can also save your slide show.

Adding Sound to Your Slide Show

You can use sound several ways in your slide show. You can use it just to spice up the process of going from slide to slide, so that as each slide comes up it sets off a chime, or some other sound effect (breaking glass, a gunshot, a bird call—whatever seems appropriate). If you prefer music

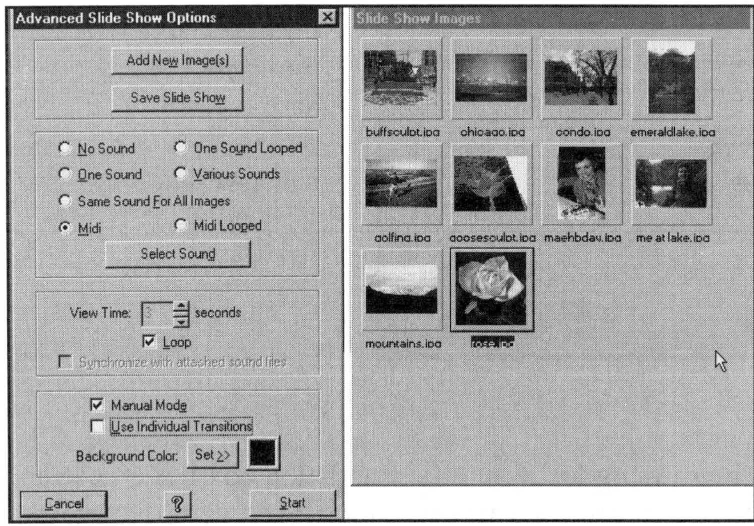

Figure 7-5 Add polish to your slide show with the advanced options.

to sound effects, you can set up your slide show with a musical background in MIDI format.

Here's how to add sound to your show:

1. Select the kind of sound you want to add. You have several options:
   - **No sound.** That's what you have right now.
   - **One sound.** This lets you set up a single sound that plays whenever you start the slide show.
   - **One Sound Looped.** This plays a single sound over and over, for as long as the slide show is being shown.
   - **Same Sound for All Images.** This repeats a single sound each time a new image is displayed.
   - **Various Sounds.** Choose this if you want to make different images trigger different sounds.
   - **Midi.** Choose this to play a single MIDI file once when the slide show begins.
   - **Midi Looped.** Choose this one to play a MIDI file over and over, for as long as the slide show is being viewed.
2. Click Select Sound. This brings up a dialog box that lets you browse your computer for the sound you want. If you've chosen One Sound, One Sound Looped, or Same Sound for All Images, only .wav files will show up as you browse. If you choose Midi or Midi Looped, only MIDI files will show up. Choose the sound you want and click OK. (You can preview any sound file by clicking Play.)

Figure 7-6 Record your voice as a .wav file with Windows' built-in Sound Recorder.

3. When you're browsing for .wav files, the dialog box has an extra button: Record. You can use this option to record your own voice-over for your slide show. Clicking it opens Windows' standard Sound Recorder (see Figure 7-6). The controls work just as they do on any cassette recorder. Provided your microphone is hooked up properly to your sound card, you can click the red record button and record whatever it is you'd like to say. Then choose File, Save and save the new .wav file somewhere on your computer. Close the recorder, browse for the file you just created, highlight it and click Select, and it's attached to your slide show.
4. If you clicked Various Sounds, you have to select a sound for each slide. To attach a particular sound to a particular slide, click on the slide. This opens the Image Options dialog box, whose third button currently reads Attach Sound. Click the Attach Sound button, and locate or record a sound just as you did in Steps 2 and 3. To continue adding sounds to slides, click on each slide and repeat the process.
5. Once you've attached a sound to a slide, all the buttons in the Image Options dialog box become active (see Figure 7-7). You can play the attached sound, remove it, or change it at any time. Click Finish when you're done.

Editing Your Slide Show

You've already seen the Add New Image button in the Advanced Slide Show Options dialog box. Notice that in addition to its sound-related buttons, the Image Options box in Figure 7-7, which appears after you click on a slide, also lets you remove a slide or change its position.

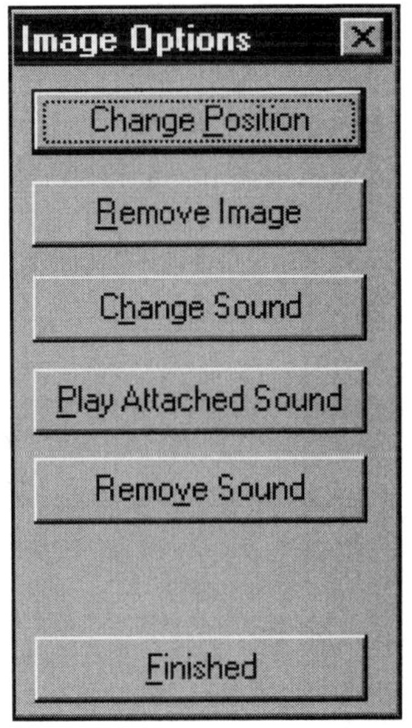

Figure 7-7
Change or remove the sounds attached to images using the Image Options dialog box.

When you click Change Position, another dialog box opens with a single control in it that allows you to assign a new position to the selected slide.

In the Advanced Slide Show Options dialog box you have some additional options:

- **View Time.** You can set a fixed time that slides will be displayed, or you can synchronize the image view time with attached sound files. This is a great option if you've created a complete slide show narration by recording comments for each slide in the show. Each slide will be displayed for as long as the recording lasts, and then the next one will come up.
- **Manual Mode.** As noted earlier, Manual Mode displays each slide until you click a mouse button. Clicking the left mouse button advances the show to the next slide; clicking the right mouse button returns it to the previous slide.
- **Use Individual Transitions.** This lets you attach specific transitions to specific images a lot more easily than carefully arranging the transitions in the same order as the slides during the initial set up. When this box is checked and you click on a slide in the show, there's a new button in the Image Options dialog box: Add Transition. Clicking it opens the Transitions dialog box, shown in Figure 7-8.

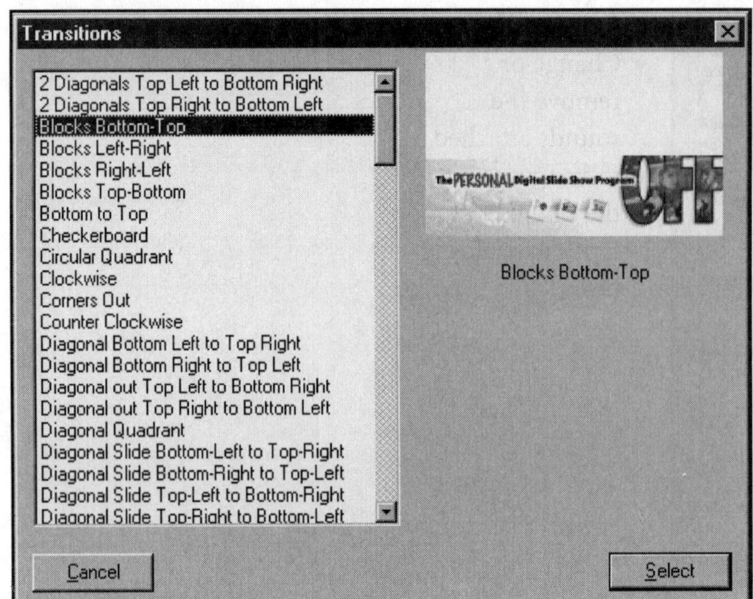

Figure 7-8
You can make each slide in your slide show appear in a unique fashion.

Simply choose the transition you want from the list at left. Don't worry if you don't know what it does: As you highlight each transition, it's previewed for you. (The transitions you set here, by the way, override any transitions you established during the initial setup.)

- **Background.** To set the background color that will appear outside your slides' boundaries, click Set. Choose the color you want from the palette, or create your own custom color by moving the crosshair over the large color box at right. If you create a new color you like, click Create Custom Color to make it available.

Running Your Slide Show

When you're ready to view your slide show, click Start. You'll be prompted to save your show, and then it's off and running (see Figure 7-9).

If you're running your slide show in Manual Mode, remember to click the left mouse button to advance to the next slide and click the right mouse button to go back to the previous slide. To stop the show and return to ShowOff, press Esc.

Figure 7-9 Here's a slide of the beautiful Canada Geese sculpture I saw on my recent trip to downtown Regina, Saskatchewan. (Okay, so it's only four blocks from my home—it still counts as a trip!)

Creating a Runtime Project

A regular slide show is fine if you're planning to have people over to see your show, but what if you want Aunt Ethel in Omaha to see it, and you live in Nova Scotia?

If Aunt Ethel also happens to have ShowOff, you could e-mail her the slide show and all the sound and picture files that go with it, but that would be a major undertaking. Fortunately, ShowOff has a solution. Instead of creating a slide show, create a Runtime project.

Runtime takes the images and sounds you specify and turns them into a single, compressed executable file. All you have to do is e-mail that file to Aunt Ethel; she starts it like she would any other program and can enjoy your slide show, and even your voice, if you attached sound files, at her own computer in Omaha.

Creating a Runtime project is almost exactly the same as creating a slide show, but with slightly fewer options:

1. Start ShowOff.
2. Choose Tools, Create Runtime.

3. Select the images for the Runtime project just as you did for the slide show, from the dialog box in Figure 7-10. When you're done, click OK.

4. The next screen also looks very similar to what you saw while creating a slide show. Again, all of the images you selected are displayed as thumbnails at right, while controls for fine-tuning your project are at left (see Figure 7-11). These controls are almost-but-not-quite the same as those for slide shows. They include

   - **Add New Image(s).** Use this to browse for additional images to add to your Runtime project.
   - **Save Current Project.** Click this to save your project to disk.
   - **Create Runtime Player.** Click this when you're ready to create the executable Runtime file with the current image and settings.
   - **Select Sound.** This works exactly the same as the Select Sound options for slide shows.
   - **View Time.** You can set a specific length of time for slides to be displayed or synchronize them to attached sound files. You can also set the project to run as a continual loop or to play through once and then stop.
     If you want images to start flipping automatically as soon as the Runtime file is launched, select Auto play on startup.

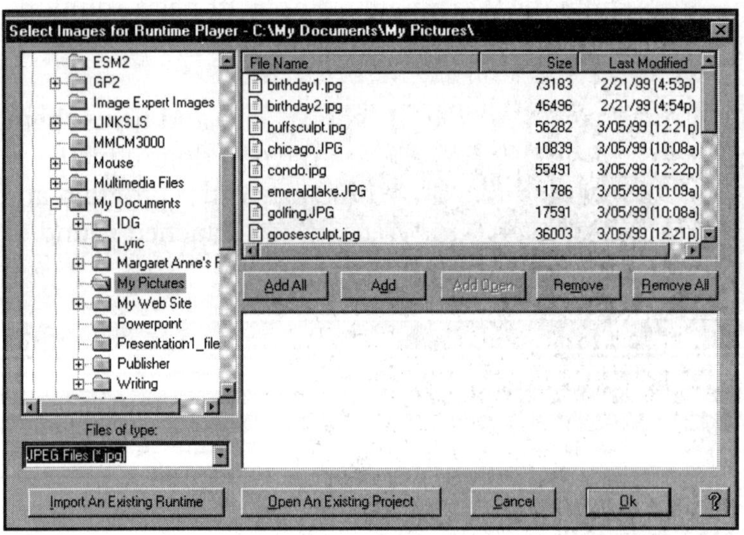

Figure 7-10 Choosing images for a Runtime project is almost the same as choosing images for a slide show . . .

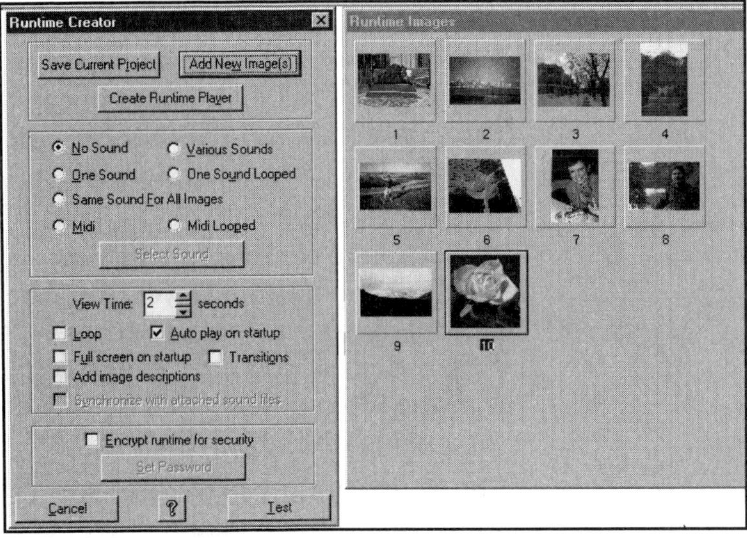

Figure 7-11
. . . and the next screen is very similar, too.

If you want to add a description to each image—a caption—activate Add image descriptions. You can then click on any thumbnail, click Add image description from the Image Options dialog box, and type in a caption up to 60 characters long.

Full screen on startup automatically maximizes the Runtime window whenever the project is started.

Runtime projects, alas, don't have as many transitions to choose from as slide shows. If you activate Transitions, two different transitions called horizontal blind and vertical blind are alternated.

- The final option is Encrypt runtime for security. If you only want people who know the correct password to be able to view your Runtime project, check this, and then click Set Password and enter the password you want to attach to it.

Five Ways to Spice Up Your Slide Show

Here are a few ways you can liven up your slide show. You want to keep them awake, right?

- **Add a title slide.** Use PhotoSuite's Project tools to create a title slide by adding text over an interesting background photo. If your trip included several destinations, create a title slide for the photos from each place. You can even add a "The End" slide so your victims—um, viewers—know when it's all over. Just remember to save the title slide not as a project but as a single image (I'd recommend .JPG format) so you can use ShowOff to add it to your slide show.
- **Choose your sounds carefully.** You have two ways to add sounds to a slide show, if you're not already using pre-recorded narration. One would be to add appropriate sounds: bird calls for that slide of your visit to the aviary or the sound of surf for the pictures from the beach. The other approach is to be funny (my personal choice!).

Five Ways to Spice Up Your Slide Show (Continued)

- **Improve upon nature.** These aren't regular film-based photographs, and you shouldn't treat them as such. In PhotoSuite II SE, you have a powerful imaging-editing tool: Don't be afraid to use it. Create artistic effects. Crop pictures to improve them. Change the colors. Increase the contrast. Create slides that are collages from several different pictures. In other words, do the sorts of things that you used to need several thousand dollars' worth of equipment and your own darkroom to achieve. It will make your slide show more interesting and memorable for both you and your viewers.
- **Tell a story.** PhotoSuite II SE provides you with word balloons for a reason—use them! You can insert the actual comments people in a picture were making at the time you were taking it, or, if you're more interested in humor than truth, stick in the comments they should have been saying!
- **Edit.** The trouble with most slide shows is that they include everything—every single slide that was taken, good, bad, or indifferent. Don't do that. Only use your best and most interesting pictures. Combined with the other techniques I just mentioned, that simple principle will ensure that people look forward to seeing your pictures, instead of trying to avoid them.

5. When you've set all the options you want, and added sounds and image descriptions as required to the various slides, preview your project by clicking Test.
6. When you're completely satisfied, click Create Runtime Player. You'll be prompted to save your project as a project first, so you'll be able to edit it in the future; then you'll be asked for a name for the player.
7. Run your Runtime player like you would any other program on your computer (see Figure 7-12).
8. Notice that the recipient of the player can now reset many of the display options, such as whether it will show full screen. He can even use one of the pictures as his wallpaper!

Once that big trip is over, the memories start to fade. But digitize those memories and they'll stay fresh and sharp. Thanks to ShowOff, you can share them more easily, too—even with people who you could never drag into attending a showing of slides at your house.

Go to keyword Travel Photography to find lots of good tips for taking better photos while you're traveling (or any other time).

Go to keyword MIDI to find MIDI files you can use for background music.

Figure 7-12
Once you've saved your slide show as a Runtime player, you can e-mail it with ease as a single executable file.

CHAPTER 8

PROJECT: Create Your Own Animated Cartoon

What You Need:

- Access to a scanner or digital camera
- GIF animation software (downloadable from Internet)
- Paper and pencil

Introduction

Once upon a time, I dreamed of becoming an animator for Disney. I wanted to draw wonderful adventures like *The Jungle Book* and *101 Dalmatians*.

It never happened. I decided to tell my stories with words instead of pictures. But I've never lost my love of animated films; and now, with the advent of the personal computer, it's possible for anyone to create his or her own animated cartoons at home.

Not, I hasten to add, that what you're going to create in this chapter will pose any threat to the Disney empire. But you can use animation to spruce up your family Web page (which you'll create in the next chapter), and you can have a lot of fun doing it!

What Is GIF Animation?

The kind of animation you're going to create in this chapter is called GIF animation because the individual drawings that comprise it are stored in GIF format. GIF is one of the two most common formats for images on the Web (see sidebar).

Animated GIFs are great for viewing on the Web because they don't require any special plug-ins or complicated programming. You can simply insert the finished animation into your Web page like you would any other graphic; your visitor's browser takes care of displaying it properly.

How Does Animation Work?

In the early 19th century scientists discovered that a sequence of still pictures, viewed rapidly one after the other, can given the illusion of movement. They called this "persistence of vision," which is just a fancy way of saying that your eye hangs on to an image for a fraction of a second after the object you're looking at is gone. The lingering of each image between the time it's removed and the next image in the sequence is displayed somehow fills in the gap between the two, so that instead of seeing each picture jerkily appear, you see a smooth illusion of movement.

If too much time elapses between seeing one image and the next, the illusion of movement is disrupted, and eventually you realize that you're really just watching a high-speed slide show.

Regular movies run at 24 frames per second, plenty fast enough to create the illusion of smooth movement. Video in North America runs at 30 frames per second. However, the illusion of movement holds down to about 1/10th of a second, which is about the time persistence of vision lasts.

None of the programs on the CD that accompanies this book lets you create animated GIFs, but that's not a problem: You can download dozens of easily accessible shareware and freeware programs on the Web.

Whatever program you choose to use (you may even have a graphics program already on your computer that can create animated GIFs), the basic process will be something like this:

1. Create a series of still digital pictures, each of which advances the action a little bit (more on this a little later).
2. Save each picture in GIF format. You can do this in PhotoSuite II SE. Open the file in PhotoSuite II SE, and then choose File, Save As. Give the picture an easily recognizable name, such as cartoon1 (the first frame of the cartoon, get it?). Then, from the Save as type listbox, choose CompuServe image (*.gif), and click OK (see Figure 8-2).
3. In your GIF animation software, insert the pictures one after the other.
   Most software allows you to preview your animation as you work, so you can see if it's turning out all right. If it's not, you may have to rearrange the order of the pictures or add or delete pictures. (See the sidebar at the end of this chapter for more information on how to make your animations look better.)
4. Save the completed animation. Like the pictures that make it up, it will have a .gif suffix. To view it, just open that .gif file using your Internet browser.

A good place to look for GIF animation software is in AOL's Download Software area (keyword Download Software). Under the Shareware tab, double-click on the Graphics folder and choose Graphics Utilities (see Figure 8-1). You can find animation software in the A&V & MM Creative Tools software library, the Draw & Paint-Windows library, and the Graphics Utilities-Windows library.

One excellent package available in AOL's Download Software area is called the GIF Construction Set; it's also probably one of the most popular programs for creating GIF animations.

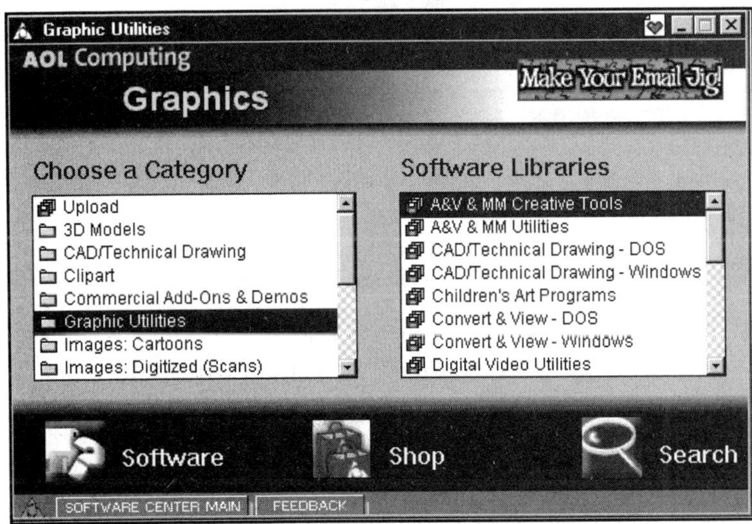

Figure 8-1 AOL's Download Software area has several graphics utilities libraries where you can find programs to help you create GIF animations.

Drawing Images for Your Animation

If you, like me, have had a hankering to try your hand at traditional hand-drawn animation, the computer makes it possible. Here's how:

1. Get out some paper and something to draw on it with—pen, pencil, or paintbrush; it doesn't matter.
2. Draw the first image of your cartoon.
3. Draw the second image, advancing the action just a little bit, and trying to make your second drawing exactly the same size as your first (although you can correct some problems with size, and so on, on the computer, it'll save time if you get it right from the beginning).
4. Continue drawing images until you've created the entire cartoon.

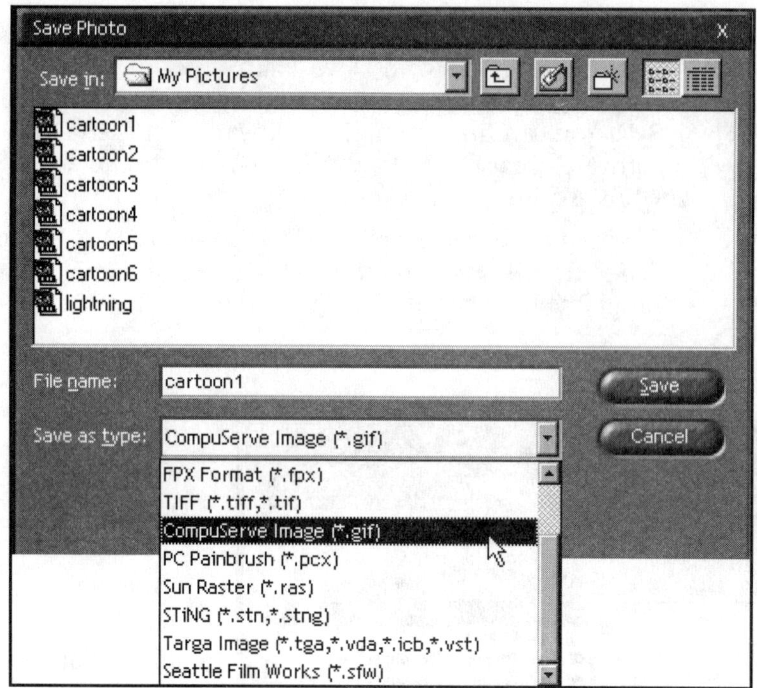

Figure 8-2 The first step to turning a series of digital images into an animated GIF is to save them as GIF files.

5. Place the first image into your scanner. In PhotoSuite II SE, click Photos, Get Photo, and then Scanner (TWAIN). Scan in the photo (see Figure 8-3).
6. Place the second image into your scanner. Scan it in (see Figure 8-4).

Figure 8-3 Here's the first frame of my animated GIF . . .

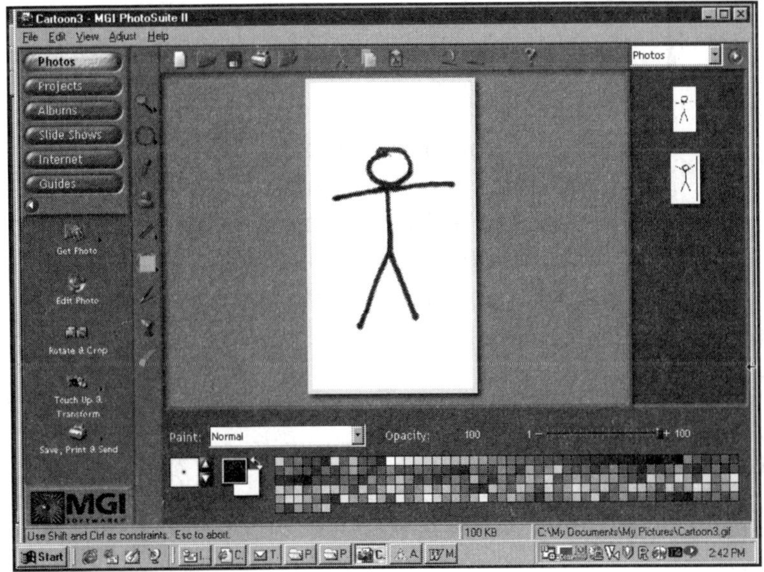

Figure 8-4
. . . and here's the second. Notice how the position of the arms has changed slightly.

7. Continue scanning until you've opened each image of your cartoon in PhotoSuite II SE. Now follow Steps 2 to 4 from the earlier description of how to create an animated GIF.

8. Once your GIF is created, view it in your browser by choosing File, Open, and then the name of the animated GIF file (see Figure 8-5).

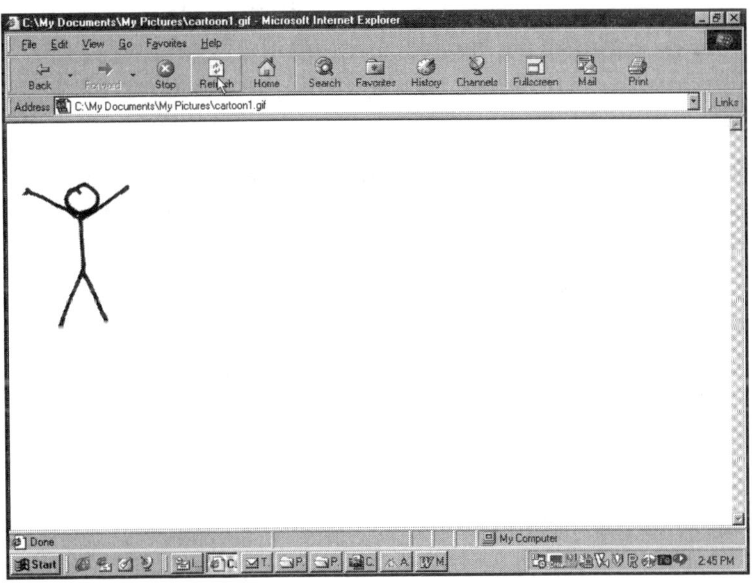

Figure 8-5
In my browser, my little animated stick-figure flaps its arms wildly (you'll have to trust me on that).

What's a GIF?

The most common graphic formats on the Web are GIFs and JPEGs. Essentially, they're both methods of compressing graphics files so they don't take as long to transmit over the Internet.

GIF stands for *Graphic Interchange Format.* It was popularized by CompuServe (now owned by America Online) in the 1980s, which is why PhotoSuite II SE calls it "CompuServe image" in the Save as type listbox. It was well-established by the time the World Wide Web appeared in the early 1990s, and as a result, the majority of the first pictures on the Web were GIFs.

The method of compression used to create GIF images limits them to 256 colors. That limitation helped JPEG (an acronym for *Joint Photographic Experts Group*) become popular: JPEGs can display millions of colors.

JPEG files are also often smaller than GIF files because the JPEG compression system lets you decide how much you want to compress a picture file (although the smaller it gets, the poorer the quality).

JPEG compression makes photographs look great but can make diagrams and text blurry. As a result, most Web pages use GIF for most graphic elements involving text, while reserving JPEGs for photographs.

Photographing Images for Your Animation

You don't have to draw your own images, of course. If you have a digital camera (or if you have a regular camera and are willing to wait for the film to be developed before creating your animation), you can take photographs that, in turn, you can use to create an animated GIF.

For example, I created a simple animation of a dancing knife using my digital camera, PhotoSuite II SE, and my GIF animation software. Here's how:

1. I took a series of photographs of the knife, moving it slightly between each photo.
2. Next, I downloaded the pictures into PhotoSuite II SE (see Figure 8-6).
3. I saved each picture as a GIF file, naming them knife1, knife2, and so on.
4. Next, I inserted each picture into my GIF animation software, in this order: knife1, knife2, knife3, knife4, knife3, knife2, knife1. By moving backward through the sequence, I create the illusion that the knife moves, then moves back to where it started from.
5. Finally, I use my GIF animation software to make the animation loop endlessly and adjust the timing of the animation to make it look as smooth as possible (to make it really smooth, I'd need to take several more pictures so the movement from one frame to the next isn't as large).
6. I save the animation and then use Internet Explorer to watch it (see Figure 8-7).

Figure 8-6
Here's the initial photograph of my "dancing knife" series. You can see the others, each with the knife slightly repositioned, in the Photo Library at right.

If you're planning to post your GIF animation to the World Wide Web, you'll probably want to stay away from large photographic images like my knife picture. Although the computer is capable of displaying the images quickly enough for the animation to be effective, it first has to load them. That doesn't take long when you're loading off of your hard drive, but each frame of my knife animation is almost one megabyte in size, making the full GIF animation almost four megabytes in size. Nobody is going to stick around long enough to see your animation if it's that large and consequently takes several minutes to load. Most GIF animations posted to the Web are very small for that reason. In the case of my animated knife, I could reduce the file size by using PhotoSuite II SE's tools to remove the background from each picture, leaving only the knife. I could also make the image itself smaller.

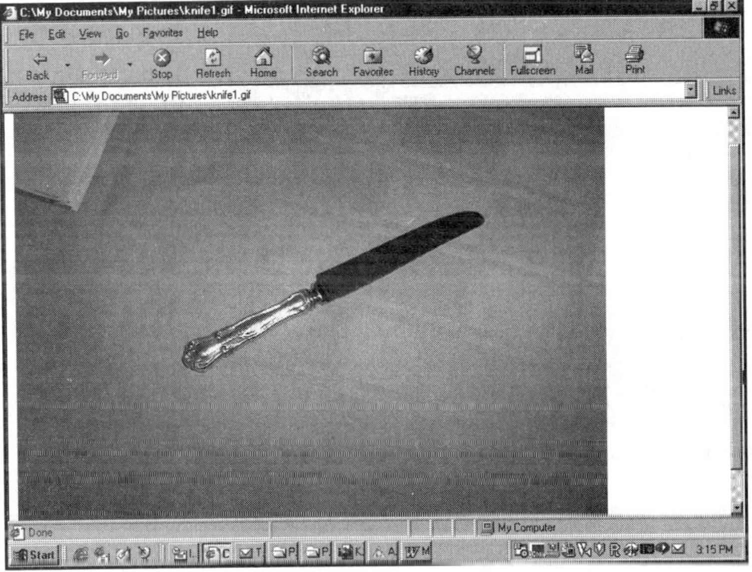

Figure 8-7
I know you can't see it, but this knife is actually dancing up a storm.

Tips for Better Animation

Here are some basic principles to keep in mind whenever you're creating animations:

- **Ease into movements.** Suppose you're animating someone lifting his arm. The first couple of frames of the arm lifting should vary less than the following frames. For some reason, we perceive a series of equidistant movements as jerky. Easing into the movement—and out of it—makes it smoother.
- **Use key drawings.** Professional animators draw the high points of movements first and then add the in-between movements. The high points are called "key drawings." Getting those down first makes your animation look more dramatic and allows you to ease into and out of the high points, as described above, for a smoother effect.

Creating Animations from Existing Images

Another fun way to approach animation is to edit existing images, using PhotoSuite II SE's editing tools. For instance, the Wind effect added to my knife images (see Figure 8-8) could add a nice feeling of speed.

Another possibility is to simply use a static photo, but alter it little by little, saving each intermediate stage as a separate GIF file. Figure 8-9 shows the photo I started with, and Figure 8-10 shows the photo I finished with. My saving a number of stages in between, I

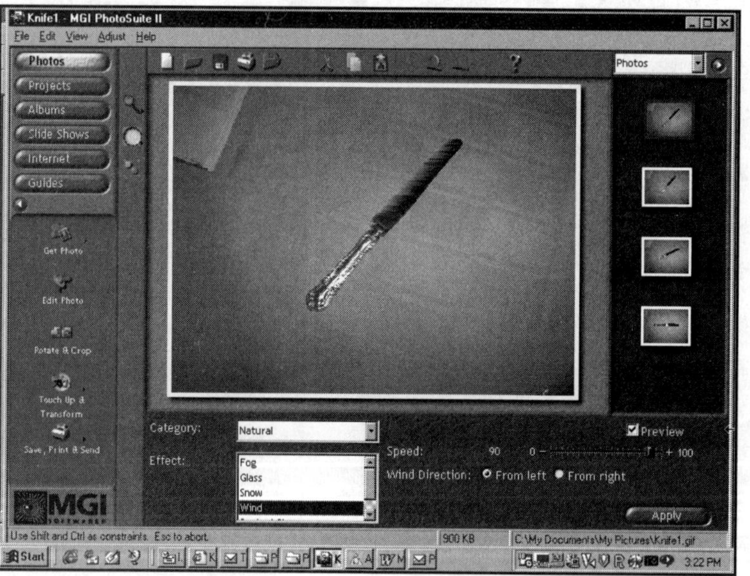

Figure 8-8
You can almost hear this knife whistling as it cuts the air.

created a rather unsettling GIF animation of my head going in and out like a balloon.

Use your imagination and all of PhotoSuite II SE's special effects, and see what interesting animations you can create!

Tips for Better Animation (Continued)

- **Plan ahead.** Know where you're going with your animation, or you probably won't get there. Sketch it out roughly before creating the final images. Even if you're taking photographs, thinking carefully about what you hope to accomplish ahead of time can save you a lot of fixing up later.
- **Emphasize movement.** There are several tricks to this. If the person or object you're drawing is going to make a big move, go backwards first. This gives a quick hint of what's going to happen and makes it more believable. Then, after the move, let the object go slightly beyond the final point—like a pitcher's arm staying in motion after the ball is released. Finally, let objects squash and stretch. A ball hitting the floor doesn't stay round, for instance: It squashes into an oval shape and then springs out, actually stretching beyond round into another oval shape, as it leaps back into the air. Emphasizing this in your animation makes it look more fluid and believable.
- **End where you began.** Most GIF animations play as an endless loop, so you need to have your final drawing lead smoothly back into your initial drawing. That way the animation continues without missing a beat. This is what I did in creating my knife animation.

Figure 8-9 I created an animation that shows my head going from its normal (more-or-less) appearance . . .

Figure 8-10 . . . to this— and back again.

CHAPTER 9

PROJECT: The Family Web Site

What You Need:

- Personal Publisher 3 (keyword PP3)
- NetGraphics Studio 2 (on the CD)
- Hemera Photo-Objects SE (on the CD)

Introduction

You've already created several digital projects and learned how to create your own digital images. You've also spent quite a bit of time on the World Wide Web. By now, you're probably hankering to create your own Web page and post some of your projects and images for the whole world to see—or as an easier way of sharing them with friends and loved ones than individually e-mailing everyone.

In this chapter you'll learn how to do that using AOL's own easy but powerful Web-page creation program, Personal Publisher 3, and how to use two of the programs on the CD that came with this book, NetGraphics Studio 2 and Hemera Photo-Objects SE, to enhance your page even more.

Ready? Let's get started.

Some early versions of AOL 4.0 do not support Personal Publisher 3. If you get an error message telling you Personal Publisher 3 is not available, you need to upgrade to the latest version of AOL 4.0. To do so, use keyword Upgrade and follow the instructions. Also note that Personal Publisher 3 only works with the 32-bit version of AOL 4.0 for Pentium or better computers and that parental controls must be set to 18+.

Creating a Web Page with Personal Publisher 3

Before you can begin using Personal Publisher 3, you have to access it. To do so, you have to be logged onto AOL and using AOL 4.0.

Once you're logged on, just use keyword PP3 (the formal keyword is Personal Publisher, but PP3 is shorter and easier to type).

This opens the introductory screen for Personal Publisher 3, shown in Figure 9-1.

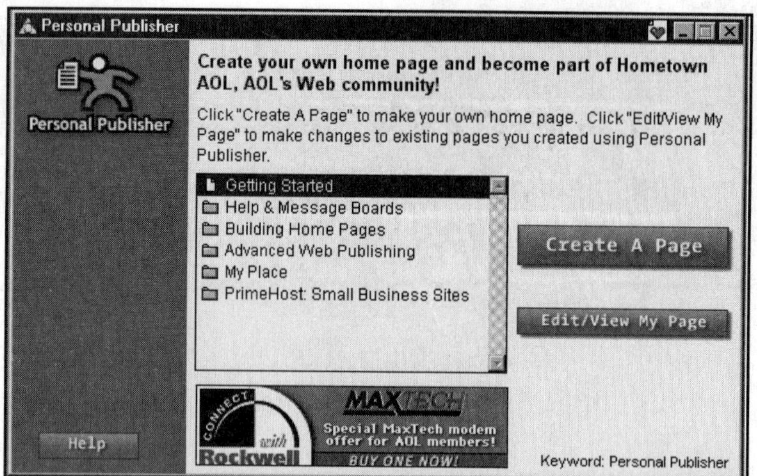

Figure 9-1 Whenever you open Personal Publisher 3, you'll see this screen.

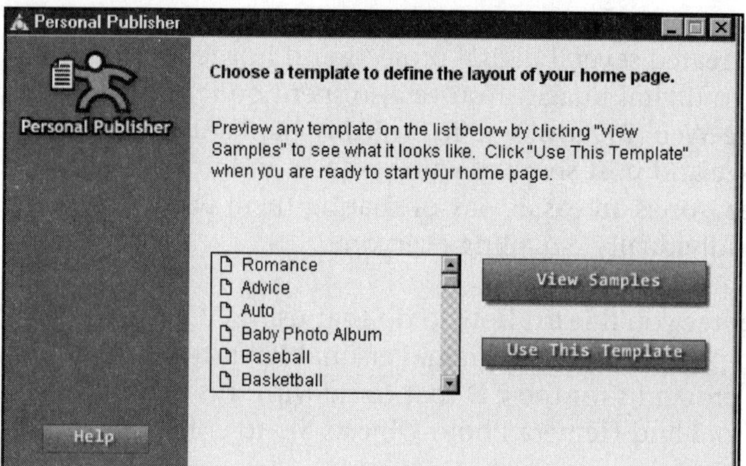

Figure 9-2 Choose a template from the list . . .

Once PP3 is up and running, you're ready to begin creating your family Web page.

1. Click Create a Page.
2. From the screen that appears (see Figure 9-2), choose a template—a pre-designed Web page that you will modify with your own text and images. Templates run the gamut from Romance to Wrestling, so you have lots to choose from. Of course, you can't tell what a template looks like just by its name, which is why AOL also provides you with a View Samples button. In Figure 9-3 I've clicked this button to preview the Family template.
3. If you like the preview, click Begin to start the process of creating your page. If you'd like to look at some other templates, click

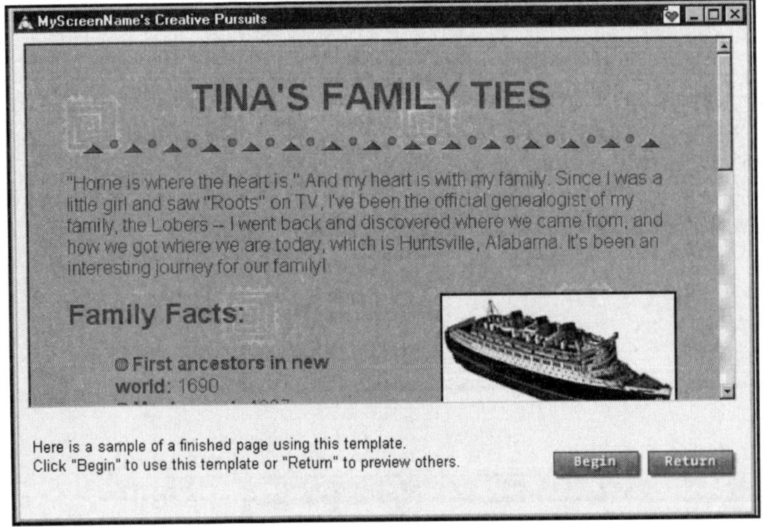

Figure 9-3
. . . and preview it to make sure it's what you want.

Return to go back to the template selection screen. From there you can also begin creating a page from any template without going to the preview screen by clicking Use This Template.

4. AOL loads a copy of the template you selected onto your computer and then presents you with an introductory screen explaining that that's what it just did and reminding you that your job is to customize the page's content. Click Next when you're ready to proceed.

5. On the next screen (see Figure 9-4) you're asked to give your page a title, which will appear at the top of your visitors' browser window and also in their list of Favorite Places if they add your page to that list. Because this is a Web page about my family, I'm entitling mine "The Ed Willett Family." Click Next.

6. Next, choose a background style or color. The style you saw when you previewed the template is the default, but Personal Publisher 3 offers you several others to choose from (see Figure 9-5). The big advantage to using one of these preset styles is that they're designed to be legible and pleasing to the eye—something that can't be said about every color combination people use on the Web!

7. If you don't like any of the preset styles or colors, click the Custom Colors button to open the dialog box in Figure 9-6. Here you can choose your own text and background colors by clicking the Text and Background buttons. Each opens a standard color palette from which you can choose the colors you want to use.

The exact number and order of the steps that follow will vary, depending on which template you chose, but these, from the Family template, are pretty typical.

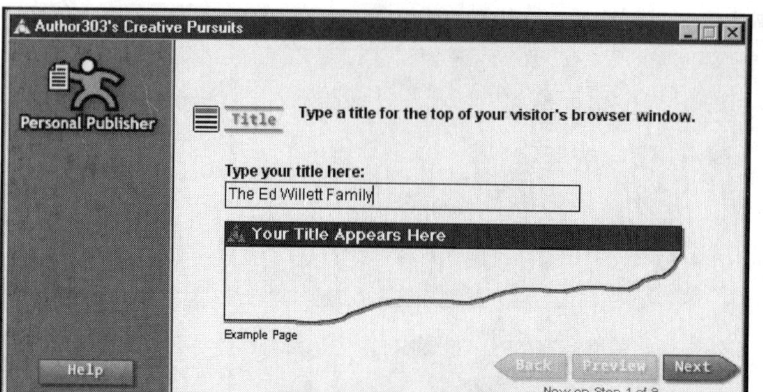

Figure 9-4 Give your page whatever title you want.

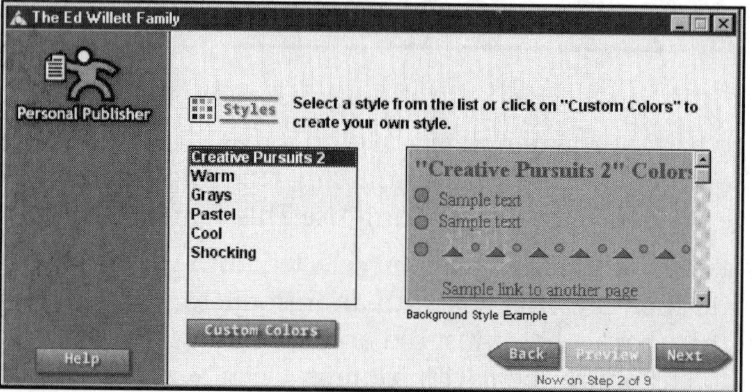

Figure 9-5 There's more than one way to color a Web page.

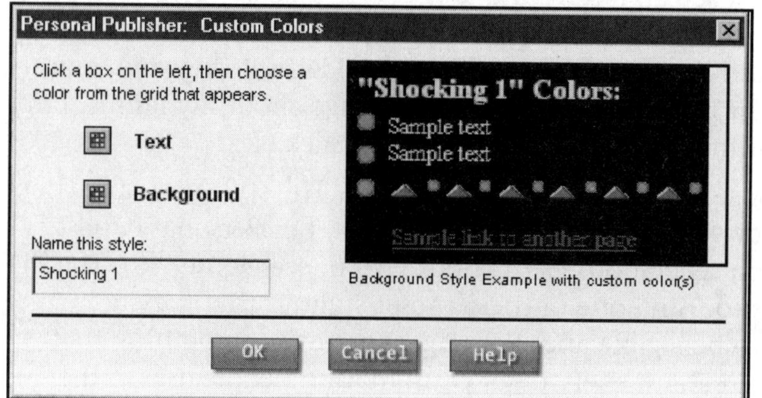

Figure 9-6 If you prefer, you can create a custom color scheme.

You can also give your custom color scheme its own style name, so it will show up on the list of styles as you create future pages. When you're done, click OK to return to the Styles screen and then click Next to proceed.

8. Now you can begin entering text, beginning with a header—the large, eye-catching text that appears at the top of the page (see Figure 9-7). You can format this text using the standard tools across the top of the text window (see sidebar).

9. Next you're asked to enter body text—perhaps a paragraph or two welcoming people to your site and explaining what it's about or whatever else you want to enter (see Figure 9-9). Again, you can format it and add links to it as you see fit. When you're finished, click Next.

10. The next step is to add a list (see Figure 9-10). The template includes a number of list items: to edit them, highlight them, and type in your own information, formatting and adding links to it as you would any other text. You can rearrange items by highlighting the item you want to move and moving it up and down in the list using the Move buttons, or you can remove an item entirely by

Formatting Text in Personal Publisher 3

Formatting text in Personal Publisher 3 is straightforward but not quite the same as formatting text in, say, a word processor. To begin with, you'll notice there's no provision for setting a specific point size. That's because text on Web pages must be displayed in one of several preset sizes. (In a word processor, text height is measured in *points,* an old printers' measurement. One point is approximately 1/72 of an inch.)

The leftmost buttons on the formatting toolbar alter the text's size based on those pre-existing restrictions. The button on the left reduces the size of highlighted text one notch, the one in the middle makes the text the standard size, and the one on the right increases the size one notch.

The three buttons at the center of the toolbar set the text's alignment. Click the left button to align the text with the left side of the Web page, click the middle button to center it, and click the right button to align it with the right side of the Web page.

The remaining three buttons let you make highlighted text bold (the leftmost button), italic (the center button), or both. You can also change the text's color by clicking the rightmost button and choosing the color you want from the palette that appears.

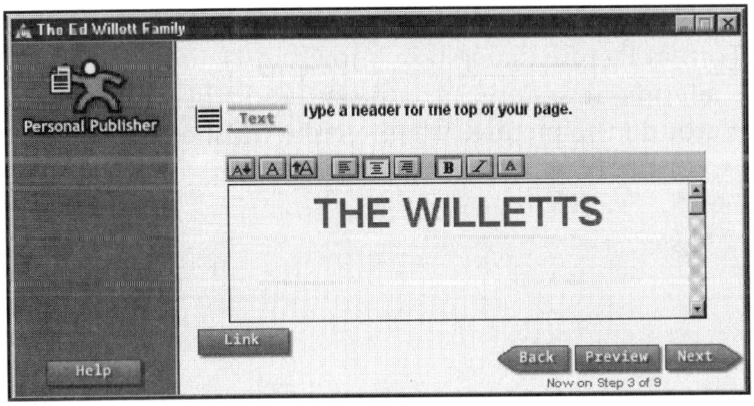

Figure 9-7
Enter the main header for your Web page here.

Adding Links to Text

It's *hypertext* that makes the Web the Web. Hypertext lets you click on one word or phrase to zip to another part of the Web related to that word or phrase.

All the screens in Personal Publisher 3 that let you add text also provide you with a Link button. To add a link:

1. Highlight the text you want to attach the link to.
2. Click Link. This opens the Link Choices dialog box, shown in Figure 9-8.
3. Choose the type of link you want: AOL's Hot Links (links AOL recommends), Your Favorite Places, Type any URL, or Send E-Mail. In the first two cases, you can pick any of the links on the Hot Links or Favorite Places lists to link the text to. If you choose Type any URL, you can do exactly that—type in the address of the Web page you want the text to point to. Send E-Mail lets you create a link to any e-mail address. Clicking on it will open a window into which your visitor can type a message and then automatically send it to the specified address.
4. When you've chosen the kind of link you want, click OK.

highlighting it and clicking Delete. Add new list items by clicking New. When your list is complete, click Next.

11. Now it's time to add a picture. Each template comes with a sample picture (or pictures) already in place. You can use that picture if you want, but you can also select a piece of clipart provided by Personal Publisher 3 or use any digital photograph or other image you've created yourself and stored on your computer. To add a picture from your computer, simply click Get My Picture and locate the picture on your hard drive using the standard Windows browsing box that opens. If you can't remember what it's called but you know where it's stored, you can highlight the file folder where you think it is and click Open Gallery to open a display of thumbnail images of all the pictures in that folder. That makes choosing the one you want simple. Double-click on a thumbnail to add that image to your Web page (see Figure 9-11).

12. To add Personal Publisher 3 clipart, click Get Clip Art and choose the art you want from the pieces provided (see Figure 9-12).

13. Once you've chosen a picture, type a caption for it in the space provided.

14. To adjust the picture's size and position, click Format Picture. This opens the Format Picture dialog box, shown in Figure 9-13. You can change alignment, indenting, and size, and add a thick or thin border around the picture. When you're finished, click OK.

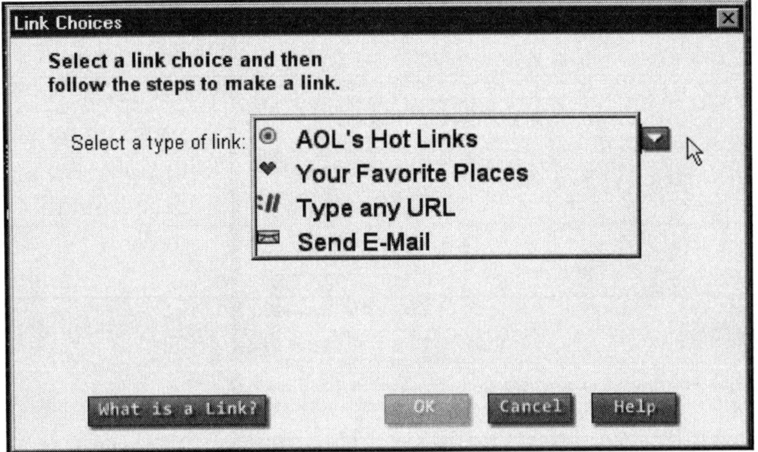

Figure 9-8
You can add a link to any text on your Web page.

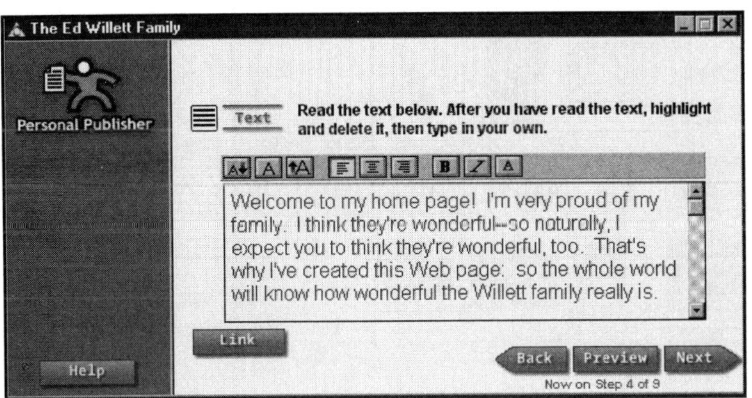

Figure 9-9
Add body text to your Web page.

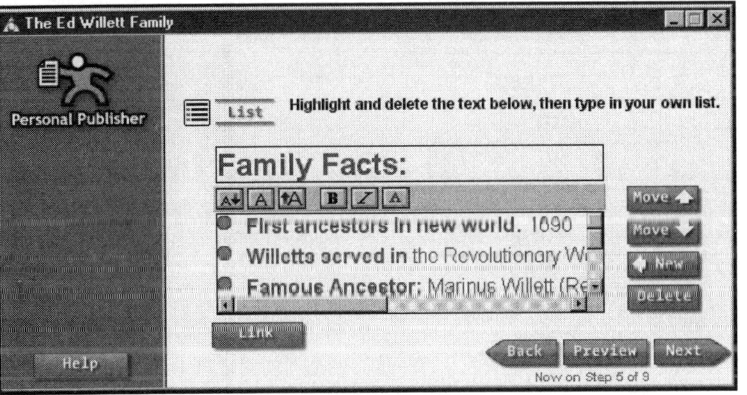

Figure 9-10
"I've got a little list . . ."

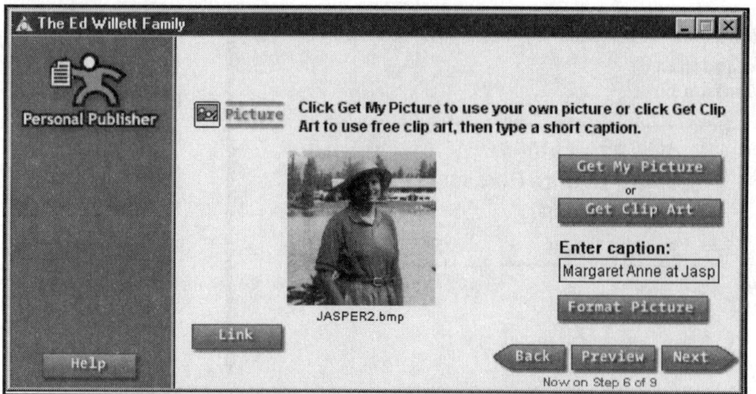

Figure 9-11 You can add any image on your computer to your Web page from this screen.

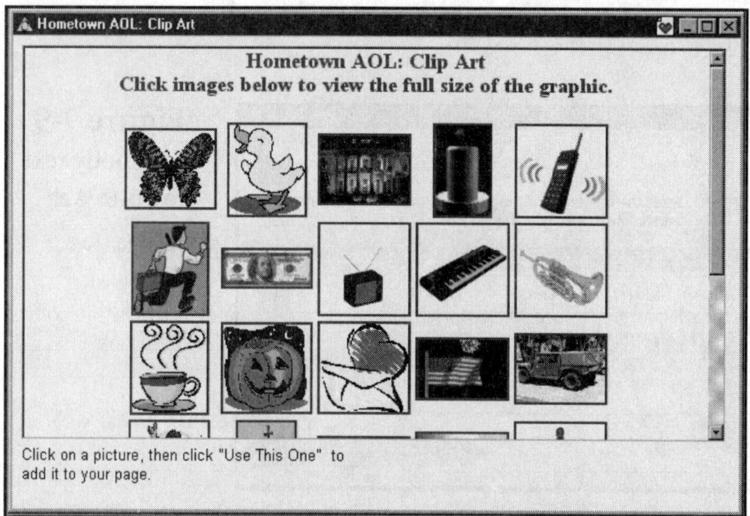

Figure 9-12 Personal Publisher 3 also provides lots of ready-to-use clipart.

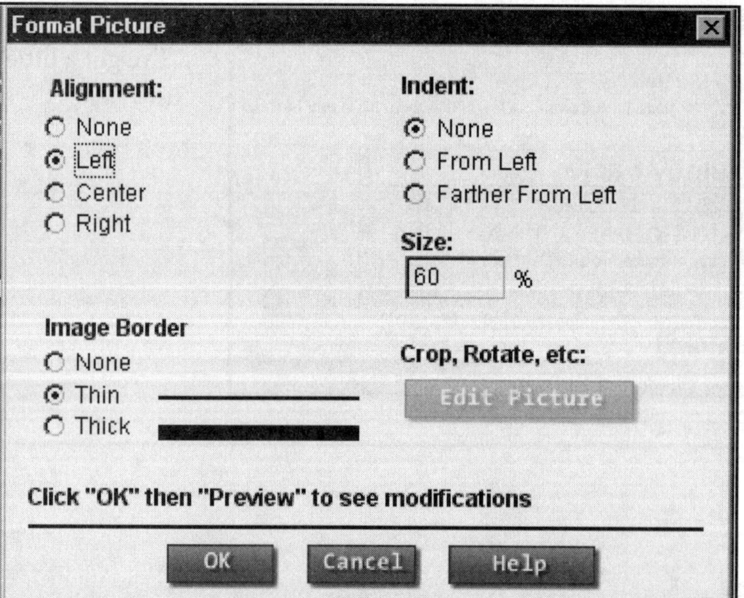

Figure 9-13 Basic formatting of your picture can be carried out here.

15. By this time you may be wondering how your Web page is shaping up. You can find out from any screen by clicking Preview. A preview of my Web page is shown in Figure 9-14. Click Return to go back to creating it.

16. The next step in this template is adding more text; type in your text, format it as before, and then click Next.

17. Next, you're invited to add a list of links (see Figure 9-15). The template suggests some likely links and shows you your list of Favorite Places. You can move any Favorite Place into the list of links by highlighting it in the left box and clicking Copy. You can also create an entirely new link by clicking New and typing in a description and an Internet address in the spaces provided. You can move items around in this list just as you did in the earlier list, by highlighting them and clicking the two Move buttons. When you're finished, click Next.

18. The final step is to add a couple of extras, if you want them. One is a link to your e-mail address, so people can tell you what they think of your page and ask you questions; the other is simply a logo that tells anyone visiting your page that you made it yourself using Personal Publisher 3. By default both are added, but you can remove them by unchecking the box next to each one.

19. You'll see a preview of your Web page. If you're happy with it, you can go ahead and publish it to AOL's computers for display on the Web. Just click Publish. Personal Publisher 3 will take a minute to communicate with your Web space and will show you the address for your new page.

Pictures and text don't just appear by magic: They're created by someone, and that someone has the right to decide how those pictures and text are to be used. If you're using pictures you've taken yourself or text you've written yourself, then you can generally reproduce it at will. If you're using a picture you scanned in from a book or magazine, though, or something you copied from another site on the Internet, you may not have the right to reproduce it at all.

Before using any material such as that, you must get permission from the copyright owner. On a Web site, look for a link to the webmaster, a mailing address or a phone number. E-mail, write, or call that person to ask permission before using any images or text from that site. Don't use it on your own site until you have written permission to do so. Using copyrighted material without permission is illegal and could result in a stern letter from someone's lawyer—or an even sterner lawsuit.

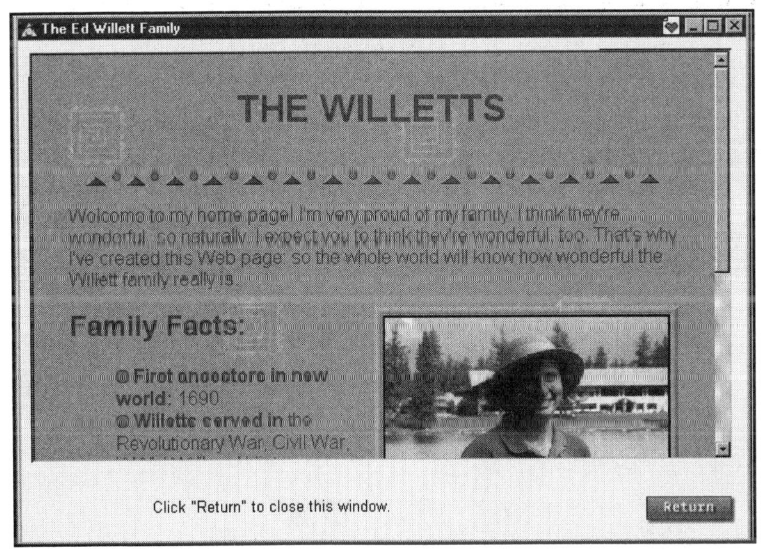

Figure 9-14
My Web page is shaping up nicely.

20. Click Options, and you can have Personal Publisher 3 create a menu of all the pages you've created (if you've created more than one; if this is your first page, this option won't do anything). The menu lets visitors jump from page to page of your site with a single click. The Options box also tells you how many graphics files appear on the page and their total size, which gives you a clue to whether the page will load quickly or slowly. Click OK when you're done, and then click OK again.

21. If you chose to add the menu of your other pages, a new screen (see Figure 9-16) shows you the existing pages in your Web space. It also lets you choose which ones to include (just check the box by their names) and lets you rearrange their order (by highlighting the one you want to reposition and using the Move key).

22. Click OK and off your page goes to the World Wide Web!

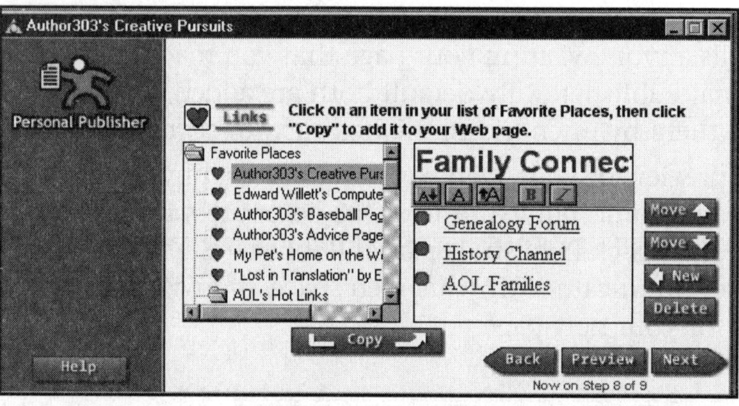

Figure 9-15 Add a list of links to your Web page.

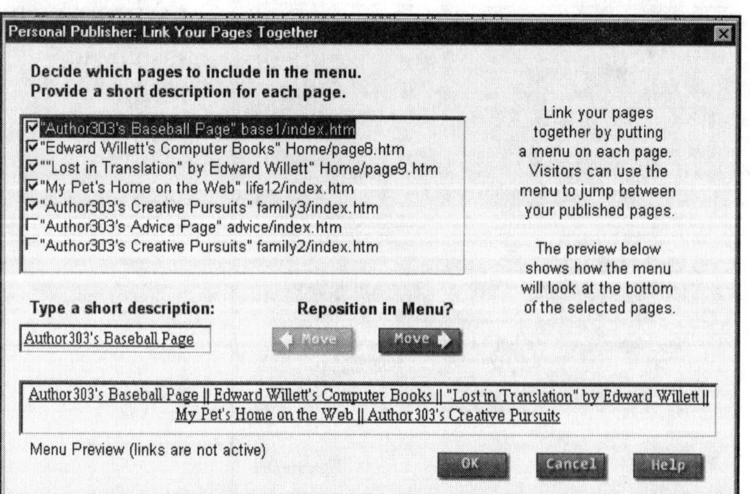

Figure 9-16 If you create more than one page, you can add a menu to each page that provides an easy way to navigate among them.

Editing Your Web Page

The steps outlined above are fine if all you want to do is follow an existing template. Odds are, however, you want to add additional items to your Web page, especially more of those wonderful digital images you've been creating for all of your digital projects.

Don't worry: Your Web page isn't written in stone. You can use Personal Publisher 3 to edit as well as create.

To add more pictures (or anything else) to your Web page:

1. Open Personal Publisher as before, but this time choose View/Edit My Page. After a moment, you'll see a screen something like the one in Figure 9-17.
2. Highlight the page you want to edit, and click Edit. (Notice that you can also use this dialog box to move items from your computer to your Web space and rearrange items within their folders.) This opens the dialog box in Figure 9-18.
3. Notice the list at the top of all of the items on your Web page. Each bit of text, each graphic, each list, and so on, appears here. To edit any item, using the same basic tools you used to insert them in the first place, just click on the item and then click Edit Item. To add items—additional pictures, in this case—click Add. This opens the Add an Item dialog box, shown in Figure 9-19.
4. Choose the type of item you want to add—in this case, a picture. You'll see pretty much the same dialog box you saw while you were using the template and reached the point where you added a picture. Find the picture or clipart you want to add just as you did before.
5. The new picture will be added just below whatever item you had highlighted on the Edit screen. Once it's inserted, you can move it around until you've positioned it where you want it.

Submitting Your Page to Hometown AOL

Hometown AOL is a virtual community of Web sites created by AOL members. Although your page is published as soon as you finish Step 22 above and can be accessed by anyone who knows its address, Hometown AOL gives your site added exposure by allowing you to place it within a virtual neighborhood of similarly themed sites.

Whenever you publish a page on AOL, you'll see a screen that invites you to select a community for that page. Click the link provided, and you'll be presented with a number of categories of communities to choose from, from Careers & Money to Sports & Recreation. Each category features a number of subcategories. By following the instructions, you can submit your site to up to five different communities.

Pages in Hometown AOL have a common banner across the top that lets viewers search the various communities for the pages they're interested in. Hometown AOL also offers links to lots of tips on building better home pages and even highlights "Top Picks" from the ranks of the Hometown dwellers.

You don't have to join Hometown AOL to get your site on the Web—but why on Earth wouldn't you want to?

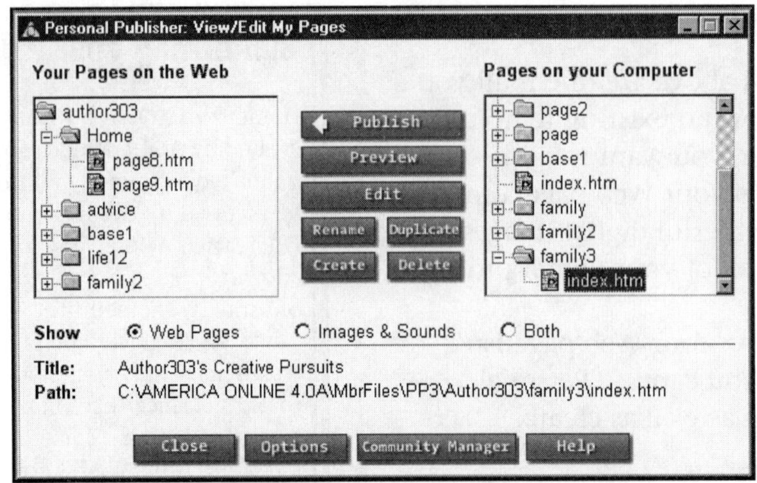

Figure 9-17 All the pages you've created, both the ones you've published to the Web and those you've kept on your computer, can be edited with Personal Publisher 3.

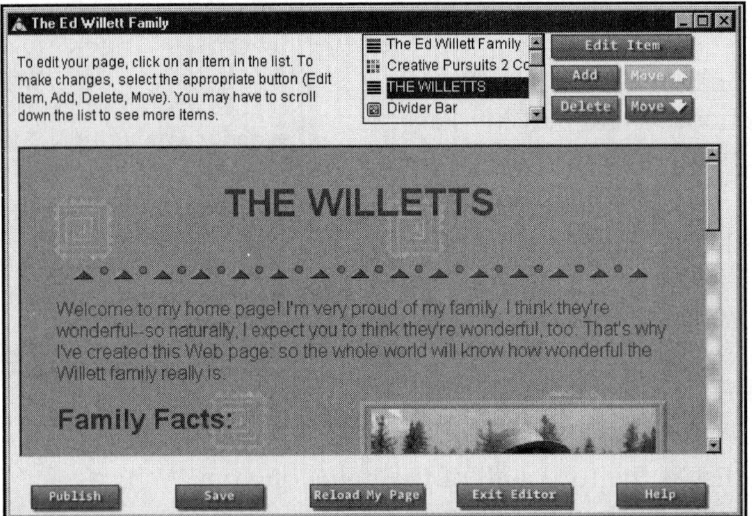

Figure 9-18 Use these controls to fine-tune your Web page and add additional items.

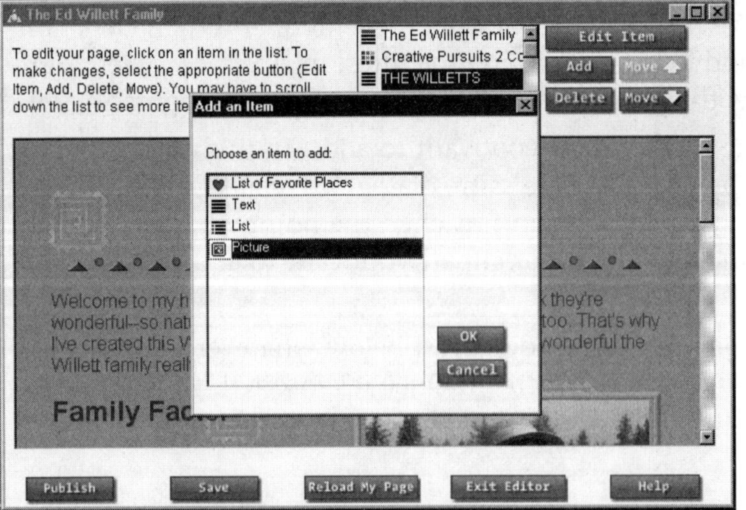

Figure 9-19 Choose the type of item you want to add from this menu.

6. You may have noticed that when you're inserting a picture and you choose Format Picture, the resulting screen includes another button, Edit Picture, which is grayed out. Once a picture is inserted into your Web page, you can select it from the Edit menu, click Edit Item, then Format Picture, and you'll find that the Edit Picture button is now active. Clicking it calls up AOL's standard picture-editing controls, described in detail in Chapter 1.
7. Once you've added the pictures you want, click Save to save them to your computer or Publish to send them to your Web space. If you want to revert to the latest-saved version of your page, click Reload My Page. To stop editing, click Exit Editor.

When you're selecting the background color for your Photo-Object or (in the next section) PhotoFont, you can match it exactly with your Web page by using the Pick Color from Document button. Arrange your windows so you can see both your Web page and Photo-Objects. Click Pick Color from Document. Your mouse pointer changes to an eyedropper. Place the eyedropper on the background of your Web page and click once. This automatically changes the background of the Photo-Object or PhotoFont to the background color of your Web page.

Using Hemera Photo-Objects in Your Web Page

Hemera Photo-Objects SE is one of the products on the CD included with this book. A *Photo-Object* is an object that combines the look of a photograph with the ease of use of clipart. Photo-Objects SE includes hundreds of Photo-Objects on all subjects, any of which you can use in your Personal Publisher 3 Web page. In addition, Photo-Objects SE lets you create PhotoFonts, which apply photographic textures of various sorts to any font you have installed on your system.

To find and use the Photo-Object you want:

1. Open Hemera Photo-Objects SE. You'll see a screen like the one in Figure 9-20.
2. To find a Photo-Object that suits your needs, you can search by keywords. Just plug in a word or two that describes the topic you want to illustrate into the box labeled Enter keywords that describe the image(s) you want. Hemera Photo-Objects SE searches automatically as you type; you don't have to hit Enter. By the time you're finished typing in your keyword, it's already displaying any matches it found (see Figure 9-21).
3. Next, choose File, Export To. This opens the dialog box in Figure 9-22 and also opens up a lot of options regarding how you want the final Photo-Object to look.
4. As you can see, you can use your Photo-Object in various other types of software, including graphics applications like PhotoSuite II. For now, choose Web Authoring and click Next.
5. The next screen lets you specify the final size of the image and flip it horizontally or vertically, if you like. Click Next again, and you can select a background color for the image or a background

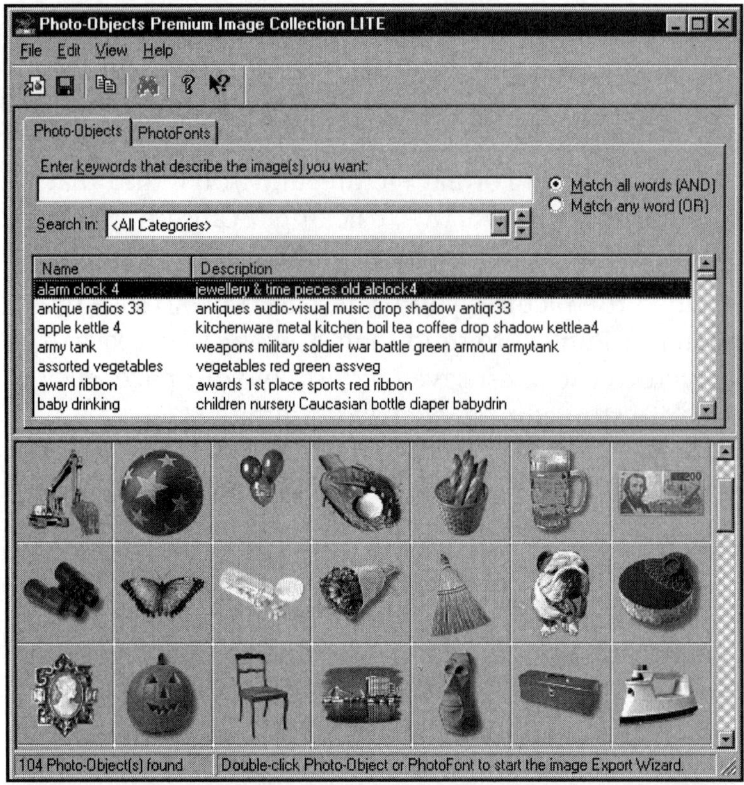

Figure 9-20 Photo-Objects of every description are available for your use.

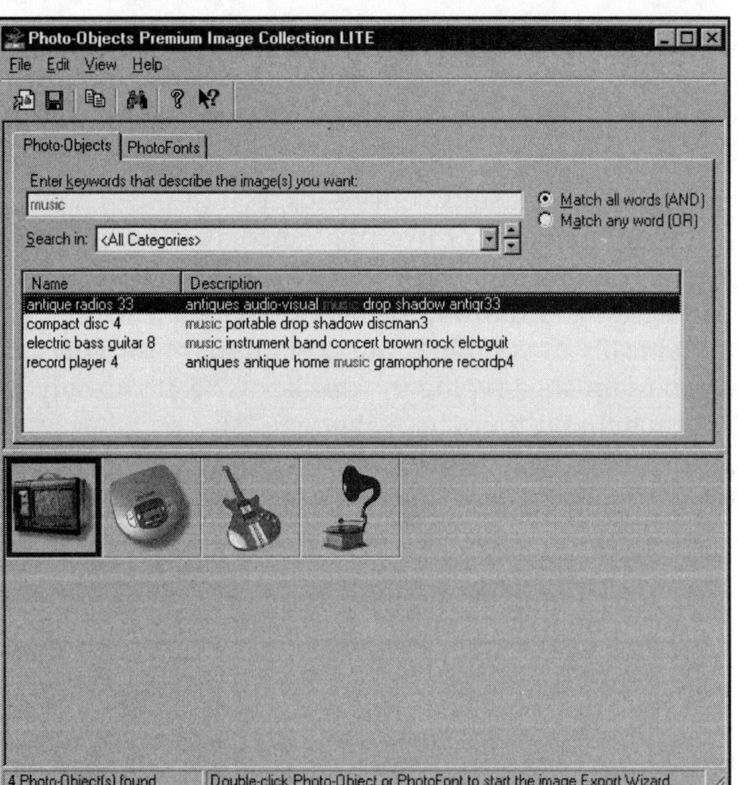

Figure 9-21 Entering the keyword *music* produced these four matches.

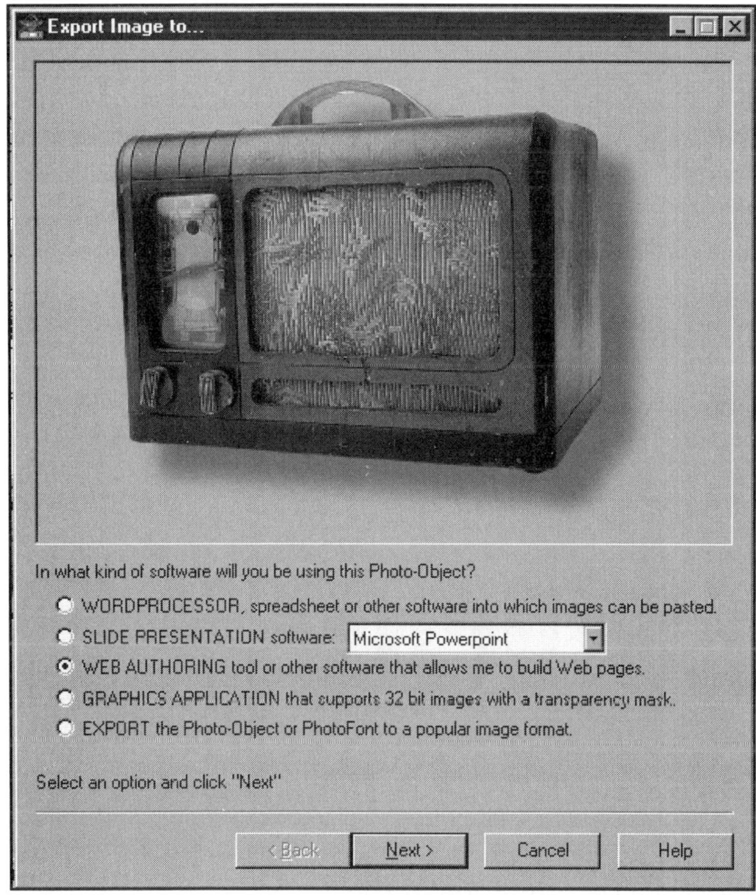

Figure 9-22 Photo-Objects SE gives you tremendous control over how your Photo-Object will look on your Web page.

texture. Click Next one more time, and you're asked to specify where you should save the file. Put it wherever you're keeping the graphics files you're using in your Web page.

6. Now add it to your page just as you would a new photograph (see the previous section on editing your Web page).

Using a PhotoFont is very similar:

1. Return to Hemera Photo-Objects SE and choose the PhotoFonts tab instead of the Photo-Objects tab.
2. Enter the text you want to put into a PhotoFont, and choose a font, style, and size for it. Finally, choose one of the textures (see Figure 9-23).
3. Now export the PhotoFont image just as you did the Photo-Object, by choosing File, Export To. Now add it to your Web page as you would any other image. Figure 9-24 shows my Web page with the Photo-Object and PhotoFont both installed.

Figure 9-23 You can achieve many interesting effects with PhotoFonts.

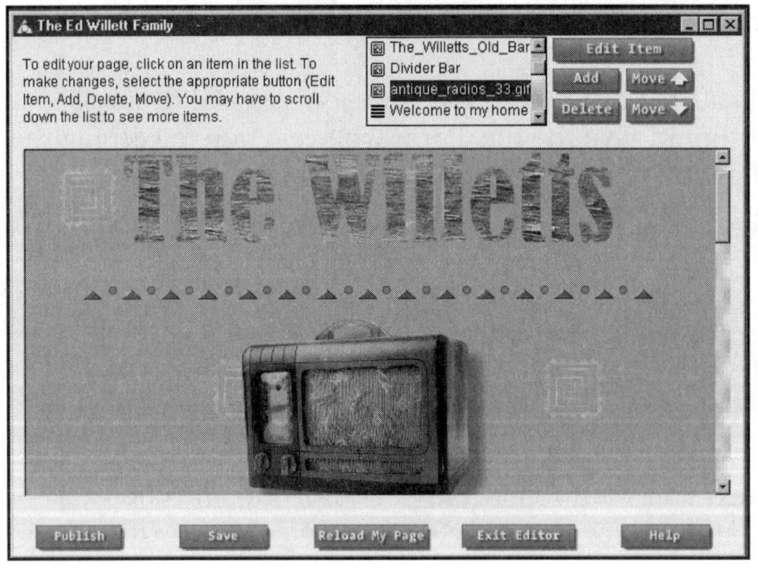

Figure 9-24 Here are my Photo-Object and PhotoFont in place on my Web page, looking very snazzy.

Optimizing Your Graphics with NetGraphics Studio 2

You've probably visited plenty of Web pages that took so long to load you lost interest in them before you could even see what they looked like. The culprit was probably graphics files that were too big.

Obviously you don't want your Web page to suffer the same sad fate; at the same time, you do want to make use of all your spiffy new digital images. What to do?

What you need to do is optimize your graphics using the NetGraphics Optimizer that is included on the CD as part of the NetGraphics Studio 2 program. The Optimizer removes unnecessary data from your graphics so that they look good on the Web while taking up much less space.

To optimize a graphic:

1. Open the Optimizer.
2. Open the graphic you want to optimize by entering its location, browsing for it, or simply arranging your windows so that you can click on it and drag it into the Optimizer. That's how I moved the photo in Figure 9-25.
3. Click Next. As with Photo-Objects, you can specify the size of the graphic and flip it horizontally or vertically, if you wish. Click Preview in Browser if you want to check how the size you've chosen will look to someone visiting your page.
4. Click Next again, and the Optimizer analyzes the graphic and recommends either GIF or JPEG format. You can save it as the other if you prefer, however.
5. Click Next once more. Now you're in the heart of the Optimizer. Use the slider to choose between a small file (and hence lower quality) or a large file (and higher quality). The Optimizer

What Should I Put on My Web Page? Ten Ideas

- Lots of pictures of your family doing interesting things.
- Creative things family members have done: kids' stories and artwork, for instance, or Mom's fancy Christmas candles.
- Links to sites that relate to things your family is involved in.
- Your family history and ancestors for as far back as you can research. Genealogical researchers will bless you for it.
- Cute or funny pictures of your pets.
- Your family's reviews of books they've read, movies they've seen, amusement parks they've visited, computer games they've played.
- Things you have learned that have helped your family get through difficult times: illness, a house fire, and so on. Your experience could help others.
- Your annual Christmas newsletter. Your relatives can pick it off the Web so you don't have to mail it to them. (Besides, that way only the ones who are really interested have to read it!)
- Your family's favorite recipes—and least favorite!
- Your family's favorite jokes.

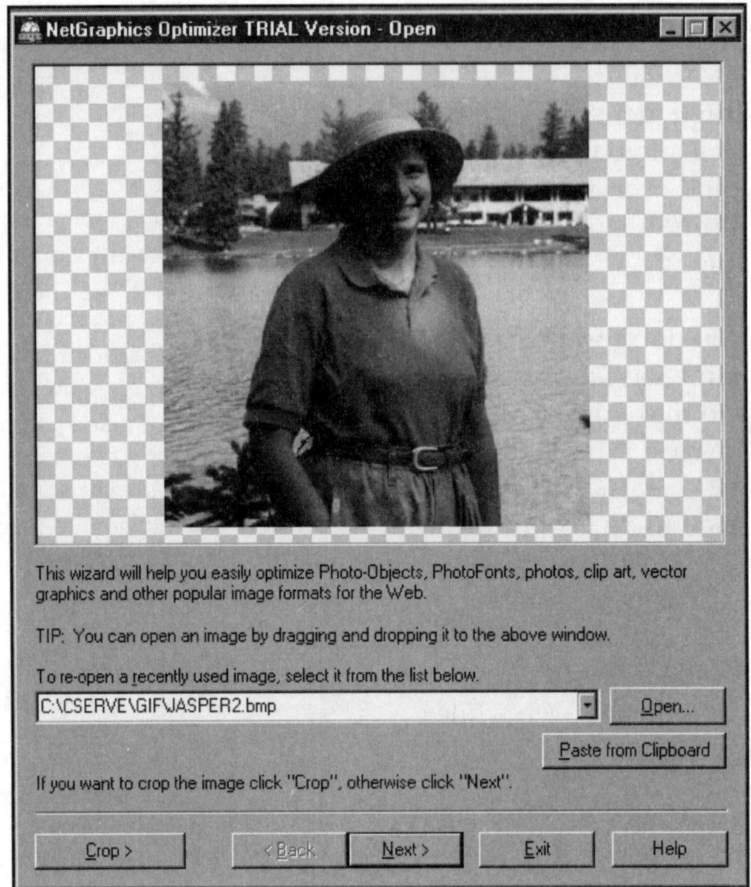

Figure 9-25 You can simply click and drag images from your Web page into the Optimizer, if you organize your windows right.

automatically calculates how big the file will be if you accept the new settings and, even better, gives you some idea of how long the file will take to load using a 28.8 or 56.6 modem. Generally, the faster the better, as long as the image doesn't deteriorate too much. Even five seconds can seem like a long time to someone in a hurry.

6. Click Next again, and choose whether you want the image to be "interlaced" or not. Interlaced images don't load any faster, but they give that perception because a fuzzy image appears almost at once and then clears up as the rest of the information about it arrives. You can view a simulation of each type of download by choosing them in succession and clicking View Download Simulation each time.

7. Finally, you can save your revised image. If you're willing to save it over top of the original version click Save; you can also save it under a different name by clicking Save As. If you save it under

Resources for Web-page builders

Go to keyword BuildingHomePages to find tips for adding many other features to your page, including sound, counters, and more. AOL also has links to sources of graphics and many other useful resources.

For more tips and information about using Personal Publisher 3, I recommend *America Online's Creating Cool Web Pages,* published by IDG Books and available from AOL. (I have to recommend it—I wrote it!)

the same name, you won't even have to go back to your Web page to edit it further; the new image will be used the next time the page is called up (unless you've already published the page, in which case you'll have to go back to Personal Publisher 3 and publish it again to get the new image into your Web space).

8. If you want to work with other images, click Back to Beginning and start the whole process all over again.

Chapter 10

PROJECT: The Baby Book

What You Need:

- Regular camera and access to a scanner or access to a digital camera
- PhotoSuite II SE
- Personal Publisher 3
- Access to a color printer
- A baby (you're on your own!)

Introduction

As a kid, I remember looking through the baby books my parents had created for my two older brothers and me. I was fascinated by the pictures of what seemed like ancient history. It was hard to believe that someone as grown up as I was had ever been a tiny baby like the ones in the pictures.

I also confess to feeling just a little bit short-changed. My oldest brother's baby book went on forever, full of details like "baby's first visit to the doctor" and "baby's first tooth." My second-oldest brother's baby book contained less, but was still quite complete. Mine, however, began promisingly and then quickly petered out. I'm afraid, by the time the third boy in the family arrived, the novelty had worn off.

Those baby books were nothing more than glorified photo albums, with preprinted pages on which you could note important events in the baby's life and add a few pictures. To see them, we had to dig them out of my parents' closet. It wasn't very often we made the effort.

That's the biggest advantage of a digital baby book. It's always at your fingertips on your computer and, if you post it on the World Wide Web, it's always at the fingertips of doting grandparents, aunts, and uncles, too. Your whole extended family can watch your baby grow up on the Internet.

In this chapter, you'll look at making a digital baby book for home use with PhotoSuite II SE and creating and posting an on-line version with Personal Publisher 3.

Tips For Photographing Babies

Here are eight tips for getting better baby pictures:

- **Photograph your baby when he/she is at his/her best.** You know when your baby tends to be happiest—after a bath, maybe, or after first getting up in the morning. That's the time when photography will be fun for both you and the baby.
- **Don't overdress the baby.** Simple clothes and colors photograph best on small children.
- **Try different camera angles.** Don't just shoot at eye level: Try shooting from above or below.
- **Keep backgrounds simple.**
- **If you're shooting outdoors, stick to the shade and/or use a flash to fill in the harsh shadows.** Early morning and late afternoon light gives a nice warm touch.
- **Get close!** One of the most common mistakes amateur photographers make is standing too far away from their subject.
- **Don't photograph your baby in a vacuum.** Get him or her interacting with other people and playing with favorite toys.
- **Take more than one photo at a time to be sure of getting a good one.** (Of course, with a digital camera, you can check each photo as soon as you've taken it to see whether it's a good one or not.)

Deciding on What to Include in the Baby Book

First and foremost, you need to include pictures—lots of them. Again, you can take pictures with a regular film camera and scan them (or have them scanned by your photo developer), but if there's one subject the digital camera was really made for, it's taking pictures of babies. It's always ready and it's never out of film—and the pictures are instantly available for e-mailing to Grandma and Grandpa, who are as anxious as you are to see baby's first smile.

Pictures by themselves aren't enough, though. It's important to take good notes, so you know when the pictures were taken and what they're of. Once you start turning your digital images into a baby book, you can attach your notes directly to the pictures, so you can readily look it up.

The special occasions that are typically memorialized in baby books range from the first smile and first haircut through a record of growth to first birthdays and holidays. One good idea you might like to try is keeping a detailed record of a typical day in your baby's life, from getting up to bedtime. Keep the camera handy and photograph everything from sleeping to eating to crying to bathing.

Make full use of your scanner. Scan in baby's birth certificate, for instance—even his or her hospital bracelet. Yes, you'll want to keep those keepsakes in a box somewhere, but for everyday viewing and showing off, a digital image is much handier. You could even scan in the congratulatory cards you received and the birth announcement from the newspaper. Anything that you want to remember that fits in the scanner, scan. Anything that doesn't fit in the scanner, photograph.

Finally, makes sure you include all of the basic vital statistics of the birth: length, weight, hair color, eye color, date and time of birth, place of birth, doctor's name, length of delivery, and so on.

Hey, do me a personal favor: Remember that the third child eventually will be just as interested in this stuff as the first child, even if you aren't!

Creating Your Baby Book

In PhotoSuite II SE, you can use several of the existing templates to create a lovely baby book. To do so:

1. Open PhotoSuite II SE.
2. Click Photos.
3. Click Get Photo, and get the digital images you want to use, either from where you've stored them on your computer or by scanning them in or downloading them from a digital camera. Opening the photos adds them to the Photo Library, which you can access by clicking the button at the far right of the top toolbar (see Figure 10-1). Putting photos in the library before you start your baby album makes assembling the album easier.

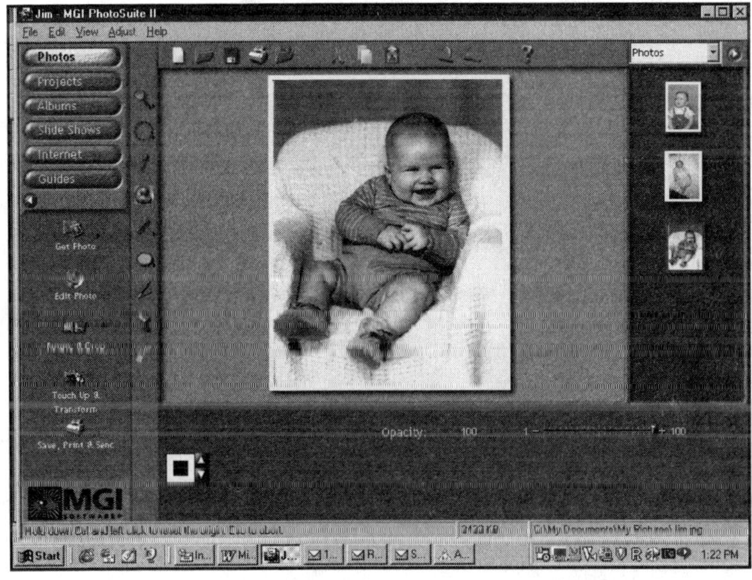

Figure 10-1 Opening the pictures you want to use first in the Photo area of PhotoSuite adds them to the Photo Library at right and makes it much easier to use them in assembling your baby book.

4. The first step is to create a cover for your baby album. A fun idea is to make the cover look like a magazine cover—and PhotoSuite II SE makes that possible. Click Projects, then choose Fun, Magazine Covers. Look over the available covers until you find one you want (see Figure 10-2). Click on it and click Select to open it.

5. When the magazine cover project template opens, drag the photo you want to use on the cover from the Photo Library at right into the gray box (it'll automatically replace the gray box). See Figure 10-3.

Figure 10-2 A fun idea for the cover to your baby album is to make it look like a magazine cover.

Figure 10-3 Drag the picture you want on the cover of the magazine onto the project template, and your baby will look like big news indeed!

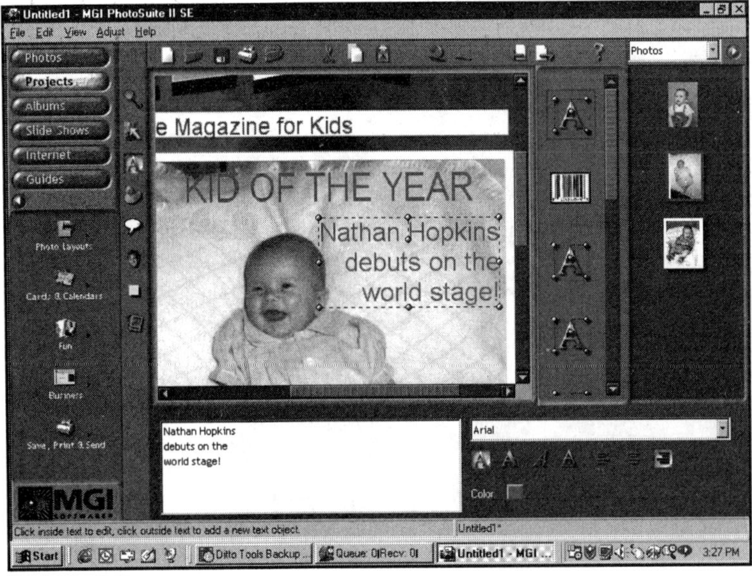

Figure 10-4
A suitable headline finishes off your baby album's cover.

6. This magazine cover includes several text boxes, but you can change them or add more. To add a text box, click the text tool on the left toolbar, then click wherever on the template you want the text to appear. Type the text into the box in the settings area below the workspace, and adjust font, alignment, font style and color using the controls at right (see Figure 10-4).
7. Save your cover by choosing File, Save.
8. Now you're ready to begin creating the inside of your baby album. Several useful project templates are available. Using any of them follows the same procedure you used to create the cover: Open the template, drag any pictures you want to use into the gray boxes, and then add text. Figures 10-5 and 10-6 show some of the kinds of baby album pages you can create using various PhotoSuite project templates.

You can also spruce up baby albums using PhotoSuite's props and speech balloons. Refer to Chapter 4, "Create a Calendar!", for more detailed information on those tools.

Printing and Sharing Your Baby Album

Because your baby album is really made up of several different project templates, you'll have to save each page as a separate project file. The only way you'll be able to view the album as a whole is to print each project and then assemble them by hand. That makes it very important that they're all printed on the same size of paper.

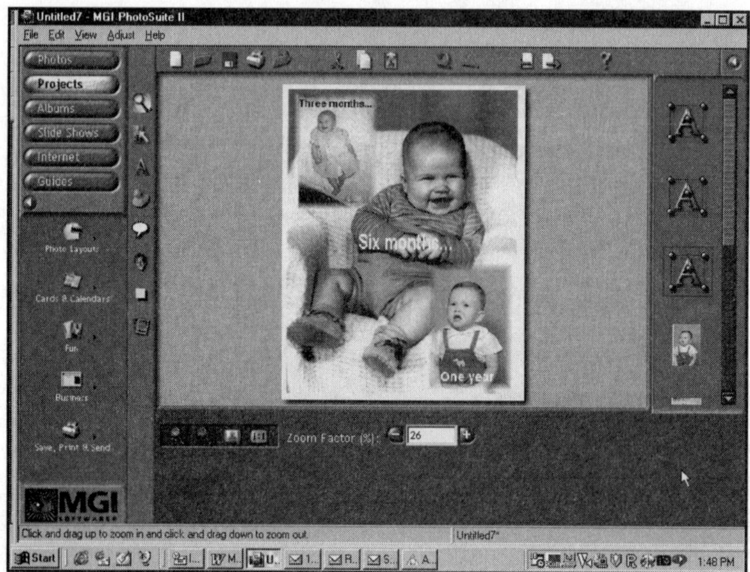

Figure 10-5 This page uses the Collage from Current Photo option found under Photo Layouts.

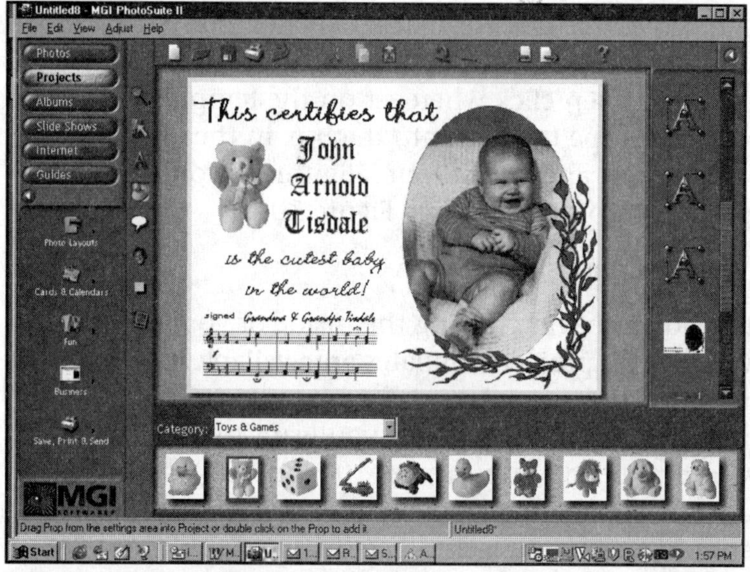

Figure 10-6 This page uses one of the Certificate templates included with the Business projects (note that the teddy bear is one of PhotoSuite's Toys & Games props, shown at the bottom of the screen).

Printing Your Baby Album

To print a page of your baby album:

1. With the page open, choose File, Print. This opens the Print Settings area, as shown in Figure 10-7.

Figure 10-7
Specify print settings for your baby album using the controls at the bottom of the page.

2. Choose the printer, orientation, and so on, as usual. Make sure Fit To Page is chosen under Print Size. When this is selected, PhotoSuite makes sure the project fits on the paper you're currently using in your printer, which, in turn, ensures that each page of your baby album will be printed on the same size paper.
3. Click Print.

E-mailing Your Baby Album

Because each page of your baby album is a separate project file, you can't e-mail the whole thing to Grandma and Grandpa. You can, however, e-mail each file separately. Save each page as a separate picture file in whichever format you prefer (JPG is usually a good choice, because it makes photos look the best), and then attach the file to an e-mail addressed to whomever you wish to share your baby album with.

For detailed information on how to attach a file to an e-mail, see Project 3: E-mail a picture to a friend in Chapter 1, "Let's Get Started."

Sharing your Baby Album on the Web

An even better way to share your baby album is to turn it into HTML files—Web pages, in other words. Then you can either e-mail the whole thing as a series of HTML files to your friends and families, or publish it to your personal Web space on AOL so they can view it online.

To turn your baby album into a series of HTML files:

1. Open the page's project file.
2. Choose File, Create Web Page. You'll immediately get a message telling you where the new Web page has been saved; make a note of it.
3. Repeat until you've turned all of your baby album pages into Web pages.

By default, PhotoSuite saves each page in its own directory as two files: an HTML file and a JPG image. In order to use Personal Publisher 3 to create links among the pages and publish them to your AOL Web space, you need to move those files to the same directory as the Personal Publisher 3-created Web pages are stored in, which typically is C:/America Online 4.0/MbrFiles/Pp3/YourScreenName.

The easiest way is to use Windows Explorer (which you can find by going Start, Programs, Windows Explorer), locate the files in your PhotoSuite directory, highlight them, and drag them into the correct directory (see Figure 10-8).

Now you're ready to use Personal Publisher 3 to add links among your baby pages and publish them to the Web, turning your baby album into a baby Web site!

To do so:

1. Sign on to AOL.
2. Go keyword PP3.
3. Click Edit/View My pages.
4. If you have the PhotoSuite pages in the right place, you should be able to find them in the list of Web pages on your computer on the right side of the screen, as shown in Figure 10-9. Click the Both radio button so that both the .html files and the .jpg files you moved into the directory are visible.

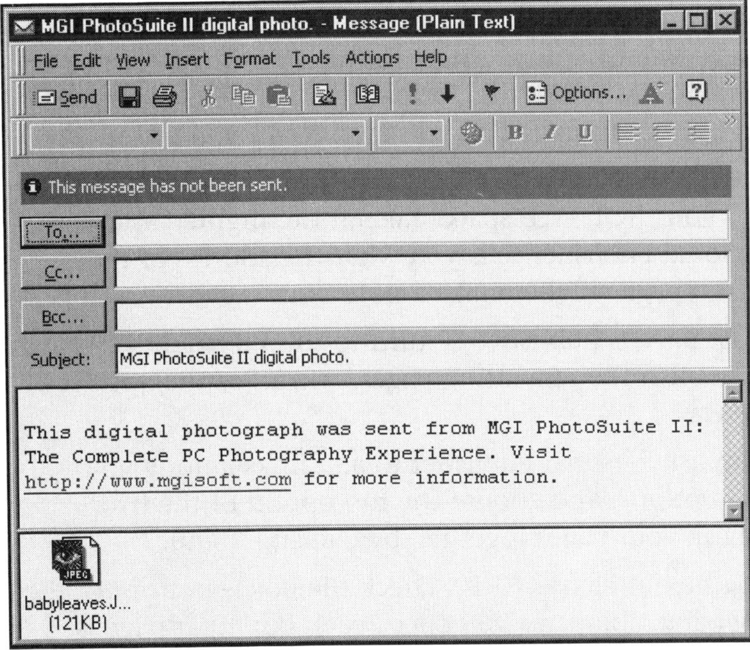

Figure 10-8
The easiest way to move your PhotoSuite-created Web pages into your Personal Publisher 3 directory is with Windows Explorer.

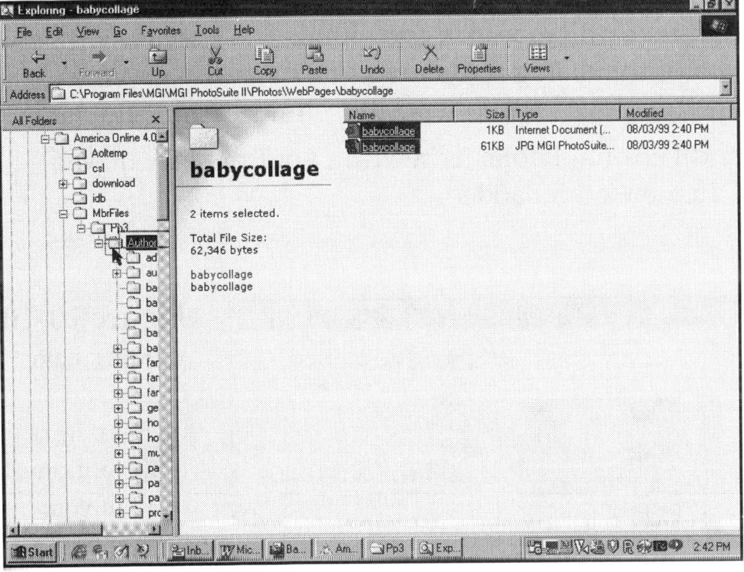

Figure 10-9
Your Photo-Suite-created Web pages now show up in Personal Publisher's list of Web pages on your computer.

5. For your Web site to work properly, you need to change the name of your baby album's cover from whatever it currently is to index.html. To do so, highlight it, then click Rename. You'll be warned that this may break any links to the page; since there aren't any links to worry about yet, ignore that warning and enter the page's new name when prompted.

6. If you'd like, you can edit the pages as you would any Personal Publisher page (see Chapter 9, "The Family Web Site," for more information). You can add text, format the picture, add additional pictures, and so on. Click Edit if you wish to do so.
7. Once you're happy with your page's appearance, you're ready to publish it to your AOL Web space. Keep it highlighted and click Publish. Personal Publisher tells you what the address of the published Web page will be; make a note of it.
8. Once the first page is published, return to the View/Edit My Pages screen and publish the remaining pages, and all of the .jpg files, in the same way.
9. Now you can ask Personal Publisher to add links among your pages. Click Options, and choose the top option of the two presented, Link your pages together, by clicking Menu.
10. In the dialog box in Figure 10-10, check the boxes in front of the pages of the baby album. As you check each box, that page is added to the menu of links that will appear on the bottom of all your pages. Type a short description of the link in the box provided; that text will appear in the menu. The preview window at the bottom of the dialog box shows you what the menu will look like; use the Move keys to reposition links within the menu.
11. Click OK, and Personal Publisher rewrites your published Web pages with the new menu added.

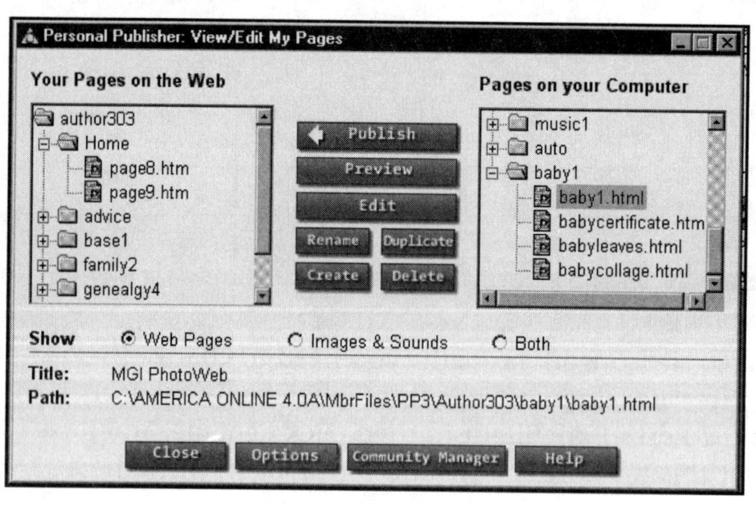

Figure 10-10 Use this dialog box to add a menu of links to the bottom of all of your baby album Web pages, finally bringing all the pages of the album together into a unified whole.

Figure 10-11 Your digital baby album is complete and ready for viewing on the World Wide Web!

If you want something a bit simpler than a custom-designed PhotoSuite II-built baby album, try using the Baby Photo Album template offered by Personal Publisher 3. It lets you get a few pictures and the basic information about your baby's birth up and on the Web in minutes.

That's it! Your baby album is now available for grandparents, uncles and aunts, nieces and nephews, brothers and sisters, and all the in-laws to coo over (see Figure 10-11). All you have to do is provide them with the address!

Keeping It Going When Baby's No Longer a Baby

The great thing about a Web-based baby album is that it has no time limit on it. Traditional paper-based baby albums run out of space for entries in a year or two at most. But a digital baby album can evolve as baby grows into a toddler, a preschooler, an elementary schooler, a high schooler, and even a university student. You can change it from a baby album into a personal history and scrapbook that anyone in the family with an interest in your child's progress can access to find out what his or her favorite grandson/nephew/cousin is up to.

Best of all, it's a project that the child can eventually take over, turning it into their own personal Web site.

Just make sure you don't let them delete all those "embarrassing" baby pictures. Keep a copy of the original digital baby album on your computer and on a floppy disk or Zip disk—or, better yet, on a CD-ROM, if you have access to a CD-writer. Sometime around his or her 30th birthday, your son or daughter will be glad to have it to show his or her kids.

CHAPTER 11

PROJECT: Create Your Own Storybook!

What You Need:

- Access to a scanner or digital camera
- PhotoSuite II SE
- The Home Gene-Splicing Kit (on the CD)
- A good imagination!

Introduction

I write computer books, but that's not all I write. I'm also the author of three young adult fantasy and science fiction books (*Soulworm* and *The Dark Unicorn*, published by Royal Fireworks Press, and *Andy Nebula: Interstellar Rock Star*, published by Roussan Publishers.)

I love writing stories more than anything else, and when I was a kid, I not only wrote them, I illustrated them, filling page after page of scrap paper with detailed drawings of knights and dragons and spaceships and airplanes and castles and—well, you get the idea.

My drawing skills were never quite up to my imagination (which is why I concentrated on writing instead of art), but I had a lot of fun. And if I'd had a computer, I could have had even more fun because I could have turned my artwork and stories into complete on-line storybooks.

Where Do You Get Your Ideas?

Every writer eventually gets asked this question. The correct answer is "everywhere," but that doesn't usually help the person who wants to know. Here are a few places you can find ideas for stories:

- **Your own experiences.** This is a safe, if somewhat dull, choice. "Write what you know" is something many beginning writers are told, but if you're interested in writing science fiction and fantasy, like me, it sounds like you're being told not to use your imagination. Nevertheless, if something exciting has happened to you, why not turn it into a story?
- **Experiences you wish you'd had.** Have you always wanted to go skydiving? Snowboarding in the Alps? Snorkeling? Fire up AOL, search the Web for all the information you can find on the topic, and then write a story about the day you went skydiving, snowboarding, or snorkeling. Imagining doing something is almost as much fun as doing it!

> **Where Do You Get Your Ideas? (Continued)**
>
> - **Your friends' and family's experiences.** Is Uncle Tim always telling that story about the time he went hang-gliding and landed in a tree? Turn it into a story, complete with illustrations. Maybe he won't have to tell it again.
> - **The landscape.** My novel *Soulworm* came about because the town I was living in at the time, Weyburn, Saskatchewan, has a prominent hill, called Signal Hill, that provides a great view of the surrounding flat-as-a-tabletop prairie. One day when I was up on that hill, I thought, "Wouldn't this be a great place for a castle?" I ended up writing a book just so I could put one there.
> - **People you meet.** Have you ever passed someone on the street rushing in the opposite direction and wondered, "What's his hurry?" Or maybe you've seen someone who looked a little odd or dressed a little differently. Write a story that explains it.
> - **Phrases you hear.** My second novel, ***The** Dark Unicorn,* started when my niece got the titles of two movies, *The Dark Crystal* and *The Last Unicorn,* mixed up. As soon as she said, "Let's watch *The Dark Unicorn,*" I thought, "What a great title for a book!" And so I wrote it.
> - **Current events.** You can find dozens of story ideas in every newspaper. My most recent novel, *Andy Nebula: Interstellar Rock Star,* resulted from an article I read about teen pop stars in Japan, one-hit wonders who are groomed to be a sensation and then disappear. I just took that idea, transplanted it to the far future, and threw in a few orange, multitentacled aliens for good measure.

Well, that's exactly what I'm going to do in this chapter. (Better late than never!)

Creating Your Storybook

To create a storybook, you need a way to combine pictures and text. If you have a word processor that allows you to insert images or if you have regular desktop publishing software such as Microsoft Publisher, you'll probably want to use those programs to create your storybook. But you can also create it using PhotoSuite SE II. Here's how:

1. Write your text in your favorite word processor, or even in NotePad.
2. Create the digital images to illustrate it (more on that later).
3. Open PhotoSuite SE II.
4. Click Photos, Get Photo, and open all the images you want to use to illustrate your storybook. This adds them to the Photo Library, visible at right when you click the button at the far right of the top toolbar.
5. Now click Projects.
6. Click the New button in the top toolbar, or choose File, New.
7. In the New dialog box (see Figure 11-1), choose inches from the Units listbox and set the dimensions of the page to 8.5 inches wide by 11 inches tall. Now click OK. This creates a blank project like the one in Figure 11-2.

Figure 11-1
In this dialog box you can specify the dimensions . . .

8. Now you're ready to begin creating your storybook. Start with a title. Click the Text tool on the left toolbar and then click on the page where you want the title to appear (hint: it's generally at the top). Type your title into the box in the Settings area, and choose a font, font style, and color. Add a second text box beneath it and put in your byline (for example, "By Edward Willett." After all, you want everyone to know who created this masterpiece, don't you?)

> **Where Do You Get Your Ideas? (Continued)**
>
> - **Pictures.** A picture is worth a thousand words, or it can generate a thousand words. A picture in a magazine or newspaper, on a Web site, or even in a television ad can spark your imagination. So can a picture you create yourself—such as the mutants you can create with The Home Gene-Splicing Kit, which you'll experiment with later in this chapter.

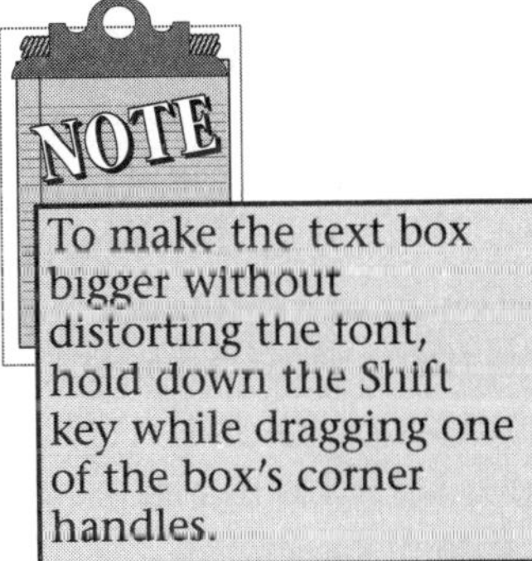

To make the text box bigger without distorting the font, hold down the Shift key while dragging one of the box's corner handles.

In PhotoSuite II SE text boxes, text only wraps (starts a new line) where you've pressed Return. To make a long section of text fit on the page, you'll have to manually enter a number of returns. For example, in Figure 11-3, I entered a return after the word *geese*.

Figure 11-2
. . . of a brand-new blank project.

Creating Images for Your Storybook

You have two ways to create images for your storybook: Draw them by hand and scan them in or use digital photographs.

If you've got an artistic bent and really like to draw and paint, then by all means create the images yourself. If you need to save space, use pencil or ink drawings, so you can scan them in black and white. However, you can just as easily go hog-wild and create full-fledged paintings in glorious color.

If you're more of a photographer than a drawer, you can create the illustrations for your book from existing photographs (as I did in Figure 11-4), or you can take special photographs just to illustrate the story. They could be as simple as landscape photos to set a mood—a foggy morning or a frosty, moonlit night—or you can be much more elaborate, staging scenes from your story complete with sets and costumes.

If you're writing a storybook for your children, why not make your children part of it? Kids love to play dress-up, and here's the perfect excuse. Turn them into princesses, pirates, or policemen and get them to act out scenes from the story while you take their pictures with your digital camera. Then download the photos into PhotoSuite II SE and pop them into your storybook. You'll end up with a beautiful book that not only tells your story, but makes it very personal.

9. Continue adding the main text of your story. If you've written your story in a word processor, the easiest way to add text is to highlight and copy the text in the word processor and then paste it into the text box by choosing Edit, Paste, or pressing Ctrl+v. You can also type directly into the text box, if you prefer (see Figure 11-3)

10. Next, add your pictures by simply dragging them from the Photo Library onto the project page (see Figure 11-4). Once they're in place, you can adjust them by clicking on them and dragging them around. Resize them by clicking and dragging their handles. (For more detailed information on using the various Project tools and working with multiple objects, see Chapter 4, "Create a Calendar!")

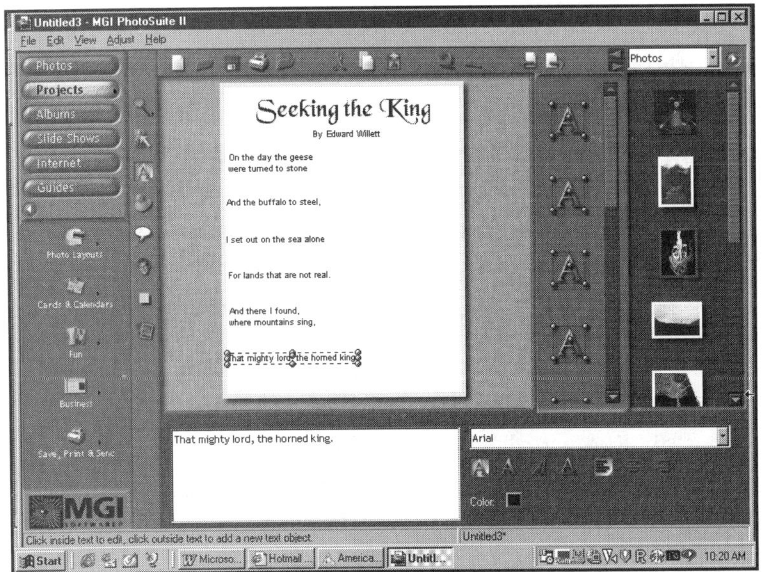

Figure 11-3
Here I've entered the text for the first part of my story.

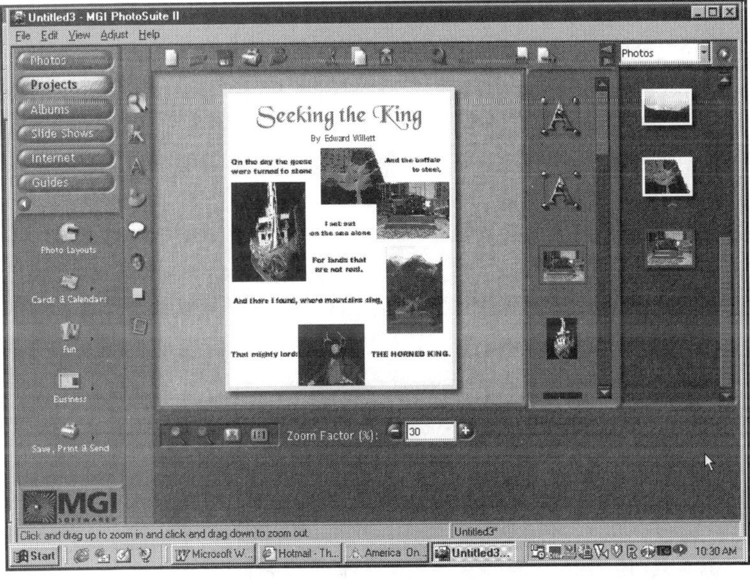

Figure 11-4
By carefully placing text and pictures, I've created an intriguing and well-illustrated storybook page.

11. To create the second page of your storybook, you'll have to click New and create a brand-new project. Continue doing so until your storybook is finished.

12. Choose File, Save for each project/page, and save each with a straightforward name like page1, page2, page3.

13. Click File, Print for each project/page to print out the separate pages of your storybook. Then you can assemble them by hand into the completed work.

Creating Images with The Home Gene-Splicing Kit

One good source for story ideas—and pictures to illustrate those stories!—is included on the CD that came with this book. It's called The Home Gene-Splicing Kit. With it, you can create fabulous creatures, part human, part animal—sort of like the popular children's book series *Animorphs*.

When you first start The Home Gene-Splicing Kit, you'll see something that looks a bit like an old-fashioned refrigerator. To get started, press the flashing red Start button. The gene-splicing machine comes to life, and a strange face floats to the surface of the washing-machine–like window at the bottom (see Figure 11-5).

Here's how to create your own mutant faces with The Home Gene-Splicing Kit:

1. Click either the Back or Forward button to the right of the TV screen. Two labels will appear, saying something like "Donor 01" on one and something like "Humans" on the other. At the same time, an image matching the bottom label appears in the TV screen—in this case, a human. Below the image a control panel appears with four different areas in it: a head, an eye, a nose, and a mouth. Below that are two arrows, one pointing left and one right (see Figure 11-6).

Figure 11-5 The Home Gene-Splicing Kit is ready for action!

Figure 11-6
Use these controls to choose the donors you want to splice together.

2. Use the Forward and Back buttons to the right of the TV screen to move forward and backward through the available donor groups, which include animals, boys, girls, men, and women. Use the arrows in the control panel beneath the TV screen to move forward and backward through the available images within each donor group. When you see a donor you'd like to use, choose which part you want to splice into your mutant from the control panel under the TV screen: head, eye, nose, or mouth. You can also click on that part of the image in the TV screen. That feature is added to the mutant in the bottom window. For example, in Figure 11-7, I've given the mutant the head of the boy in the TV screen.
3. Continue building your mutant by adding other features from other donors. Experiment as much as you like. Try animal heads with human features, human heads with animal features, boy heads with girl features, and animal heads with features from other animals. In Figure 11-8, I've given my mutant the eyes of a dog, the nose of a bear, and the mouth of a little girl.
4. When you're satisfied with your mutant's appearance, click Save. This opens the "lab notebook," shown in Figure 11-9, in which you can enter more information about your mutant. Give your mutant a name, enter your own name as the mutant's creator, enter the date of creation, and provide any other information about the mutant. Some suggested questions are given, such as "Does it have a job? Go to school?" and "What are its favorite foods?" As you start to think about what your mutant would be

Figure 11-7 I've begun to build my mutant.

Figure 11-8 My mutant may look a little odd, but he seems to be friendly!

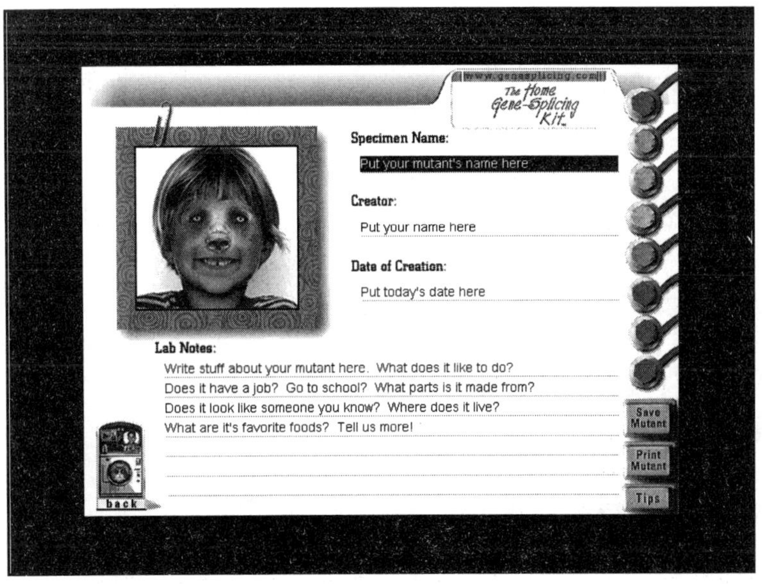

Figure 11-9 Enter more information about your mutant in the lab notebook. This is a great way to begin getting an idea for a storybook!

like if it really existed, you may also start to come up with interesting ideas for stories about your mutant's life that you can then turn into a storybook! To enter text in any of the areas, just highlight the text that's already there and type over it.

5. Change the color of the frame around the mutant's picture by clicking on the color buttons on the right side of the notebook page.
6. To print the lab notebook page, click Print Mutant. This opens a standard Print dialog box in which you can choose a printer and set its properties.
7. To save your mutant, click Save Mutant. A standard Save dialog box opens that lets you choose what name to save the mutant under and where on your computer to store it.
8. To return to the Home Gene Splicer to make more mutants, click the picture of the refrigerator in the lower-left corner.
9. To quit The Home Gene-Splicing Kit, click the Exit button in the bottom right corner of the refrigerator screen.

Using Your Mutant in Your Storybook

Once you've created and saved a mutant, you can easily use it in your storybook, because you can open it just like you would any other photo in PhotoSuite II SE, by clicking Photos, Get Photo, My Computer. Figure 11-10 shows my mutant in PhotoSuite.

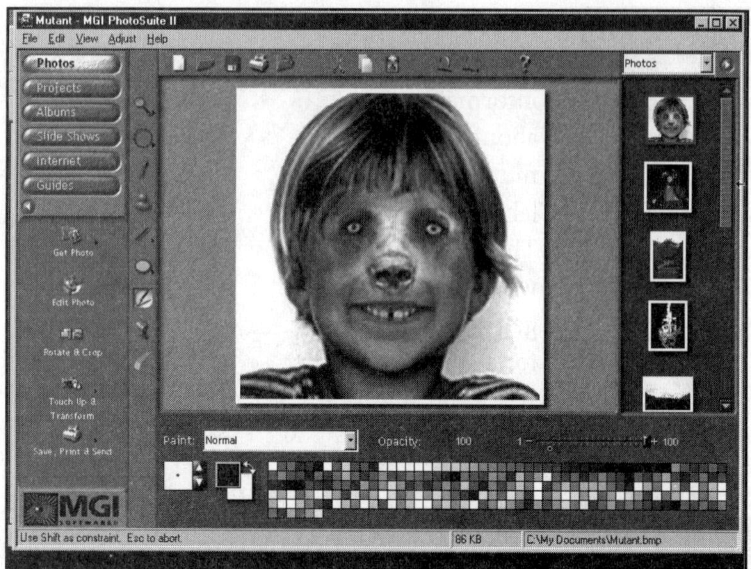

Figure 11-10 You can open and edit your mutant in PhotoSuite just like you can any other photo.

Of course, your mutant is just a disembodied head at this point. There is a fun way to give him a body, though:

1. Click Projects.
2. Start a new project as you did for each page of your storybook.
3. Click the Body Switch button on the left toolbar (third from the bottom).
4. Choose the body you want, and double-click on it. This inserts the body into your project (see Figure 11-11).
5. Drag the mutant's head from the Photo Library into the project.
6. Resize and reposition the head and the body until they match (see Figure 11-12).
7. Save the project as a single image. Choose File, Save, and in the Save dialog box, enter a name for the mutant and choose a graphic image format such as JPEG or CompuServe image (*.gif). Click Save.
8. Now click Photo, and open the image you just saved as you would any other photo.

You can put your storybook on the Web, with a menu of links on each page leading to every other page, in exactly the same way as you put a baby album on the Web in the last chapter. Refer to the section in Chapter 10 entitled "Sharing Your Baby Album" for detailed instructions.

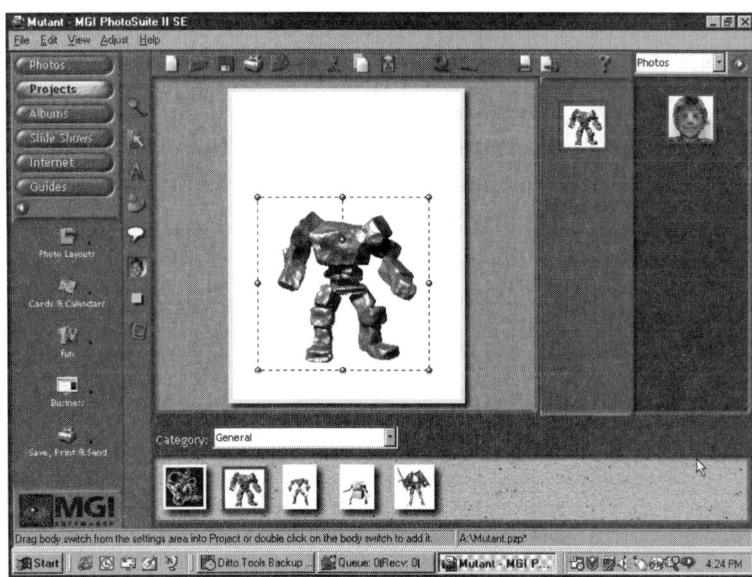

Figure 11-11
This is the body I've picked to attach my mutant's head to.

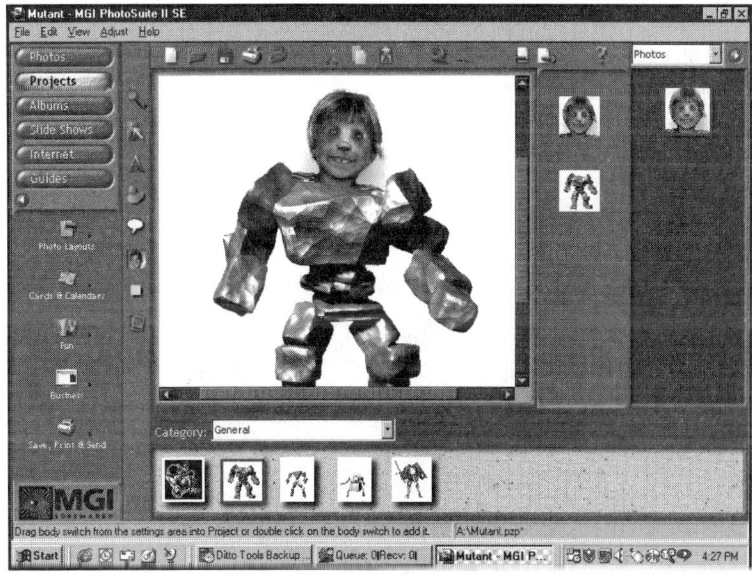

Figure 11-12
Okay, so he's a little weird-looking: What did you expect from a mutant?

9. Use the photo-editing tools to make the head and body match a bit better. For instance, in Figure 11-13, I used the Clone tool to make the mutant's shoulders match the shoulders of the body, whiten some of the gray areas around the head and round the top of the head, which was cut off slightly.
10. Save your picture one more time to lock in the changes. Now it's available for use in a storybook any time you want.

Figure 11-13
The photo-editing tools can make your mutant's head and his new body fit together better.

Everyone, it's said, has a story to tell. With digital images, your story can be one that you, your family, and friends will remember and enjoy for years to come!

Chapter 12

Project: Add Spice to Your School Reports

What You Need:

- Access to a scanner or digital camera
- PhotoSuite II SE
- ShowOff (on the CD)

Introduction

Back when I was in school—in that ancient, long-ago time known as the '70s—you had basically two choices for a school report: You could write it out by hand, or you could type it on a portable or electric typewriter.

The only images you could include were drawings you created yourself, ugly black-and-white photocopies, or things you had cut out of magazines (a practice which, for some reason, the school library frowned upon).

Times have changed. With a home computer, an AOL account, a scanner or digital camera, and a good printer, your average 12-year-old can now produce a school report that rivals what a professional printing company could have cranked out 25 years ago.

Suppose, for example, you want to create a report on skiing. You could research the topic on AOL and the World Wide Web, probably finding all the information you need; scan in pictures from your last skiing trip to illustrate it and print them out again, full-color, right in the body of your report; and take your digital camera down to the local ski shop to take pictures of different types of skis and poles or even to take pictures of a ski instructor demonstrating the various maneuvers.

The basic tool for creating a school report is a word processor. But while word processors are great at processing words, they're not always that great at processing pictures. That's where PhotoSuite II SE comes in.

In this chapter, you'll create photo pages and a cover for a school report, just to give you some idea of how you can use digital-imaging software and hardware to spruce up your school work.

Illustrating Your Text

The first step in creating a school report is to pick a topic. Because I'm not actually in school any more, I can pick a topic I'm really interested in, instead of one that the teacher is interested in. I've always enjoyed looking up at the sky (maybe because here on the prairies there's so much of it!), so I decided I'm going to write about clouds.

As noted in the introduction, I'm assuming you're going to write the bulk of your report in a word processor. I suppose you *could* write it in PhotoSuite II SE, using text boxes, but text boxes are really only for small amounts of text. It would be a lot harder, and the last thing you want to do is make your homework any harder than it has to be!

The first way in which PhotoSuite II SE can be useful is in helping you illustrate your report, assuming that your word processor allows you to add images. You can use PhotoSuite II SE to find and edit the pictures you later add to the pages of your report inside your word processor.

Of course, you can simply insert the pictures as they are—or you can use PhotoSuite II SE's photo-editing capabilities to add a whole new dimension to illustrations.

For instance, in one portion of my report, I talk about birds riding the columns of warm, rising air that create clouds. I want to include a small image of a bird, just a silhouette, to highlight the point.

I don't have a silhouette like that, but I do have a picture of a bird. To turn it into a silhouette:

1. I open the image in PhotoSuite II SE. The original image appears in Figure 12-1.
2. Next, I choose Touch Up & Transform, Touch Up, and, from the list of touchups, Fix Colors. Because I'm only interested in a silhouette, I only need the bird in black and white. I can turn the picture into a black-and-white picture by pulling the Hue and Saturation sliders to zero (see Figure 12-2).

Figure 12-1
You don't have to have exactly the right image for your report with PhotoSuite II SE, as long as you have one that's close!

Figure 12-2
Second step to a silhouette: Make the photo black and white.

9. Now I click Edit Photo again so I can get at the selection tools (second button from the top in the left toolbar). From the little menu of tools that opens when you click on the tiny black triangle beside the button, I choose the Magic Wand, which selects all pixels of approximately the same color surrounding the spot where you click the Wand. By experimenting—eventually sliding the Tolerance slider up to 100—I'm able to get the Magic Wand to select the area in Figure 12-3.

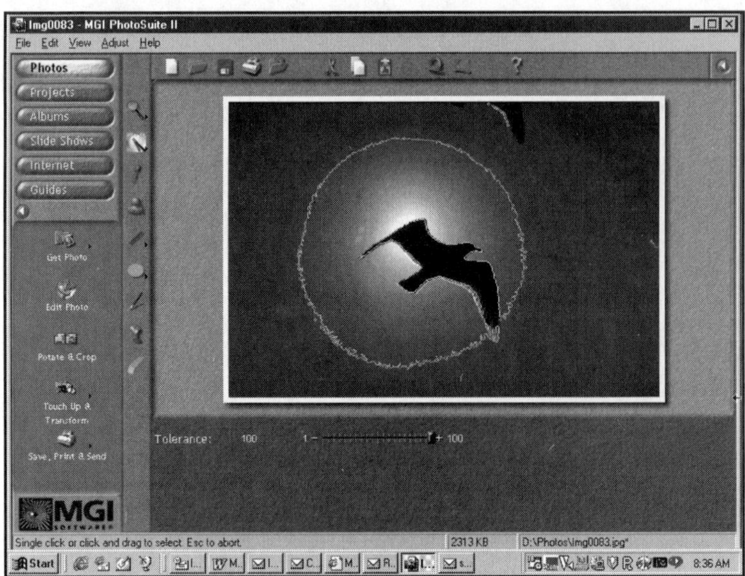

Figure 12-3
The next step is to select the area I want to create my new illustration from.

In Figure 12-3 I was really only trying to select the bird. I was quite astonished when the Magic Wand selected everything except the circle around the sun, but immediately realized that this could result in a more dramatic image. It's important to be open to serendipitous accidents like that when working with digital images. Sometimes the computer creates something that looks much better than what you originally had in mind! In this case, all the colors in the photo, except for those around the sun, were similar enough that, with the tolerance slider set to maximum, PhotoSuite II SE selected them all.

4. Now I want to turn the part of the photograph I selected into a new image. First, I choose File, Copy (or press Ctrl+C) to copy the selected portion of the photo to the Clipboard.
5. Next, I click the New button to create a new photo. This opens a dialog box in which you can specify the size, orientation (landscape or portrait), and resolution of the new photo. For my needs the default settings are fine, so I just click OK.
6. When the new, blank photo opens, I choose File, Paste (or press Ctrl+V) to paste the selected part of the original photo into the new one (see Figure 12-4).
7. I've almost got a silhouette now, but not quite. To make it more of a silhouette, I want to increase the contrast, so that I have only black and white—no shades of gray as I have at the moment. To do that, I click Touch Up & Transform, Touch Up, choose Brightness and Contrast from the list of Touchups, and move the Contrast slider all the way to the right for maximum contrast. Then I click Apply (see Figure 12-5).
8. The final step is to get rid of parts of the photo I don't want. I click Edit Photo, then choose the Elliptical Selection tool and draw an oval around the portion of the photo I want to use as my final illustration. Then I repeat Steps 4–6. The final step is to get rid of as much of the unwanted white space as I can. To do that, I click Rotate & Crop, then click the Crop tool from the left

Figure 12-4
Here's what the selected part of the original photo looks like when pasted into a new photo.

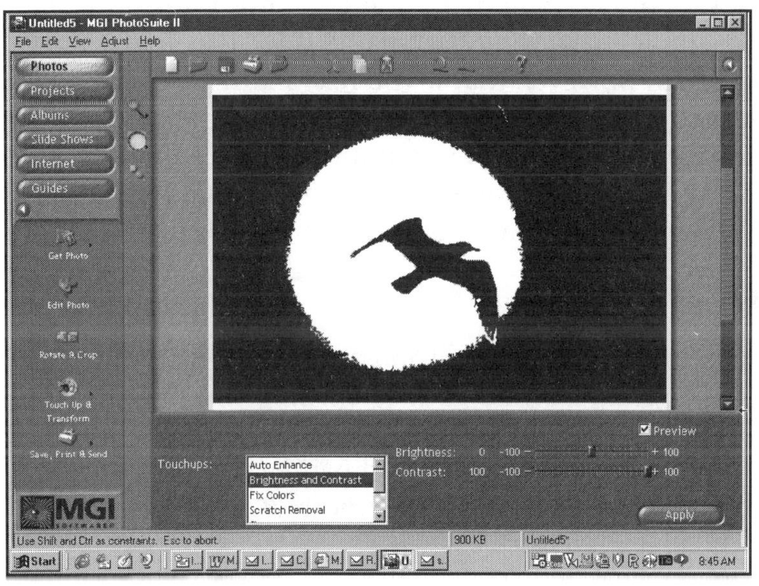

Figure 12-5
By heightening the contrast, I turn my photo into a stark black-and-white image.

toolbar, drag in the sides of the cropping frame until they are as tight to my oval as I can make them, and finally click Crop. The final image is shown in Figure 12-6.

9. Now I can save this image under a new name in whatever picture format I like and place it directly into my school report's word processor file using my word processor's normal picture-importing tools.

Figure 12-6
Here's my final illustration, ready for pasting into my word processor.

This is obviously only one of many ways you can transform a photographic image into clipart using PhotoSuite II SE. Use your imagination! (Remember, however, that if you're working with a copyrighted image, you have to change it drastically—essentially, create a completely new image—to be sure you're not infringing on the copyright. It's always best to use pictures that are in the public domain, free for anyone's use, or pictures that you took yourself.)

Creating Photo Pages

As the saying goes, "A picture is worth a thousand words" (although, unfortunately it doesn't count toward your total when you have to write a 2,000-word essay on, say, common garden snails). A photograph, presumably, is worth more words than mere clipart because it conveys more information, which makes it that much more useful in a school report.

To print photographs effectively, however, you need to use glossy photographic paper in your inkjet printer—paper you probably don't want to waste on ordinary text. So how can you add high-quality photographs to your school report?

The solution is to create special photo pages, which you can insert into your report once both the photo pages and the regular text pages are printed. PhotoSuite II SE provides you with a number of different layouts.

Figure 12-7
For my photo page, I've chosen a layout with room for three photographs and plenty of room for captions, too.

To create a photo page:

1. Open each of the photographs you want to put on the page. This places them in the Photo Library.
2. Click Projects.
3. Click Photo Layouts, and choose Photo Albums.
4. From the selection offered (see Figure 12-7), choose the one you want. Click on it to select it, and click Select.
5. If the Photo Library isn't showing, open it by clicking the button at the far right of the top toolbar.
6. Drag each photo you want to use from the Photo Library to the proper space in the layout. If you wish, you can also move the photos around on the page by selecting them and dragging them (see Figure 12-8).

PhotoSuite II SE treats text as just another graphic element. That means that if you resize the box in just one direction—say, making it taller without making it wider—the text inside is distorted just like a picture would be if you did that. To ensure that the text isn't distorted, resize using the corner handle and hold down Shift. This keeps the contents of the text box proportionally the same.

Once the photos are in place, you can add other elements. For instance, I want to add a page title and a caption for each photo. To do so:

1. Click the Text tool in the left toolbar, and click where you want the title of the page to go. I'm placing my title, "Cumulus Clouds," to the right of the first photograph.

Sources of Photos for Your Reports

So where do you find the photos and images to use in your school report? They're all around you!

The Internet is a good place to look. You're probably using it for research anyway, and in the process, you're sure to come across a lot of images relating to your topic. Right-click on any image on any Web site and choose Save Picture As, and you can tuck that image away on your computer for later use in your school report.

Just one word of warning, though: Copyright still applies. Many images are free for everyone to use—NASA, for instance, allows pretty much unrestricted use of its photographs —but others are not. When in doubt, ask. Almost any Web site you visit will have an e-mail address listed. A quick, polite note asking for permission to use a particular image in a school report will usually result in a yes. If you receive permission, it's usually a good idea (in fact, it may be required) to place a notice with the image saying that it is reprinted with the permission of the copyright owner.

If you have a scanner, you can turn any photograph you find into a digital image for use in your school report. Most families have hundreds or thousands of photographs of everything under the sun. An old vacation photo of the seashore can become an illustration for a report on wave action; a photo of Great-Grandma can highlight a report on aging. Steer clear of scanning in photos from magazines and books, however, again because of copyright.

Finally, if you have a digital camera, you can take your own photographs to accompany your report. If you're writing about something with a strong local connection, this can be particularly effective. A report on pollution has more impact if the images of pollution come from your city's river or even your own schoolyard. The best thing about taking your own photos is that you end up with exactly what you need, instead of just approximately what you need!

2. Once the text box appears, type your text in the box in the settings area, replacing the text that's already there, and choose a font, style, alignment, and color (see Figure 12-9). If you want to make the text bigger, just resize the box.

3. Create a caption in exactly the same way. It's a good idea to reference the picture somehow within the caption (left, below, above, and so on) so that readers are certain which caption belongs to which picture. Also be aware that PhotoSuite II SE text boxes don't automatically wrap text: You'll have to insert any line breaks by hand. In Figure 12-10, for example, I've hit Return after every three or four words so that my text box would fit comfortably in the space available. Without those returns, it would become one long, skinny box stretching across and beyond the photo layout.

4. Create captions for the remaining photographs. The final photo page appears in Figure 12-11.

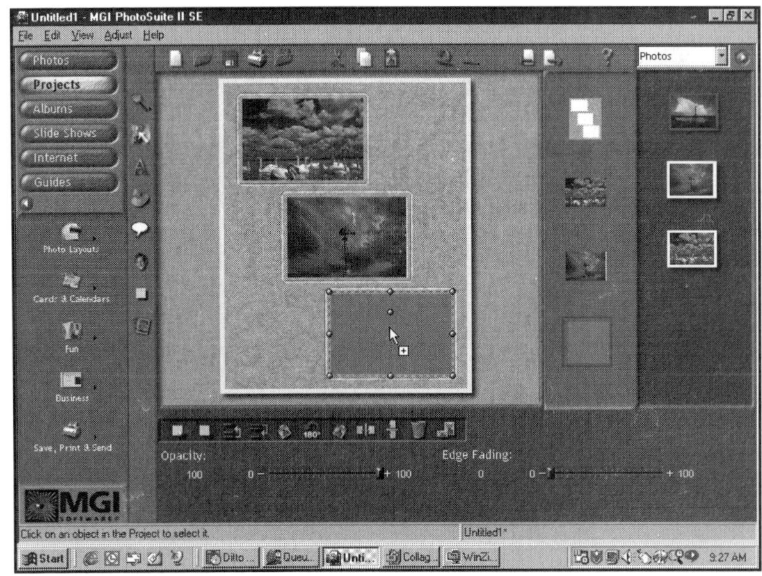

Figure 12-8
I've dragged two photos into place in the layout and am in the process of dragging the third.

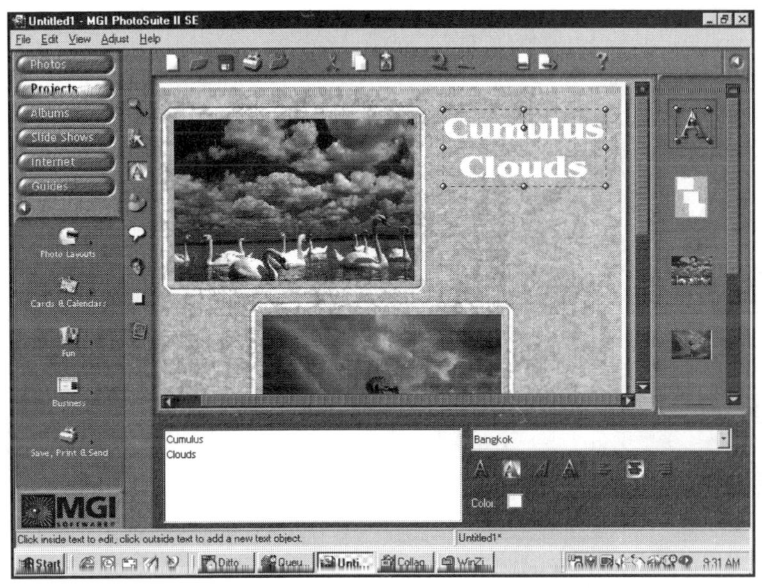

Figure 12-9
Choose your text font and color to match your topic and content of your photos.

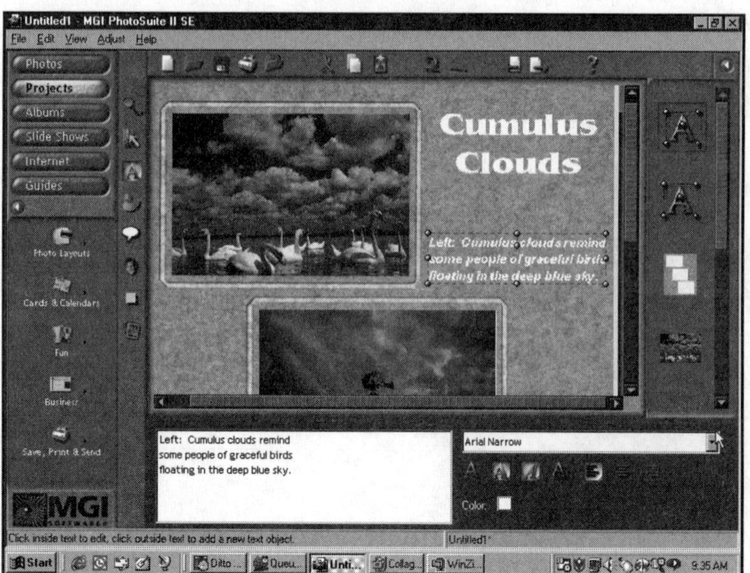

Figure 12-10
It can take some work to make your text fit properly into the space you have available.

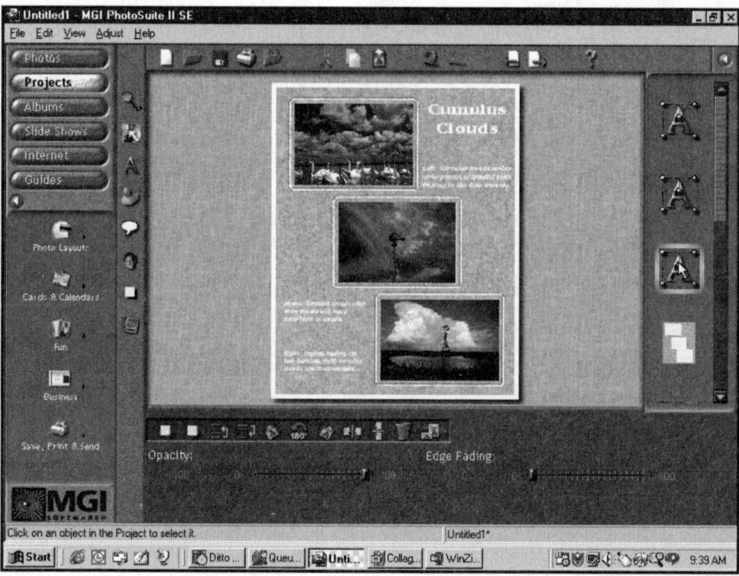

Figure 12-11
Here's my completed photo page, complete with title and captions, ready to be printed out on high-quality paper and added to my school report.

Creating a Report Cover

You can't judge a book by its cover, we've all heard, and you certainly can't judge a school report by its cover, either—but that's no reason not to have an attractive one. We've also all heard how important first impressions are, and that's what your report cover provides. A good cover may make the teacher more interested and positive about what's inside, and every little bit helps!

You might be able to find a template that you think would work well for a report cover. However, for my report, I've decided to create one from scratch. Here's how to go about it:

1. Open any photographs you might want to use on your front cover so they're in the Photo Library.
2. Click Projects.
3. Click the New button, or choose File, New from the menu bar. You'll see the dialog box in Figure 12-12.
4. First, decide if you want to use portrait or landscape orientation for your report cover.

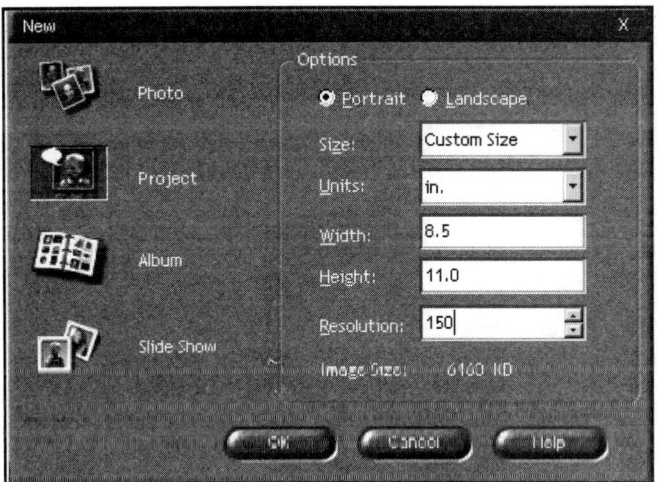

Figure 12-12
Set the size and resolution of your project using these controls.

5. Next, set the size. Since you most likely want your report cover to be 8½ × 11, the same as your text pages, you'll need to choose Custom Size from the Size listbox, then select inches from the Units listbox and finally enter 8.5 for the width and 11 for the height.

6. Resolution determines how sharp the images on your report page will be. I suggest choosing a minimum of 150. (If you're unhappy with the quality after printing, you'll have to rebuild the cover again using a higher resolution, so it's better to go high than low on the resolution. Be aware, however, that the higher the resolution, the more disk space your report cover will take up.)

7. Click OK to open your new project. Now you can drag any pictures you want to use on your cover from the Photo Library. Once I've done that, my layout appears as it does in Figure 12-13.

Figure 12-13
Using a single large-scale photo on the front of your report can be a very dramatic and effective technique.

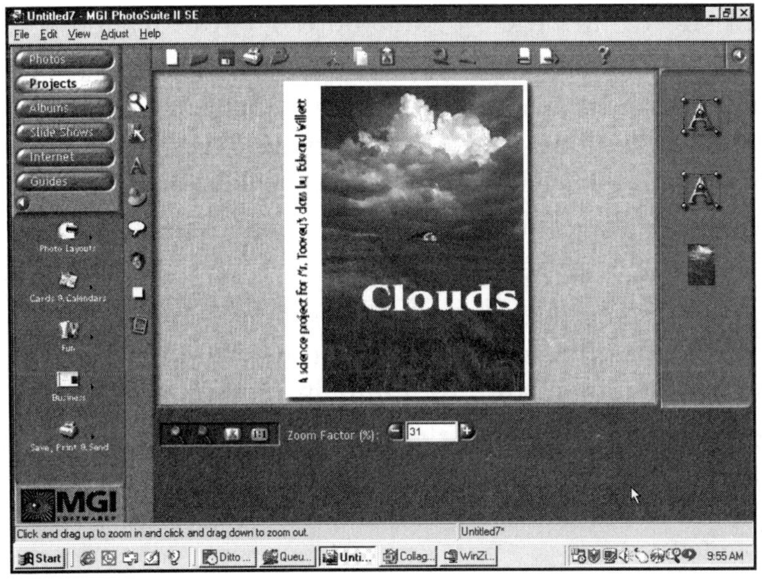

Figure 12-14
Any teacher would be impressed upon receiving a report with a title page as dramatic as this!

8. Now you can add text. Click on the Text tool, click anywhere in your layout that you want the text to go, and enter the text you want into the resulting text box. For my report, I created two text boxes. One, which states this is a science report and I wrote it, I string down the left-hand side of the page. I rotated the box by clicking on the handle that appears inside it, near the center. The other text box contains the title of the report. Once I've positioned both text boxes, my final report cover is one I'm very happy with (see Figure 12-14).

Creating a Digital Presentation with ShowOff

If there's one thing many people fear more than anything else, it's public speaking. For many that fear dates back to the horrible experience of having to make an oral presentation in school. That's because those people lived in those long-ago benighted days when personal computers and programs like ShowOff weren't available.

With ShowOff, you can create a visual presentation to go along with your talk. When people have something to look at besides you, you'll find a lot of the pressure is off you.

Creating a slide show with ShowOff is described in detail in Chapter 7, "The Vacation Slide Show," but briefly, here's how you do it:

1. Open ShowOff.
2. The ShowOff Wizard starts. Click Next.

3. On the next screen, click the top radio button, Create a Slide Show, and click Next again.
4. Choose the location where ShowOff should initially look for pictures for the slide show. Click Change image location to browse your computer; highlight the directory you want, click OK, and click Next.
5. When the next screen appears, click Finish.
6. Choose the images you want from the directory displayed, highlight them, and click Add. The order in which you add pictures is the order in which they'll initially be displayed.
7. If you want to use animated transitions between slides, click the Use Transitions checkbox. To choose which transitions you want to use, click Select Transitions and pick the ones you want from the list provided.
8. Click the Loop checkbox if you want the slide show to start over from the beginning when you reach the end.
9. Select the Manual Mode checkbox to advance slides manually by clicking a mouse button (clicking the left mouse button advances the slow to the next slide, while clicking the right calls up the previous slide). If you want the show to run automatically, uncheck Manual Mode and use the View Time scrollbox to set the number of seconds you want each slide to be displayed.
10. To set the color that appears behind any images that don't fill the screen, click Set.
11. Click Next. Thumbnails of your slides appear. To add an additional slide, click Add New Images in the Advanced Slide Show Options box. You can also add sounds to individual slides or background music to your whole show.
12. To remove or reposition a slide, click on it to bring up the Image Options box. Click Change Position to enter a new position for the slide; click Remove to delete it.
13. When you're ready to view your slide show, click Start. You'll be prompted to save; now the show will begin.

I can't promise you that applying your newfound digital projects expertise to your homework will ensure that you'll get an A, but it should certainly help!

CHAPTER 13

PROJECT: Inventory Your Valuables

What You Need:

- Regular camera and access to a scanner, or access to a digital camera
- PhotoSuite II SE
- NetGraphics Studio 2 SE

Introduction

I just got married a few months ago and, for the first time in my life, now own the place where I live. (Well, the bank and I do.) Not only that, but my wife and I now own a whole bunch of other stuff we didn't own before, thanks to the generosity of wedding guests and the mix of my accumulated possessions from several years of bachelorhood with those of my wife.

I have a vague notion of everything that's tucked away in the condo but not a detailed one. And that could be bad in the event of (God forbid!) a burglary, a fire, or some other disaster because insurance people frown on you trying to claim you have to replace a Picasso when what you really had was a Red Skelton.

Fortunately, digital images are a great way to keep a record of your belongings—and keep that record organized.

What to Include in Your Inventory

I use two criteria when deciding what should be included in my inventory of valuables.

The first is, of course, value. Anything that would be very expensive to replace should be included. (Tallying your most expensive belongings in this fashion can also help you determine whether you have enough insurance!)

The second is irreplaceability. Everyone owns things that, while not valuable in a monetary sense, are priceless in a personal sense. It might be the poster for the play you took your wife to the night you proposed or a drawing your daughter gave you for Mother's Day. You can't get an insurance company to pay what those things are worth to you, but at least if you record a digital image of them, you'll still have something tangible even in the event a disaster robs you of the actual item.

Creating Your Inventory

Using whatever criteria you use to decide what is valuable (my personal criteria are listed in the sidebar), choose the items to be inventoried. I suggest taking a slow walk through every room of the house, making notes as you go.

Capturing Your Valuables Digitally

Once those items are chosen, make a digital record of them. There's more than one way to do that; which method you use depends on the item being inventoried.

The three methods are

- **Take digital photographs.** This is the easiest way to capture images of three-dimensional objects such as china, sculpture, and furniture and can also be used to capture two-dimensional but hard-to-scan things like framed posters, paintings, and drawings.
- **Take regular photographs and scan them or get them copied to a CD.** The disadvantage with this method is that you need to have the film developed and then scan the prints one at a time, which takes a lot longer and is more expensive than just downloading images from a digital camera; the advantage is that, in addition to digital images, you also have a set of prints and, more importantly, a set of negatives—physical objects that you can store in separate, safe locations as additional backups of the digital images. If you don't have a scanner, or even if you do, you might want to consider an online photo service such as Kodak PhotoNet Online (AOL keyword Photonet), which develops your film and digitizes it at the same time, presenting you not only with a complete set of prints and negatives but a complete set of digital versions of your images.
- **Scan objects directly.** Obviously you can't scan your grandmother's antique dining table, but valuable documents such as deeds, bonds, stamp collections, letters, and so on can be scanned in directly. You'll capture a much better digital image of them that way than by photographing them.

Using PhotoSuite II SE to Create Your Inventory

Once you have your digital images created and stored on your computer, you can use PhotoSuite II SE's Photo Album function to save and organize them and its Project function to create printouts of your inventory. (You could even create Web pages that show off your valuables, but very few people want to post a list of everything valuable they own on the Web for everyone to see, for some reason!)

Here's how to create a digital inventory in PhotoSuite:

1. Click the Albums button.
2. Choose File, New, or click the New button on the top toolbar.
3. Give your photo album a name, such as "Valuables Inventory" and choose the size of thumbnails you want. I suggest using the largest 128x128 for this album (see Figure 13-1).
4. Click OK. PhotoSuite creates a blank photo album.
5. Now you're ready to start adding pictures of your valuables. Click Get Photo. If you've already stored your images on your computer, click Computer to browser for them. If you prefer, you can download pictures from a digital camera or scan in photos directly to the album by choosing one of the digital camera options or the scanner option. (For complete information on adding pictures to a photo album, see Chapter 3, "The Digital Photo Album.") See Figure 13-2.

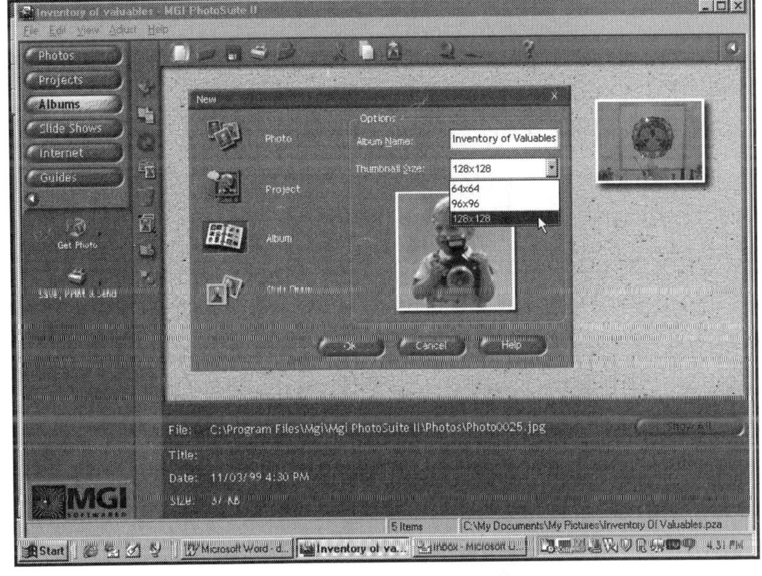

Figure 13-1
I recommend using the largest thumbnail size for an inventory album. It will make it easier to see your valuables!

Figure 13-2
My inventory is starting to take shape.

Organizing Your Inventory

To effectively organize your inventory, you need to provide complete information about each item in the pictures. The more complete this information is, the better it will be if you ever have to call on the inventory to prove a loss or try to replace an item.

To add information to a picture:

1. Right-click on the picture and choose Properties from the pop-up menu (see Figure 13-3).
2. From the Property listbox, choose the property you want to describe.
3. Type in a description in the Description box.
4. Click Add/Modify to add the property and its description to the File box.
5. If you'd like to associate a sound with the item—perhaps you've recorded a more complete description as a .wav file—use the Browse button to locate that file. Click Play to preview it.
6. Move to the next picture in the album by clicking Next, and repeat the procedure.
7. When you've added descriptions to all the items in your inventory, click OK. (Don't click Cancel; that closes the Properties dialog box without saving any of the information you've entered.)

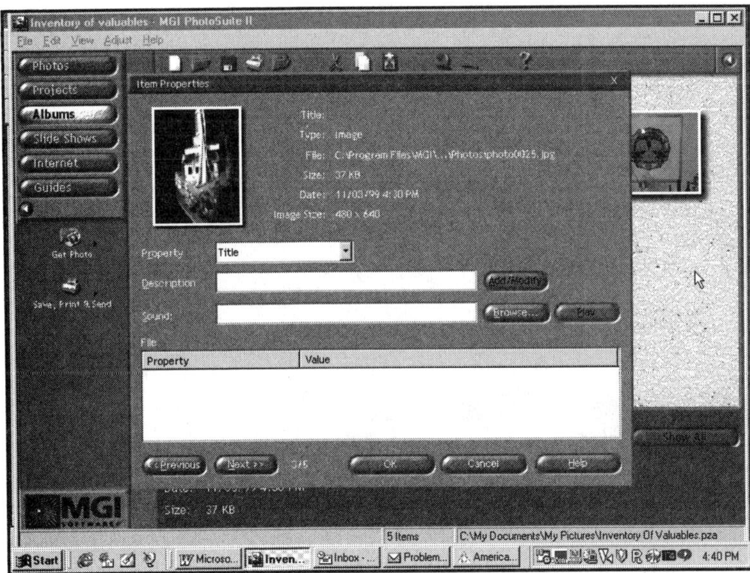

Figure 13-3 Enter detailed information about your picture in the Properties dialog box.

Once you've filled out the Properties sheet for each item in your inventory, you can use the Sort tool (third from the bottom on the left toolbar) to arrange them. Here's how:

1. Click the Sort button.
2. In the dialog box in Figure 13-4, choose the property you wish to sort by from the list provided. You can sort by all the properties you could add descriptions for in the Properties dialog box, as well as by file type, date, and size.
3. Choose whether you want to sort items in ascending or descending order.
4. Click OK.

The other really useful tool for finding your way around your inventory is the Search tool, which is the second button from the bottom in the left toolbar.

To use the Search tool:

1. Click the Search button.
2. In the dialog box in Figure 13-5, find which of the image properties you want to search through in the Search in list. Again, you can also choose to search by file name, type, or size.
3. In the Search for box, enter the word you want to look for.
4. Click OK. All items except the ones that match your criteria disappear from the screen (see Figure 13-6).

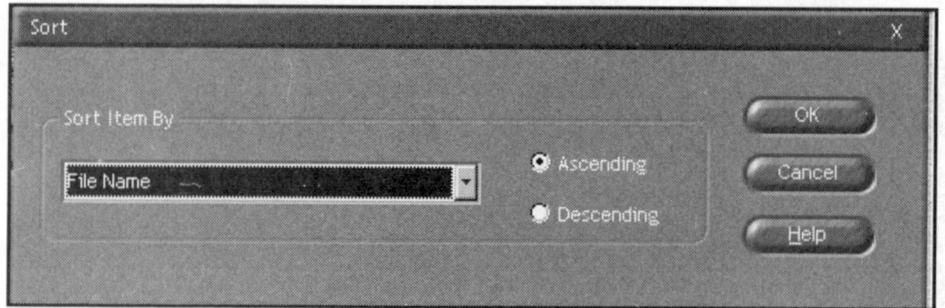

Figure 13-4
Choose which property you want to sort your inventory items by.

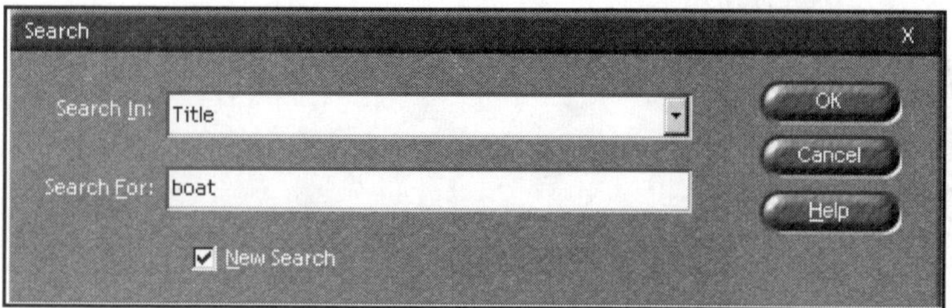

Figure 13-5
Use this dialog box to search among your inventory items for something specific.

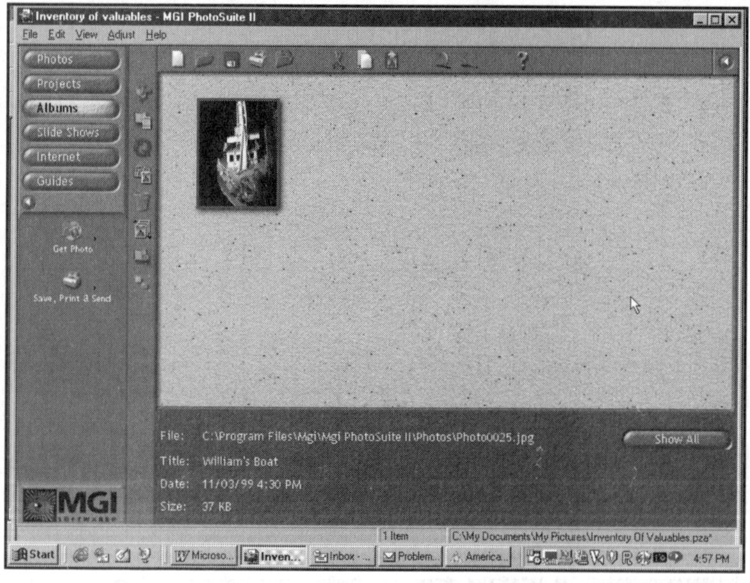

Figure 13-6
My search for an item with the word *boat* in the title turned up only one picture.

Data Storage Options

While an inventory of valuables that's readily available on your desktop computer is a good thing, you need to keep it somewhere else, as well, because if disaster strikes, your computer might not be there to bail you out.

In general, that means you need some sort of removable data storage. And because digital images can take up quite a bit of space, the data storage needs to be able to hold a lot of information.

Chapter 18 offers a complete discussion of the various kinds of data storage available, but in brief, you're looking at one of four possibilities:

- **Floppy disks.** The ordinary floppy disk has the advantage of being cheap and portable and the disadvantage of being slow and not holding all that much data. Still, if your inventory isn't all that large, this is the most readily available portable storage of all.
- **Superfloppies.** Superfloppies hold from 100 to 250 MB of data. The best-known type is Iomega's Zip drive. Superfloppies are inexpensive; the disks, though larger than a regular floppy, can easily be locked up in a nice secure safe or safety deposit box; and they're common enough that you can almost always find a machine to read them on. Unfortunately, they're also slow and sometimes suffer from reliability problems.
- **Winchester-based drives.** Winchester-based drives are faster and hold more data; they're also more expensive. The best-known are the Jaz drives offered by several manufacturers. Again, they're readily portable and can be safely stored somewhere out of harm's way. If you have a very large digital inventory, a Jaz drive might be the way to go.

Making the Most of Your Data Storage with NetGraphics Studio 2 SE

To make the most out of your data storage, whether it's your hard drive or a ZIP drive, consider optimizing the size of the images you use in your inventory using the NetGraphics Optimizer that's included on the CD as part of the NetGraphics Studio 2 program.

For complete details on using NetGraphics Optimizer, see Chapter 9, "The Family Web Site." Here's a brief reminder:

1. Open the Optimizer.
2. Browse for the image you want to optimize, or arrange your windows so you can drag it into the Optimizer and do so. Click Next.
3. Specify the size of the graphic.
4. Click Next again. The Optimizer analyzes the graphic and recommends either GIF or JPEG format.
5. Click Next once more, and move the slider to choose between a small, lower-quality file or a larger, higher-quality file.
6. Click Next yet again, and choose whether you want the image to be *interlaced.* (This is of no importance if you're just trying to save space.) Interlaced images appear all at once at low resolution when your downloading them, then gradually sharpen as more information is received. Non-interlaced images appear at full resolution, but slowly, a little bit at a time, taking shape from the top down.
7. Save your revised image.
8. To work with additional images, click Back to Beginning.

- **CD-R and CD-RW drives.** From an archiving point of view, CD-R and CD-RW drives are probably the best choice because they're likely to last longer than any magnetic-based media. Although CD writers are fairly expensive, the disks are relatively cheap and hold lots of data. And they have the added benefit of being easily stored in an ordinary CD rack!
- **Online storage.** Some online photo services now offer, or soon will, online storage, which allows you to keep your digital images safely stored on their computer. This will probably prove to be the cheapest option, since it doesn't require you to buy any additional hardware; on the other hand, it takes the security of your images entirely out of your hands, which you may or may not be comfortable with.

Using the Web to Find Out More About Your Valuables

If you've own something that you think might be valuable, or you own something you know is valuable but you're not sure just how valuable, you owe it to yourself to get on the World Wide Web and do some digging.

For instance, my father-in-law had a 1950s-era Zeiss camera. I didn't have much more information about it than what was written on the case, but on the Web I was able to find several pages devoted to Zeiss cameras that provided some information and, more importantly, the name and e-mail address of a man who was able to provide me detailed information about this particular model.

The starting place for research is AOL's NetFind. It's easy to get to: Just go keyword NETFIND.

Once you get there (see Figure 13-7), you'll find a blank box at the top, next to a button labeled Search! Simply enter a word or words that describe the item you want to find out more about, and click Search! Figure 13-8, for example, shows some of the results when I enter the words *Zeiss Camera*.

If you find yourself overwhelmed by the number of sites your search turns up, you need to refine your search. See the following sidebar, "Six Simple Steps for Finding What You Want."

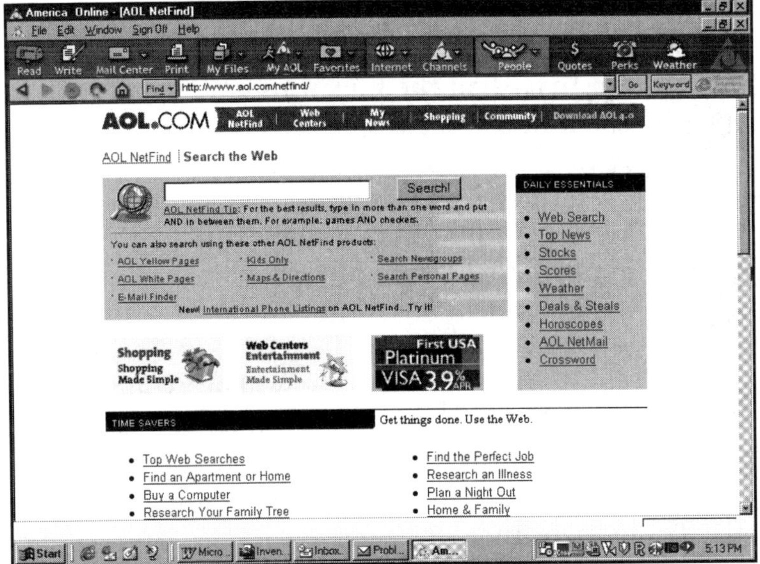

Figure 13-7
NetFind is the best place to start to find out more about your valuables.

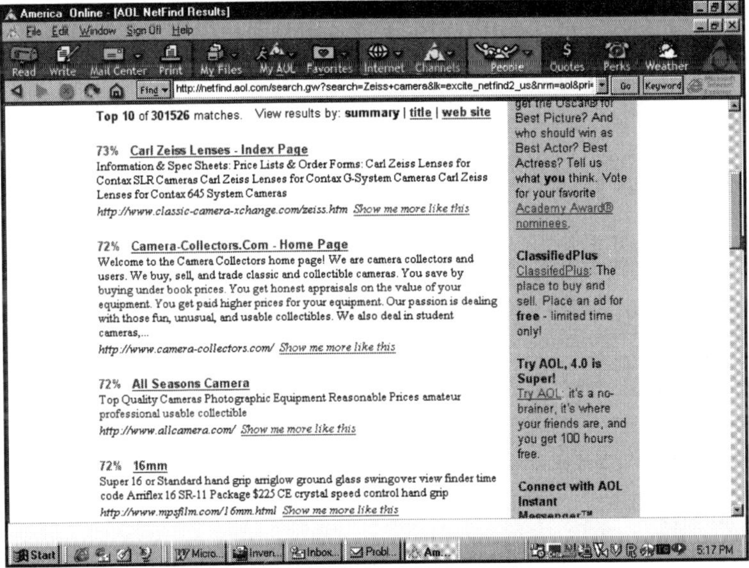

Figure 13-8
Search results appear in this format.

Six Simple Steps for Finding What You Want

- **Phrase it.** Don't use one word searches. Instead, type in multiple words or a phrase in quotes to increase your chances of finding useful results.
- **Be specific.** The more descriptive you can get, the better your results. Typing in "colonial oak dining table" is better than just "table."
- **Add it up.** Use AND or the plus sign (+) when you want to find articles that contain all of the words you enter. For example, to find articles on early American silver, try typing "early AND American AND silver," or "early +American +silver." It's important to put the plus sign directly in front of the word you want added, with no spaces ("painting +Picasso").
- **Cut it out.** Use AND NOT or the minus sign (–) to limit your results to articles with only the words you want. For example, if you want articles about chandeliers, but aren't interested in *The Phantom of the Opera,* try typing in "chandeliers AND NOT Phantom," or "pets –Phantom." Put the minus sign directly in front of the word you want left out, with no spaces ("gold –coins").
- **More like this.** If you're getting more than you bargained for in your results, be sure to click on the More Like This link next to the Web link that most closely matches what you're looking for. This tells the search engine to show you only those sites that are like the one you chose.
- **Refine your find.** If you really don't like the results you're getting, you've got a second chance. Scroll down to the "Refine Your Results" area at the bottom of the results page, and try tweaking your find a bit. If you've got too many results, get more specific by adding more words. If you've got too few results, make your find more general by removing some words.

It's easy to get sidetracked looking through all the pages most searches turn up, but that's half the fun. You never know when you'll find what you're looking for.

Keep an eye out for names and e-mail addresses for experts on the particular type of item you're looking for, too. Most people are happy to help out if they can.

The more you know about your valuable items, the more you'll enjoy them—and the more valuable they'll become, if not monetarily, then at least where it really matters, in your heart.

Chapter 14

PROJECT: Market Your Small Business

What You Need:

- Regular camera and access to a scanner, or access to a digital camera
- PhotoSuite II SE
- AOL 4.0
- Hemera Photo-Objects SE

Introduction

For a little over five years now, I've been in business for myself as a freelance writer. I quickly discovered that no matter how small your operation is (and a freelance writer is about the smallest of all small businesses, consisting of one person and, maybe, a computer), you'll get more attention from prospective clients if you present yourself like a much larger operation.

That's not as difficult as you might think. It just means you need to create sharp-looking letterhead, business cards, invoices, and so on that project an image of business-like dependability.

With PhotoSuite II SE and AOL 4.0, you can not only make your small business look like a million bucks, you can do so on-line, where you can contact prospective clients all over the world.

In this chapter you'll create a number of useful business-related projects, from business cards and flyers to an on-line photo catalog.

Ten Questions to Ask Yourself Before You Start Marketing a Business

Before you start cranking out projects that advertise your business, you should ask yourself a few questions:

- **What will I call my business?** Large corporations spend thousands of dollars selecting names for their products and subsidiaries. You probably don't have that kind of cash handy. You can still come up with a list of several possibilities and run them by friends, neighbors, family, and casual acquaintances to get a sense how the public will react.
- **What services do you want to focus on?** You may do a 101 things, but they won't all fit on your business card. For marketing purposes, it's best to focus on one or two core activities. Once they're well-established, you can begin promoting new services, and so build your business. A key rule of thumb in marketing is to keep your message tightly focused. Too much information and your audience's eyes will glaze over and they'll forget all about you.

Ten Questions to Ask Yourself Before You Start Marketing a Business (Continued)

- **Who is likely to use your services?** Identifying the people most likely to be your customers is the same thing as identifying the people you should be aiming your marketing efforts at!
- **What's unique about your services?** You probably aren't the only freelance writer, or Web-page designer, or antique silver polisher in the county. To stand out from the crowd, identify something you can offer that no one else can—some special expertise, for instance, or a better location. Then make that unique attribute a focal point of your marketing.
- **What types of marketing do you want to use?** The possibilities are almost endless: direct mailing, e-mailing, a Web page, in-person sales calls, phone calls, paid advertisements in newspapers or on radio or TV, the Yellow Pages, store window displays, and so on. Try to identify the ones that are best suited to your business (if you're a Web-page designer, for instance, you'd better be able to make a killer Web page advertising yourself).
- **How much money have you allocated to marketing?** Cross-reference the amount of money you have with the costs associated with each of the types of marketing you'd like to be able to use, and you'll quickly figure out which ones you really can afford to use and which ones will have to remain wishful thinking for now!

Creating a Flyer

One of the most basic types of advertising is a flyer. If you have the money, a flyer can be a full-color beauty on glossy paper that is mailed directly to millions of people. If you don't have the money, a flyer can be a one-color sheet stuck on public announcement boards around the city. Either way, you'll probably want one to identify your business. When I became a freelancer, it was one of the first things I created.

Creating a Flyer with PhotoSuite II SE

PhotoSuite II SE can help you create a flyer for your business, complete with digital images, which can range from a picture of your handsome (or beautiful) self, smiling at your customers from the front of the flyer, to a picture of your office (something I would never include in a flyer because my office looks like a grenade went off in it), to pictures of your products, to generic pictures distantly related to your products or services. (If you sell water filters, for instance, you could include a picture of a sparkling waterfall.)

Here's how to create a flyer using PhotoSuite II SE:

1. Click the Projects button.
2. Click Business. This opens the window in Figure 14-1.
3. Click Promotions.
4. You'll see several templates to choose from (see Figure 14-2).
5. Highlight the flyer template you want to use, and click Select. The template opens in the work area (see Figure 14-3).

Figure 14-1
PhotoSuite II SE offers you several different business-related projects to choose from.

Figure 14-2
Choose the flyer layout you want from the selection provided by PhotoSuite II SE.

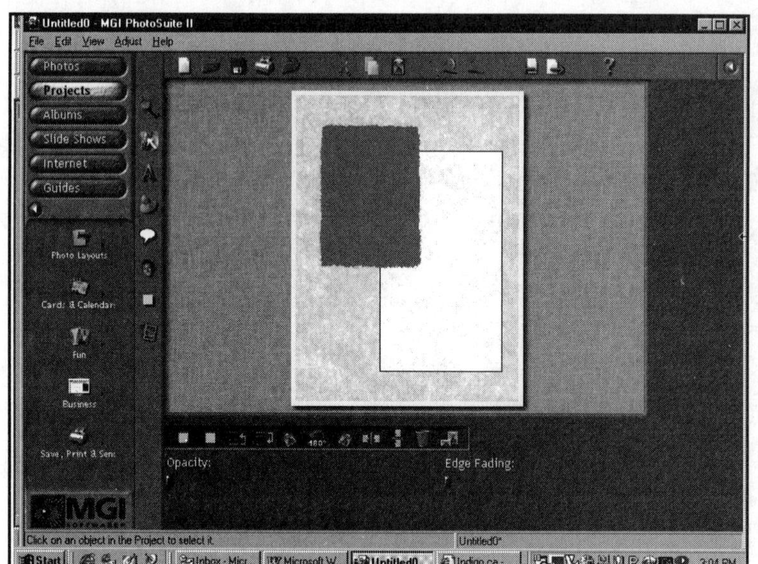

Figure 14-3
Here's a template for a one-page flyer with a picture.

6. Click Photos, Get Photo, and open the photo(s) you want to use on your flyer. This places them in the Photo Library, which you can display by clicking the button at the far right of the top toolbar. Use the Photo Editing tools to make the photos look the way you want. (See Chapter 2, "Digital Projects 101: What You Need to Know to Use This Book," for more detailed information on editing photos.)
7. Click Projects to return to your flyer template. The template I'm using has room for only one photo; some have room for more. Click on the photo in the Photo Library you want to use, and drag it into the gray square in the template (see Figure 14-4).
8. Now you can add text. I want a title, some descriptive text, a price, and a phone number. Because each needs to be a different size and sometimes a different font, I decide to put each item in a separate text box. To create a text box, click the Text button on the left toolbar and click on the project, wherever you want the text to appear. Choose font, style, alignment, and color from the Settings box; you can make the text larger by clicking and dragging one of the corner handles of the text box. Enter the text in the white box in the Settings area (you'll have to enter a return to create each additional line of text within the box).
9. Continue clicking on the project and adding text boxes until you've added the text you want (see Figure 14-5).

Figure 14-4
Here's my flyer with a picture of my new product line in place.

Figure 14-5
Here's my finished flyer.

Using Hemera Photo-Objects SE to Spice Up Your Flyer

Hemera Photo-Objects SE, included on the CD, contains dozens of *Photo-Objects*—graphics that look like photographs but are as easy to use as clipart drawings. Photo-Objects SE also lets you create *PhotoFonts*, fonts made with photographic textures. Both offer great ways to add interest to your flyer design.

Photo-Objects SE is described in detail in Chapter 9, "The Family Web Site," but briefly, here's how to use it:

1. Open Hemera Photo-Objects SE.
2. Use keywords to search the Photo-Objects for one you can use. Photo-Objects SE searches automatically as you type in the Enter keywords space; by the time you've finished typing, Photo-Objects SE is already displaying any matches it found.
3. Choose File, Export To, and choose Graphics Application.
4. Specify the final size of the image and flip it horizontally or vertically, if you like.
5. Click Next again and select a background color for the image, or a background texture.
6. Click Next one more time, and you're asked to specify where you should save the file.
7. Now add it to your PhotoSuite II SE project just as you would any other photo.

Using a PhotoFont is very similar:

1. In Hemera Photo-Objects SE, choose the PhotoFont tab instead of the Photo-Objects tab.
2. Enter the text you want to put into a PhotoFont, and choose a font, style, and size for it.
3. Choose a texture.
4. Export the PhotoFont image just as you did the Photo-Object, by choosing File, Export To. Add it to your PhotoSuite II SE project as you would any other image.

Publishing Your Flyer for Everyone to See

Once you've finished your flyer, there's more than one way to use it. Of course, you can print it (choose File, Print). If you only want a dozen or so, you can even print them all on your inkjet printer. More likely you'll want several hundred, which means taking them to a print shop. Color photocopies are reasonably cheap, and certainly cheaper than full-color printing by other methods, unless you're getting a very large quantity made. Your local printer can explain the various options to you.

You can also get PhotoSuite II SE to turn your flyer into a Web page: Just choose File, Create Web Page. Make a note of where PhotoSuite stores the page—it will tell you. Then you can preview it using AOL 4.0 by choosing File, Open and locating the Web file. (You'll be asked if you want to Browse or Edit the page; choose Browse.) Figure 14-6 shows what my flyer looks like as a Web page.

Finally, you can e-mail your flyer to as many people as you like. To do so:

1. In PhotoSuite II SE, choose File, Save As, and save your project as a JPEG image.
2. Log onto AOL.
3. Click Write.
4. Enter the addresses of the people you want to send the flyer to in the Send To box.
5. Click the Insert a Picture button on the e-mail editing toolbar and, from the submenu, choose Insert a Picture.

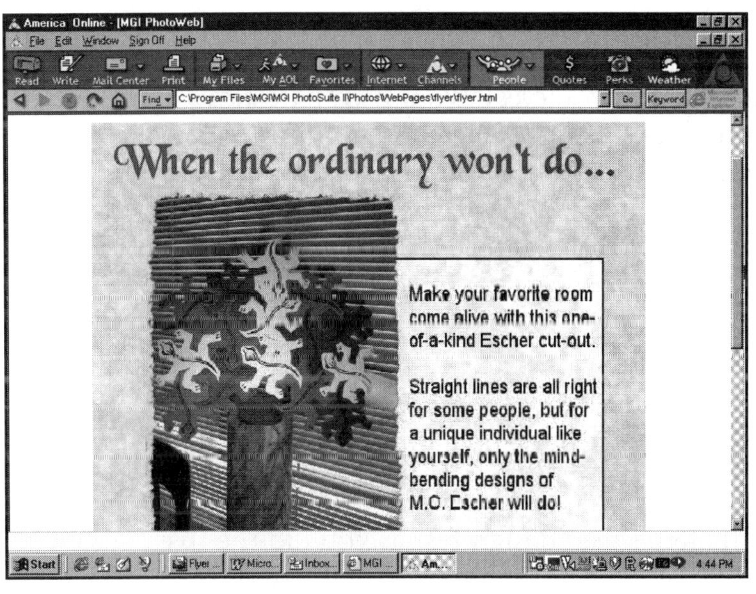

Figure 14-6
Here's my flyer transfomed into a Web page.

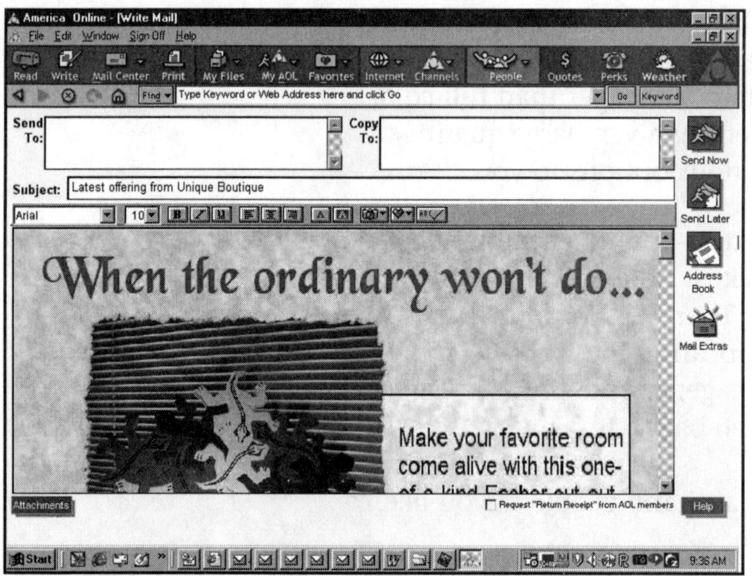

Figure 14-7
Most flyers go by regular mail, but you can also send one by e-mail.

6. In the Open dialog box that appears, locate and select the JPEG image you created in Step 1. Click Open.
7. The flyer appears in your e-mail; click Send Now to send it on its way (see Figure 14-7).

Creating Digital Letterhead

Well-designed, professional-looking letterhead is important for all your written correspondence when you're running a small or home business. It's another indicator to your customers that you, well, mean business.

PhotoSuite II SE lets you create your own letterhead. Combine it with AOL 4.0, though, and you can create something even more exciting: digital letterhead, or letterhead for e-mail!

Here's how. First, you have to create the letterhead itself in PhotoSuite II SE. To do so:

1. Click the Projects button.
2. Click the Business button, and in the resulting window, choose Page Layouts. This displays the templates in Figure 14-8.
3. Choose the letterhead design you want to use, and click Select.
4. Now edit the letterhead design just as you did the flyer, adding a photo, text boxes, and so on. My finished letterhead is shown in Figure 14-9.

Figure 14-8
You're sure to find a letterhead design that's perfect for you from the selection PhotoSuite II SE has to offer.

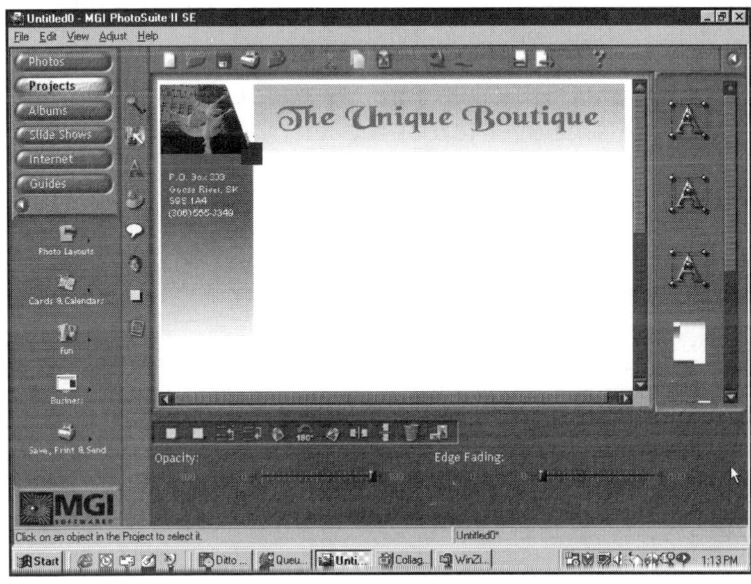

Figure 14-9
Here's a letterhead design for my fictional business, The Unique Boutique.

> **NOTE**
>
> In Figure 14-10 I used the Return key to move my text below the text and image already on the letterhead; I also used the Space key to create the illusion of an indented left margin. There's a problem with that method: It only works if your recipient is viewing the e-mail in the same-sized window as you are. You'll find digital letterhead a lot easier to use if you create it with the understanding that text will start flush against the left side of the design. Some templates are better suited to that than others.

Once you've created your letterhead, you can print multiple copies of it and use the printed letterhead over again in your printer, in conjunction with your word processor, to create letters and other documents printed on your letterhead.

To turn the letterhead you've created into digital letterhead that you can write e-mail on, however, is a little more complex. Here's how to do it:

1. In PhotoSuite II SE, choose File, Save As and save your letterhead as a JPEG image.
2. Log onto AOL.
3. Click Write.
4. Enter the address of the person you want to send e-mail to on your digital letterhead.
5. Click the Insert a Picture button on the e-mail editing toolbar and, from the submenu, choose Insert Background Picture.
6. In the Open dialog box that appears, locate and select the JPEG image of your letterhead. Then click Open.
7. Your letterhead is now the background for your e-mail. You can type your e-mail message over top of the letterhead (see Figure 14-10).

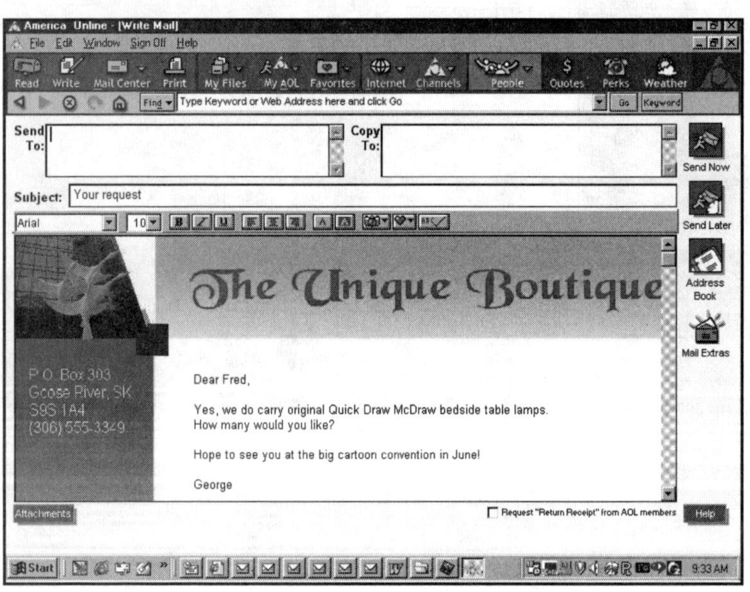

Figure 14-10
You can send an e-mail message on your letterhead, just as you would a regular letter.

Creating a Digital Business Card

One of the most basic marketing tools for any businessman is a business card. Unfortunately, I'm really bad at remembering to keep some with me at all times, but the fact I'm always looking for one and not finding it just keeps driving home to me how valuable business cards are.

Generally, you exchange business cards with a prospective client or supplier so each of you can get hold of the other if needed. In the online world, the opportunity to exchange physical cards doesn't exist, but that doesn't mean you can't exchange virtual cards!

A format called the Virtual Business Card allows e-mail correspondents to exchange the kind of information normally included on a business card automatically, but you don't have to use that format to achieve the same result, as long as you use PhotoSuite II SE to create your business card!

Creating a business card follows the same basic process as creating a flyer or letterhead:

1. Click the Projects button.
2. Click the Business button, and in the resulting window, choose Business Cards.
3. Choose the card design you like best from the templates provided, and click Select.
4. Edit the design, adding a photo, text, and so on. The finished design is shown in Figure 14-11.

Once the business card has been created, save it as a JPEG Image. Now, to pass the card along to an e-mail correspondent, all you have to do is insert it into your e-mail, like this:

1. Log onto AOL.
2. Click Write.
3. Enter the address of the person you're writing in the Send To box.
4. Write your message, and format it as usual using the editing tools on the e-mail toolbar.
5. Click the Insert a Picture button on the toolbar and, from the submenu, choose Insert a Picture.
6. In the Open dialog box that appears, locate and select the JPEG version of your business card, and click Open.
7. Your business card appears at the end of your e-mail, just as if you'd handed to the person yourself (see Figure 14-12).

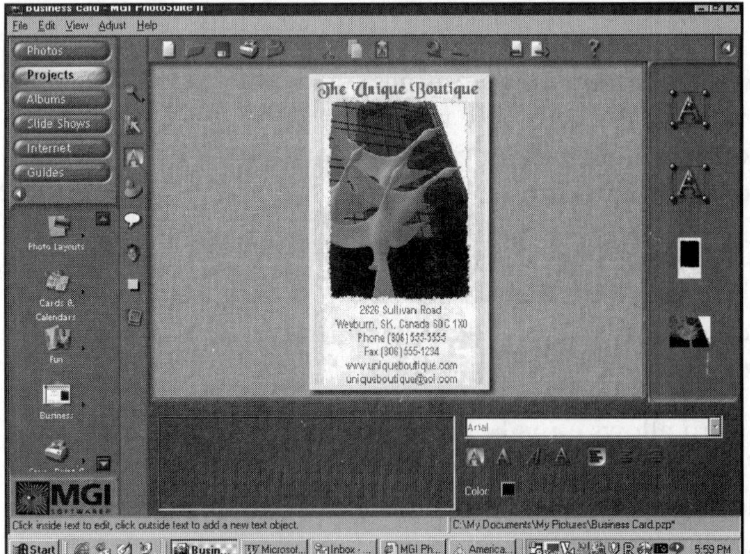

Figure 14-11
Here's a business card to match my flyer.

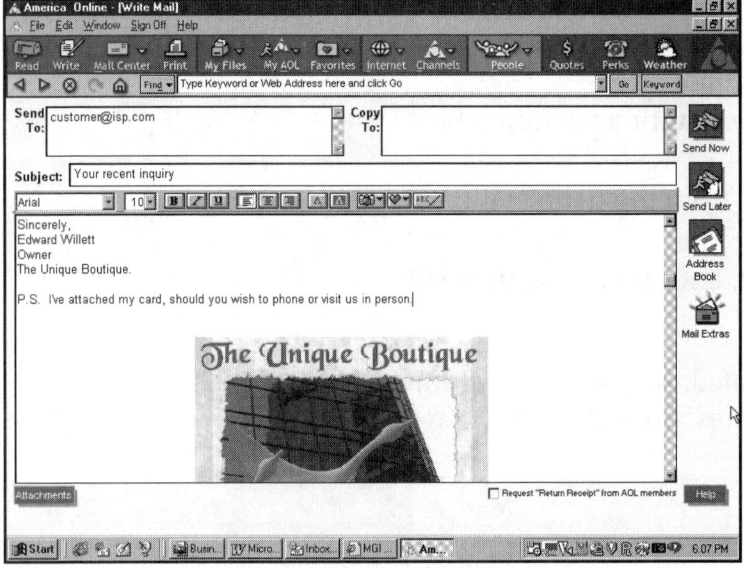

Figure 14-12
You don't have to meet someone in person to pass along your business card.

Creating an On-line Catalog

PhotoSuite II SE has many other useful business templates you can experiment with. You won't find a template for an on-line catalog, but that doesn't mean you can't create one: PhotoSuite's Album mode is perfect for the task.

To create an on-line catalog, you first have to create a separate picture file for each item in the catalog. For consistency, I'm going to make each page of my digital catalog look very much like the flyer I created earlier.

Here's how I create my catalog:

1. I create each page of my catalog as a separate project, using the flyer templates, and save each page as a JPEG Image.
2. I create a new Album (see Chapter 3 for details on creating an album), using the catalog images I've just created.
3. With the new album open, I choose File, Create Web Page. PhotoSuite creates a series of Web pages, at the heart of which is a main directory page that displays thumbnail images of each of the pages in the catalog that link to each of the images in the catalog (see Figure 14-13). Clicking on any thumbnail brings up a full-sized version of the catalog page (see Figure 14-14).

Now you can use Personal Publisher 3, if you wish, to publish your catalog to the Web. To do so, however, you first need to move all of the catalog files from the directory PhotoSuite II has put them into the same directory that Personal Publisher 3 stores Web pages.

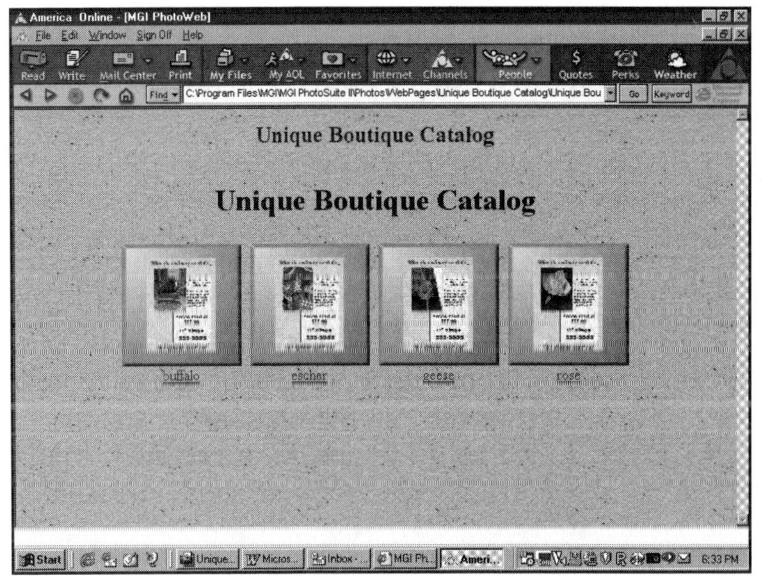

Figure 14-13
Each page of your digital catalog appears as a thumbnail on the main directory page . . .

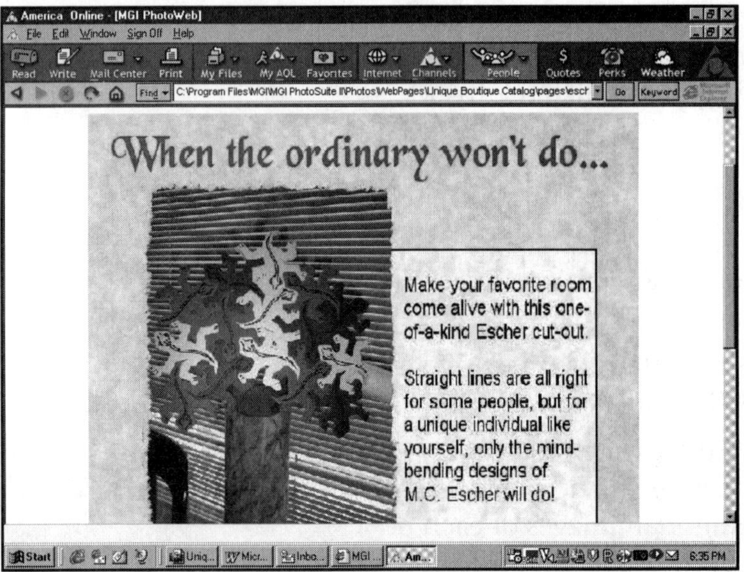

Figure 14-14
. . . which reveals a full-sized image when you click on it.

How to Promote Your Business Without Spending an Arm and a Leg

If there's one thing most small and home businesses have in common, it's a lack of ready cash. That situation won't improve until you promote your business, but it costs money to promote your business!

The solution is to make full use of low-cost promotional methods. Here are a few suggestions:

- Always use the letterhead you created in this chapter for correspondence, and always have your business cards at hand. If you can afford it, get matching envelopes made at a print shop. Business cards, letterhead, and envelopes are the public face you present to the world, and they must look professional, or you won't.
- Give your business card to everyone you meet, and pass stacks of cards along to friends and family so they can pass them along to all the people they meet.

The easiest way is to use Windows Explorer (choose Start, Programs, Windows Explorer). Locate the directory PhotoSuite has put your catalog into in the right window, highlight it, and drag it into the correct Personal Publisher directory, typically C:/America Online 4.0/MbrFiles/Pp3/YourScreenName.

To publish your catalog to your AOL Web space using Personal Publisher 3:

1. Sign on to AOL.
2. Go keyword PP3.
3. Click Edit/View My pages.
4. Your catalog directory should appear in the list of Web pages on your computer on the right side of the screen. Simply highlight it and click Publish to send your catalog to your AOL Web space. Personal Publisher 3

tells you what the URL of each page in the catalog will be; make a note of it.

Once your catalog is published, anyone can access it using the URL of the directory page, and you can add links to it from any existing Web pages you may have by using that same URL.

If you get an error message while publishing your pages, you may have used an illegal filename. Spaces aren't allowed, for instance, nor are several other characters you may have used. It's best to fix this problem back in PhotoSuite II SE; rename any offending pages or directories within the original PhotoSuite album, and then save it again as a Web page and repeat the process of publishing it to the Web described above.

How to Promote Your Business Without Spending an Arm and a Leg (Continued)

- Stick business cards and/or flyers up wherever you can. Whenever you see a place where public posting of messages is allowed, make sure your message is one of those posted.
- Use your letterhead to send out press releases to local media outlets about anything unusual or interesting you may be doing within your business. (But make sure it really is unusual or interesting: Media people don't have much use for news releases that contain nothing but self-serving puffery.) If you have a particular area of expertise, volunteer yourself as a possible source for stories related to that area. Similarly, offer to speak to local groups on the topic.
- Use your letterhead to send out letters to anyone who might be able to use your products or services, and drop a business card into the envelope, too. Do the same with e-mail, but make sure you really are targeting people who might be interested, or you'll get a name as a *spammer*—someone who sends out unsolicited e-mail advertising—and everyone hates spammers!
- Always have enough flyers, sales letters, business cards, and so on printed and ready to hand out, post, or mail, so you can reply promptly to any requests for information.

SECTION III: *Choosing Hardware & Software*

CHAPTER 15

PROJECT: Choosing a Scanner

Introduction

Now that you have seen some of the great projects you can create, you're probably interested in purchasing a scanner if you don't already have one. Scanners are more affordable than ever, and there's no reason to tear your hair out while buying one—at least not if you read this chapter first.

In this chapter I'll explain in some detail how scanners work, describe the different types of scanners, and give you some tips to help you buy the scanner that is right for you.

Then, once you have your scanner, you can go back and enjoy the rest of the book all over again!

How Do Scanners Work?

Scanners look like a pretty simple piece of equipment: just a box that is mostly empty, with a flat glass top, a bright light inside, and a lid to cover it all.

Looks can be deceiving. Scanners are actually sophisticated pieces of electronic equipment.

At the heart of any scanner is something called a *charge coupled device*, or CCD. The CCD is composed of about 2,600 photosensitive cells, even though it's only about an inch square.

As a light bar moves across the object being scanned (or, in the case of a sheet-fed scanner, the object being scanned is moved across the light bar), the light is reflected to the CCD by a system of mirrors. The amount of light that strikes each photosensitive cell determines how strong an electrical signal that cell produces. The scanner converts those signals into binary numbers that the computer can understand and manipulate—it digitizes them, in other words. Dark areas reflect less light, so they produce a weaker signal and are given lower numbers.

The very first scanners could only scan in stark black and white because each pixel had to be either on or off. Most scanners today have CCDs that can produce a range of 256 values, which correspond to that many different shades of gray (or levels of brightness). That may not sound like all that much, but it's about twice what our own eyes can manage, so it's really pretty good.

The number of cells in the CCD and the total area being scanned determine the resolution, which is measured in dots per inch (dpi). Sometimes the resolution is artificially enhanced by software, which means the software calculates what the value of a pixel that falls between two pixels that were generated by the hardware should be and then it generates a pixel that matches that value. For example, if the pixels generated by the hardware had values of, say, 5 and 7 respectively, the software would generate a pixel with a value of 6 between them in an effort to boost resolution. This works fine unless, of course, the true value of the pixel was 47!

CCDs are really good at capturing black, white, and gray images—so called *grayscale images*—because all they really measure are brightness levels. So how do scanners capture full-color images?

Scanners capture full-color images by creating three separate versions of each image: one using a red filter (so only the red component of the image is captured), one using a green filter (to capture the green light reflected from the image), and one using a blue filter. Because all other colors can be produced from these three "primary" colors, adding the information gathered through all three filters together produces a full-color image. (It's similar to the "color wheel" you may have learned about in elementary school, when you discovered you could make green paint, for instance, by mixing blue and yellow paint.)

True Color or 24-bit scanners gather eight bits of data for each color, resulting in a total of 24 bits of information about each pixel in the picture. A bit is the smallest piece of information a computer can make sense of. Just as more information helps you understand a particular subject, so more information—more bits—helps a computer understand exactly what color the object you're scanning is. Gathering eight bits of information about each of the three primary colors means that a True Color scanners can detect 16.7 million possible combinations—the total number of colors the scanner can pass on to the computer.

Some scanners require three separate passes of the light bar to capture all three colors; others can do it in one pass.

Even the best scanners produce slightly fuzzy images because it's impossible to guarantee that all three color passes will match exactly, pixel for pixel. The movement of the light bar and the fact that it sometimes has to stop and start as the computer struggles to keep up with the information flowing into it means that sometimes one or more pass is a little bit "off-register." That's a good reason to look for a scanner that only requires one pass of the light bar to capture all three colors.

Types of Scanners

You can choose from several different types of scanners. Each has its own advantages and disadvantages:

Flatbed scanners look like a box with a glass top and a hinged cover. You place the document to be scanned face down on the glass and close the cover, just as if you were using a photocopying machine. Advantages include

- **Clearer images.** Because the document being scanned remains stationery while the scanner head moves, everything is very stable and the sharpest possible image can be captured.
- **Better color.** The stability of the entire device is even more important in color scanning, especially in scanners that require three passes.
- **More flexibility.** Flatbed scanners can scan objects that aren't perfectly flat, such as books, magazines, or even your own hand.

Disadvantages include

- **Size.** Flatbeds take up a lot of space, especially if you want one that can handle legal-sized (or even larger) documents.
- **Cost.** Flatbeds are becoming quite inexpensive, but they're still more expensive than other types of scanners.
- **Hardware requirements.** For scanning that's not painfully slow, you may have to install a SCSI controller card or get a computer with a USB connection. Many scanners work through the parallel (printer) port, but that's not very speedy. (SCSI, pronounced "scuzzy," stands for Small Computer System Interface. It allows you to connect several devices—printers, CD drives, scanners, and so on—to a single card plugged into the computer. USB stands for Universal Serial Bus, which is another, newer method for connecting several devices to a single computer that's found on most new systems these days.)

Sheet-fed scanners pull the document being scanned over the light source and image head using rollers. Advantages include

- **Speed.** Sheet-fed scanners are often faster than flatbed scanners.
- **Size.** They don't take up much space. Some computers even come with sheet-fed scanners built into the keyboard.
- **Hardware requirements.** Most sheet-fed scanners plug into the parallel or serial port, so you don't need a special controller card.
- **Multiple document handling.** Some sheet-fed scanners can scan a stack of paper, which makes them well-suited for optical character recognition work, converting typewritten documents into computer-readable text. (For example, many companies use optical character recognition to convert resumes into electronic files.)

Disadvantages include

- **Less-clear images.** The document being scanned is being moved at the same time—not a recipe for the sharpest image.
- **Paper alignment.** It can be difficult to align the document being scanned properly, which means you end up with a crooked image in your computer. (PhotoSuite II can fix that problem, but it means cropping some information from the edges of the image.)

- **Poorer color.** Color from a sheet-fed scanner just isn't as good as from a flatbed, again because of the problem of lining up what are really three separate images. (See the explanation of how scanners capture color images earlier in this chapter.)
- **Flexibility.** The only way to scan pages from a book with a flatbed scanner is to tear them out of the book—not something you generally want to do.

Hand-held scanners are the least expensive of all. They're small devices, maybe four or five inches wide, that you drag by hand over the image you want to scan. You can usually "stitch" multiple scans together with software, which is useful when you have to scan a large area. The image isn't as clear because it relies on the steadiness of your hand, but the flexibility of being able to move the scanner over a surface in any way you want is something fancier scanners can't match.

Photo scanners are small scanners designed specifically for turning snapshots into digital images. Some computers even have them built in. You just stick the photo into a slot, and it pops out when it's scanned. They're small enough they can even be installed into a spare drive bay, but, of course, they're so small they can't handle anything larger than maybe a 5×7 photo.

How to Choose a Scanner

The first step in choosing a scanner is to determine what you need it for.

If you need a scanner only once in a long while, you only use it for small jobs, and you aren't that concerned about quality, a very inexpensive hand-held scanner will do the job.

If you're planning to scan mostly text, for faxing with your fax modem, for instance, or for optical character recognition, then a grayscale sheet-fed scanner may work best. If you need the added flexibility of being able to scan color photos or documents on occasion, get a color sheet-fed scanner.

If you plan to scan both text and images and need the highest quality images of both, you should be looking at a flatbed scanner.

Looking at Scanner Specifications

Once you've determined which type of scanner you need, you can start looking at specifications. Here are some things to look for:

- **Resolution.** Scanners turn images into dots. The closer together the dots are, the sharper the image. Resolution is measured in dots per inch (dpi), so the higher the dpi listed for the scanner, the better the resolution. However, as noted earlier, some scanners use software to interpolate an image to a higher resolution. The true resolution is whatever the hardware is capable of, usually referred to as "optical resolution." Don't get fooled into buying more resolution than you need, however. For example, pictures scanned for the Web are typically scanned at only 72 dpi, so if getting pictures onto the Web is your main reason for buying a scanner, any good scanner will do.
- **Pixel depth (bit depth).** Also as noted earlier, 24-bit scanners provide 16.7 million possible colors. That's all most computers can display, so that should serve you well. However, 30-bit and 36-bit scanners are becoming more common. A 30-bit scanner can produce more than 1 billion colors, but they still get sent to your computer as 16.7 million. A 24-bit scanner will suit most home users admirably. Don't settle for anything less unless you're just scanning black-and-white images or text.
- **Speed.** If you're going to be doing a lot of scanning, you'll want to find the fastest scanner you can afford. If possible, try out the scanners you're considering using the kind of documents you're likely to be scanning. A color photograph scanned at a high resolution will show you pretty quickly which scanners are the fastest. Be aware, though, that the speed of your own computer affects the speed at which the scanner scans.
- **Maximum scan size.** Again, how big a document your scanner should be able to scan depends on what kind of documents you're likely to want to scan with it. A typical home scanner can only scan a letter-sized piece of paper. If you want to scan legal-sized documents or two pages of a typical book at a time, however, you'll need one with a larger scan size. Remember, however, that a larger scan size also translates into a larger, more expensive scanner—and more space taken up on your desktop.

Looking for Recommendations

Once you've narrowed the field down to scanners you can afford that meet your needs, it's time to do some homework. Look for reviews of the scanners your considering. Consult computer magazines.

One good place to turn is the CNET Buyer's Guide, which you can access easily on AOL by using keyword Buyer's Guide. You'll see a screen something like the one in Figure 15-1.

At the bottom of the Hardware menu in the middle of this window you'll find Scanners. Clicking on that button takes you to a plethora of scanner-related information (see Figure 15-2), including news about the latest scanners being released, prices, and, best of all for the careful shopper, reviews and recommendations.

Click Compare Scanners, and you'll be shown a list of all the recent reviews of scanners (see Figure 15-3). Click on the scanner whose review you want to read.

If you want to compare several scanners side by side, check the boxes in front of them and then click Compare (see Figure 15-4). All the pertinent information, from who makes them to how they perform, is presented for you in a handy table (see Figure 15-5).

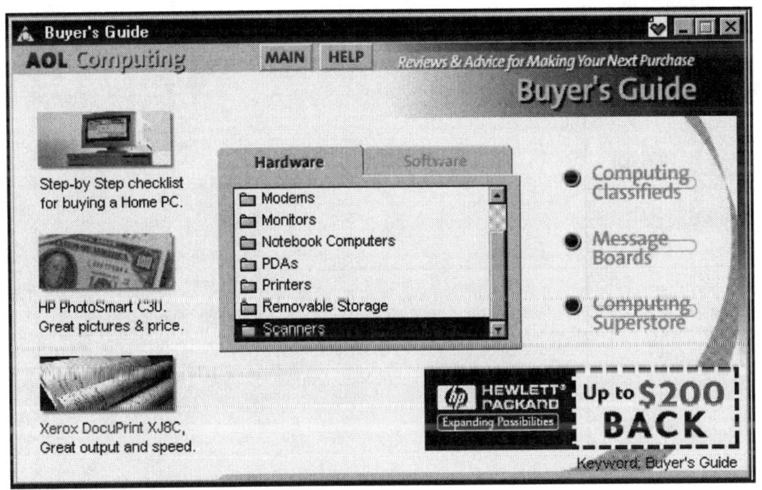

Figure 15-1
The Buyer's Guide on AOL is a good place to turn for more information about scanners.

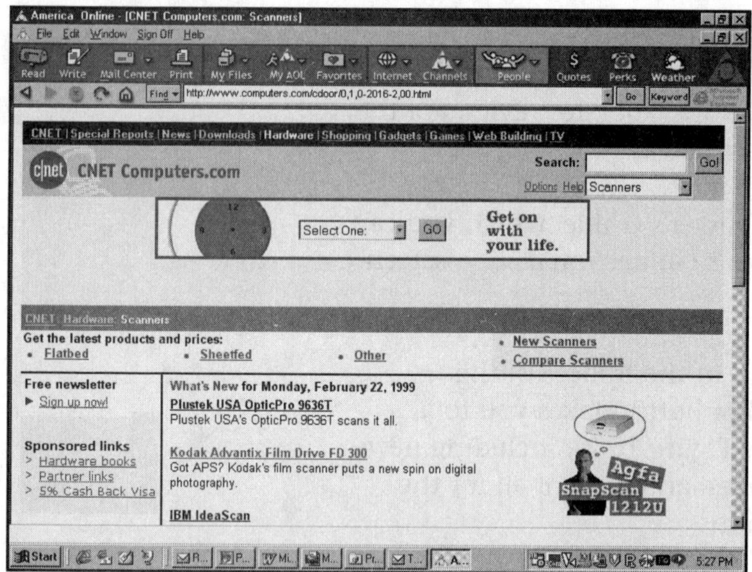

Figure 15-2 Here you can find scanner news, reviews, and recommendations.

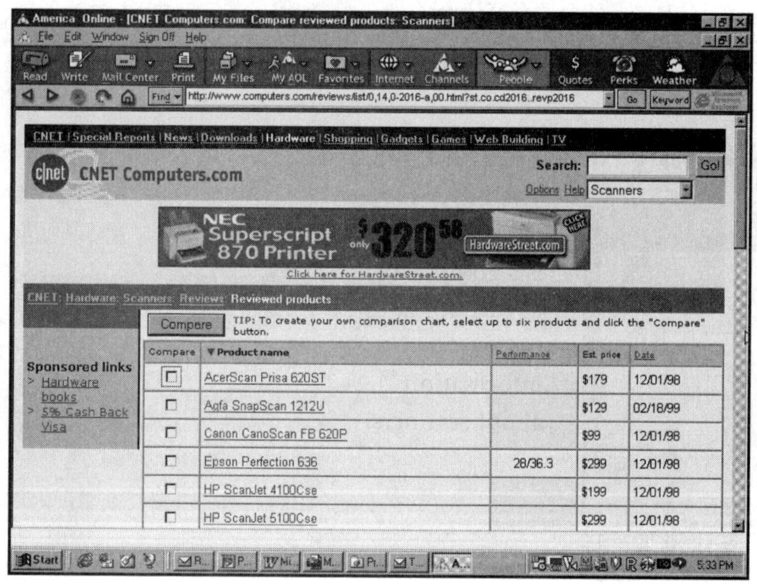

Figure 15-3 Reviews can help you decide which scanner you want.

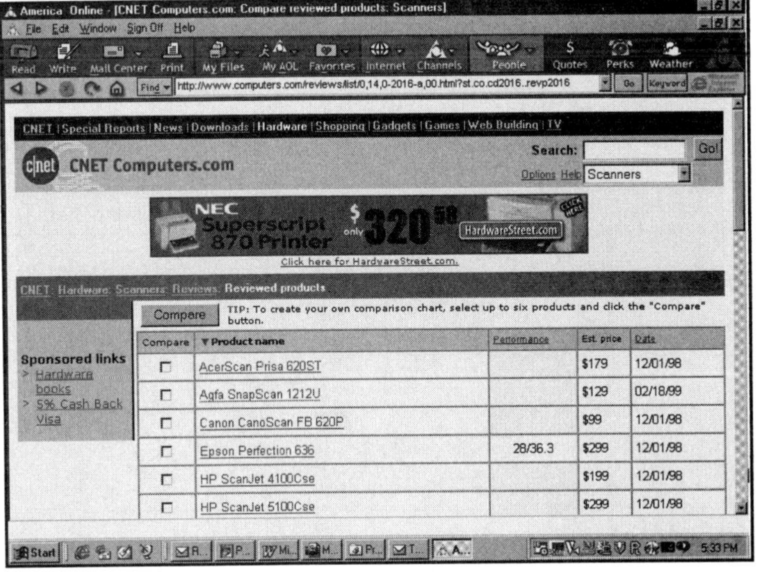

Figure 15-4
Check off the scanners you want to compare . . .

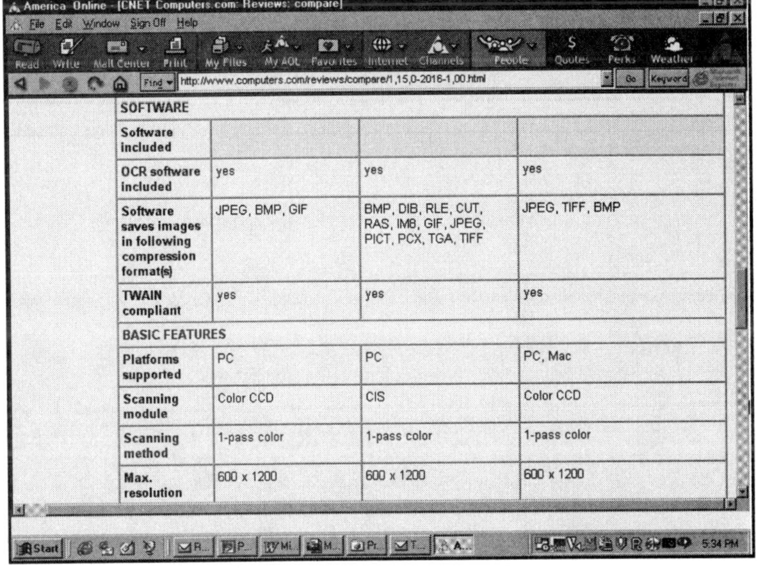

SOFTWARE			
Software included			
OCR software included	yes	yes	yes
Software saves images in following compression format(s)	JPEG, BMP, GIF	BMP, DIB, RLE, CUT, RAS, IMB, GIF, JPEG, PICT, PCX, TGA, TIFF	JPEG, TIFF, BMP
TWAIN compliant	yes	yes	yes
BASIC FEATURES			
Platforms supported	PC	PC	PC, Mac
Scanning module	Color CCD	CIS	Color CCD
Scanning method	1-pass color	1-pass color	1-pass color
Max. resolution	600 x 1200	600 x 1200	600 x 1200

Figure 15-5
. . . then compare them side by side using this handy table.

Scanners are so affordable, and of such generally high quality, that you can't really go wrong for home use. Once you have one, you'll wonder how you ever got along without it. I know I do!

CHAPTER 16

PROJECT: Choosing a Digital Camera

Introduction

Aside from a scanner (and, of course, a computer!) the one piece of hardware I've mentioned most often in this book is a digital camera. Good-quality, very usable, and useful cameras are now within financial reach of just about anyone.

In this chapter I'll explain a little bit about how digital cameras work and how they differ from regular cameras. I'll also provide some tips on what to look for when shopping for a digital camera.

How Do Digital Cameras Work?

All cameras, both regular film cameras and digital cameras, work by capturing the light reflected or emitted by objects and focusing that light onto something that can register and record that light. In a film camera, the light is focused onto a thin film covered with an emulsion that reacts chemically to light. In a digital camera, the light is focused onto either a charge coupled device (CCD), which is the same kind of sensor used in a scanner (see Chapter 16), or onto a new kind of sensor called a CMOS (Complementary Metal Oxide Semiconductor, if you're wondering) image sensor.

Otherwise, traditional cameras and digital cameras are quite similar. They both have lenses (which focus the light) and shutters (which open and close in a fraction of a second so that just the right amount of light is allowed onto the light sensing material). Most of them have built-in flashes for taking pictures in low light and autoexposure sensors that automatically set the camera's aperture (the opening through which light enters) and shutter speed for the best picture. This means that if you can take a picture with one of today's modern automated film cameras, you'll feel right at home with a digital camera.

In a digital camera, images are stored electronically. Some cameras store images onto a traditional floppy disk, but the most popular medium for storing pictures is probably CompactFlash cards, which can hold several megabytes of data. CompactFlash cards act like film, in that you can take one out of the camera, put in another, and continue shooting, but they have one big advantage over film: They're reusable!

The images from the camera can usually be previewed right in the camera, using a built-in viewscreen on the back of the camera. They can also be downloaded to your computer, where you can manipulate them using photo-imaging software, such as PhotoSuite II, and print them. Some cameras also allow you to send pictures directly from the camera to a printer.

Do I Need a Digital Camera?

Before you begin shopping for a digital camera, you need to ask yourself a few questions, beginning with, "Do I need a digital camera at all?" After all, you can create digital images just fine by taking them with a regular camera and then scanning them into your computer, or you can have your photo-processing store put your pictures onto disk or CD very cheaply when you have your regular film developed.

Film cameras and digital cameras each have their own strengths and weaknesses. The following table lists some pros and cons for each.

Pros and Cons of Digital and Film Cameras

Digital Cameras	Film Cameras

Pros Images are available instantly No film and processing costs Bad photographs can be discarded directly from the camera	**Pros** Resolution is hundreds of times higher than even the best digital camera Negatives and prints can be easily stored Negatives and slides can last a century or more Prints and slides can be viewed without special equipment User has more control over camera Wider selection of lenses available
Cons Resolution is lower than film cameras Cameras eat batteries Pictures can only be viewed electronically; no guarantee they'll still be viewable as computers change over the years Cameras lack sophisticated controls Very few lenses to choose from	**Cons** Images are only available after film is processed Film and processing cost money Bad photographs get developed along with the good ones

Questions to Ask Before You Start Shopping

Once you decide that yes, you do want a digital camera, you should ask yourself a few additional questions to help you decide which of the many different models to buy:

- **Where will I be using the camera?** If you're only going to be shooting outdoors, you don't need as high quality a flash as you'll need if you're going to be shooting indoors.
- **What will I be photographing?** Static scenes don't require as fast a shutter speed as action scenes. Your subject matter can also influence your choice of viewfinder: A viewfinder that's excellent for composing still life photos might let you down if you're trying to grab quick snapshots of the kids on the soccer field. As well, if you're shooting landscapes, you'll probably want to be able to shoot panoramas; if you're shooting wildlife, a zoom lens might be needed; if you're shooting your baseball card collection, a macro lens might be a necessity; if you're shooting large groups, a wide-angle lens might be more important. Not all digital cameras let you add additional lenses, so that's a feature you should look for if you feel you need it.
- **How much do I know about photography?** Someone who has been seriously involved in photography for years may want a lot more manual controls on a camera than someone who just wants to be able to point and click.
- **How will I use my digital photographs?** Photographs intended for the Web don't need tremendously high resolution. If you're planning to print most of your photographs, however, you should opt for a higher resolution (provided your printer is up to the task. See Chapter 17, "Choosing a Printer," for more information on printing).

What to Look for in a Digital Camera

With the answers to those questions above in mind, you can start comparing camera features. Here are some basic features to look for:

- **Resolution.** This is probably what everybody looks at first when they're shopping for a digital camera. However, as I mentioned above, it's not necessarily the most important feature. If you're only taking pictures for use on a Web site or display on your computer, a lower resolution will work just fine—there's no point in creating images with more resolution than most monitors can display. High resolution images become most important when you're planning to print your images.

The standard resolution for a digital print intended for Web publishing, e-mailing, or use in most of the digital projects in this book is 640x480. Many cameras now offer a higher resolution of up to 1536x1024, which results in about 1.5 million pixels. That's a high-enough resolution to give you a photo-realistic 5x7 print on a high-quality printer. Even an 8x10 will look pretty close to what you'd get from your corner photo developer.

Something else effects image quality: how the image is compressed. Most cameras let you choose a range of options from low (or even no) compression to high compression. The lower the level of compression, the better the final image.

- **Color Depth.** As explained in the chapter on scanners, this refers to how many bytes are used to record each color. Most cameras provide 24-bit color, or True Color. More expensive cameras provide 30-bit or, at the very top end, 36-bit. The more bits, the richer the colors appear in the final photograph. Again, for typical home use, 24-bit color will suit you fine. Professional photographers, however, might want to look for a 36-bit camera.
- **Sensitivity.** Film has an ISO number that tells you how sensitive it is to light. The more sensitive it is, the higher the ISO number. For example, 100 ISO film is fine for daylight and flash photography, while 400 ISO is better for shooting without a flash indoors. Image sensors in digital cameras also have an ISO number; the higher the ISO number, the more sensitive the sensor and the better it will be at shooting pictures in low light.
- **Storage capacity.** How many pictures a digital camera can store is as important as whether you're using 24- or 36-exposure film in a regular camera. Once the limit is reached, you can't take any more pictures until you download images from the camera to your computer. A camera with large built-in storage capability is therefore preferable.

  Most cameras also provide some kind of removable media. Some cameras still use floppy disks while others use small hard disks; the most common removable storage is a flash memory card, which comes in a variety of sizes.

Figure 16-1
Flash memory disk.

It's important to remember that the number of pictures a digital camera can hold depends on what resolution those pictures were taken at. High-resolution images contain more information and therefore take up more space than low-resolution images. Makes sure you know what resolution the salesman is talking about when he tells you how many pictures the camera you're looking at can take!

- **Output features.** You can transfer images from a digital camera to a computer in a lot of different ways. Some use cables to the computer's serial, parallel, or USB port; some use wireless connections; and some provide memory card readers into which you slide a memory card. The most important consideration is speed. Find out how long it takes the camera you're considering to transfer its images to your computer, and then decide whether you can live with that. If you're the impatient type, look for a camera that transfers its images as quickly as possible.
- **Compatibility.** Make sure your new digital camera is going to be compatible with your computer system before you take it home, and make sure it comes with all the peripherals you need to hook it up to your computer.

Figure 16-2
Camera transferring images to computer via cable.

Beyond these general features, you should consider some more technical features, most of which you'd also want to take a close look at if you were buying a regular film camera:

- **Lenses.** It's no coincidence that, in the world of film photography, camera bodies are relatively cheap, while good lenses are very expensive. The lens has a major impact on the quality of any photograph.

  The focal length of a lens determines whether it's a wide angle lens, a "normal" lens, or a telephoto lens. You'll usually see something on a digital camera like (in my camera's manual) f=5.5 mm F2.8 (equivalent to a 36 mm lens on a 35 mm camera). On a 35 mm film camera, a 36 mm lens would be a wide-angle lens. A 50 mm lens is a "normal" lens, while anything over 50 is a telephoto lens. Wide-angle lenses collect light from a wider area, so they're good for taking pictures of buildings, landscapes, and interiors. Telephoto lenses gather light from a small area, which results in an enlarged image of that area, so they're good for taking pictures of objects at a distance that you want to see more closely. "Normal" lenses are a compromise between the two. Look in the camera's manual to see how the lens compares to a 35 mm film camera lens to get a sense of how well it suits your needs.

Some digital cameras also include a *zoom lens,* a lens with a changeable focal length. Zoom lenses are usually identified by how much they can magnify images: for example, 3X. If you want this feature, make sure the magnification being quoted is for an optical zoom lens. Some cameras boast of having a "digital zoom," but all that is is a digital enlargement of a portion of the image captured by the camera. You can achieve exactly the same effect in the computer on any image by selecting a portion of a photograph and resizing it, so you don't really need this feature in your camera.

Many cameras also offer a macro mode, designed for taking pictures of objects in extreme close-up. This is great if you want to take pictures of flowers, jewelry, or other small items.

Some cameras allow you to attach additional lenses, such as a telephoto lens or an extreme wide-angle lens. This is a very nice feature that too few digital cameras permit. Additional lenses expand the capabilities of your camera and open up many new photographic possibilities.

- **Fixed focus or autofocus.** Inexpensive cameras are often fixed-focus cameras, in which images are sharp as long as the subject is within a certain predefined range of distances from the camera. Better cameras offer autofocus (some also let you focus manually), changing the focus depending on how far away the subject is.

Viewfinder. Most digital cameras have an LCD screen on the back, which many people use as their primary viewfinder. However, they typically also have an optical viewfinder just like an ordinary camera's—and that's the one you should use. The LCD screen is a great place to review the images you took, but if you leave it on all the time for taking pictures, it will drain your batteries in a hurry. If the camera has a zoom lens, the optical viewfinder should be coupled to it.

Flash. Unless you're going to take nothing but outdoor, daytime pictures, you need a flash. Most cameras provide you with one. Inexpensive cameras usually have a small flash built right in. This works fine, but it has a limited range and can sometimes cause red eye, that pink reflection that shows up in people's eyes. Better cameras have a built-in flash but also use a red-eye reduction system, which sends out a preliminary flash that causes the subject's irises to close before the main flash goes off, reducing red eye. Cameras that provide flashes that can be rotated up or down allow you to bounce the flash off the wall or ceiling, resulting in a much softer light. Some cameras also allow you to use external flashes, such as you might use with an ordinary 35 mm camera.

Finally, consider the price. Digital cameras are still fairly expensive, and you may not be able to afford one with all the features you want. If that's the case, go back to the earlier list of questions you asked yourself before you began looking, and prioritize your needs. Once you know what features are most important to you, you'll also know what features you can do without.

Then, just as when you were looking at scanners, it's time to do some homework. Look for reviews on-line and in magazines. (You'll always get a more honest opinion from a disinterested reviewer than you will from the guy in the camera store who wants to sell you the top-of-the-line model.)

Again, I recommend the CNET Buyer's Guide (keyword Buyer's Guide). Click on the Digital Cameras listing under Hardware, and you'll find a ton of information about digital cameras (see Figure 16-3).

Click See All Camera Reviews to read all the reviews currently posted about digital cameras, and click Compare Cameras to conduct a side-by-side comparison of many popular makes.

A digital camera is still a fairly major investment, but it will also make all your digital projects even more fun and easy than they are now.

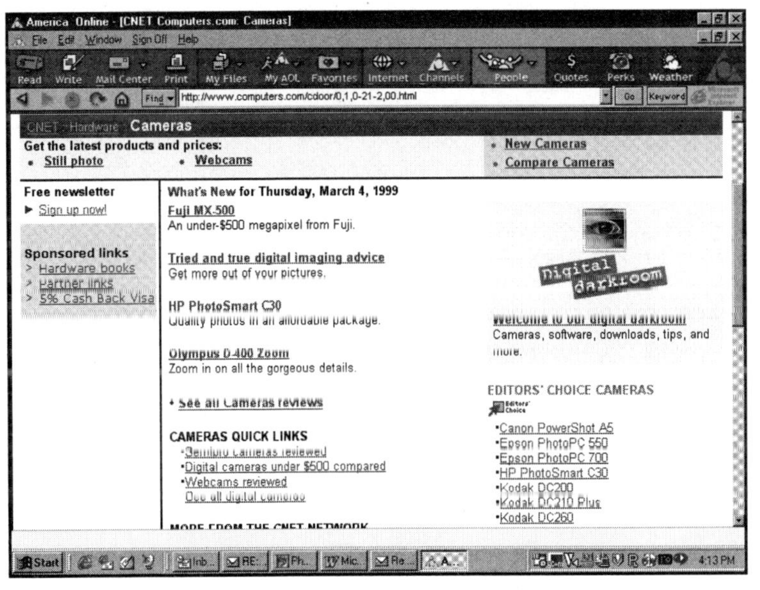

Figure 16-3
The Buyer's Guide on AOL has information galore about digital cameras.

CHAPTER 17

PROJECT: Choosing a Printer

Introduction

While it's true that you don't really need a printer to create many of the digital projects in this book, since they're intended to be displayed primarily on the computer, sooner or later you're going to want a copy of one of your digital images that you can hold in your hand, and for that, you need a printer.

Not only that, you need a printer that will meet your specific needs because nothing's more disappointing than laboring over an image so that it looks just right and then printing it out and finding the colors all wrong and everything blurry.

You can choose from several different types of printers capable of printing full-color images (see the sidebar on types of printers), but realistically, home users are going to be limiting their search to inkjet printers because they're inexpensive, easy to find, reliable, and still capable of doing a great job.

Types of Color Printers

You can choose from five types of color printers on the market, but you probably won't be looking at anything other than an inkjet printer unless (a) money is no object or (b) you're buying a printer for a business and money is no object. The five color printer types are

- **Inkjet.** Inkjet printers spray miniscule drops of ink onto paper to form an image. The quality of the output depends very much on the quality of the paper: Glossy photo-quality paper results in near-photo-quality images, while ordinary paper results in blurry, imprecise images. Inkjets are by far the most popular choice for color printing, especially for home use. In the past couple of years they have improved dramatically, now offering resolutions as high as 1440 dpi and producing photographic prints almost indistinguishable from the real thing.

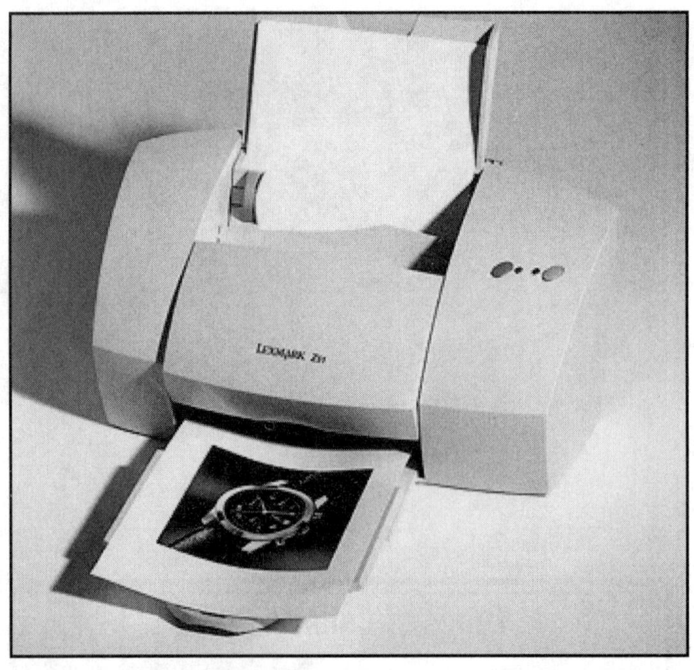

Figure 17-1
Inkjet printer.

> **Types of Color Printers (Continued)**
>
> - **Laser.** Color laser printers use toner, much like that in a photocopier. The light of a laser sensitizes an electrostatic drum. Toner is deposited on the sensitized areas, transferred to the paper, and then fused (fixed) with heat. Ordinary laser printers use a single color of toner, while color laser printers use four different colors at once. Laser printers create very crisp color images and can also be used for ordinary black-and-white text. They're fast; they're quiet; and they're expensive, easily costing 10 times as much as inkjets.
> - **Solid ink.** Solid ink printers melt solid blocks of ink and then spray the melted ink onto a page. This results in very bright colors but sometimes imprecise text and other fine lines.

In this chapter, I'll provide some tips for finding the perfect printer for your digital projects.

Asking Yourself a Few Questions

Just as with choosing a scanner or a digital camera, you need to ask yourself some questions before you head out to the store and start asking a salesperson some questions. You're much more likely to end up with the perfect printer for your needs if you know what those needs are!

Here are a few questions to ask yourself:

- **Will I just be printing images, or will I also be using my color printer to print text?** Some printers are optimized for printing pictures and are slow and/or sloppy about printing text. Some are optimized for text; still others try to do both reasonably well. If you're planning to use your color printer as your main printer for text as well as pictures, you'll probably want to opt for one of the latter.

- **What will I be using the printed images for?** If you're just printing out the occasional photograph to mail to someone who doesn't have an e-mail address or to stick on your office wall, you might be satisfied with a lower-resolution (and less-expensive) printer than someone who is producing prints for reproduction in a magazine or to frame and display formally.
- **What kind of interface do I want to use?** Most printers connect to the parallel port of your computer, but you can also get printers that use a SCSI interface, which requires a special card in your computer, or the new USB interface. Generally speaking, USB is the fastest interface, followed by SCSI, followed by the parallel port.
- **What's more important to me, speed or resolution?** You can have both a fast printing speed and a high resolution, but only by spending a lot more money. For inexpensive printers, there's always a trade-off between speed and quality. Personally, I'd go for the quality, but if you're the impatient type, or if you need the printer for business purposes, speed may be more important.
- **How much do I want to spend?** This is a very basic question, but still worth mentioning, because ultimately you have to balance the amount of money you're willing to invest with the features you want. If some of those features aren't available at the price limit you've set for yourself, you'll have to decide whether you're willing to spend more or willing to do without those features. One feature you'll particularly notice is price-dependent is speed. Typically, the more dollars you spend, the faster the printer you can afford.

Types of Color Printers (Continued)

Laser color printer

- **Thermal wax.** Thermal wax printers melt wax from ribbons and then form the image with the wax. They're best at printing transparencies, which is why businesses use them the most. However, they tend to be slow and they don't print well on regular paper.
- **Dye sublimation.** This is the best way to print color images. It's also the most expensive. Dye sublimation printers transfer dye from a ribbon to the paper, using heat. Advertising and graphic design firms often use dye sublimation printers to create final presentations for their clients, but then, they can afford the $5,000 or more a dye sublimation printer costs—not to mention the roughly $8 a page on top of that!

Understanding Printer Features of Inkjet Printers

Here are some of the basic features of inkjet printers you should take into consideration as you shop for one:

- **Resolution.** This is given in dots per inch (dpi) and influences how finely detailed the printed image will be. However, it's not the only thing that influences image sharpness. Each pixel in an inkjet-printed image isn't a single drop of ink but a cluster of many drops. This unavoidably leads to some blurring. The more accurately those drops are combined into a single pixel, the sharper the final image will be and the greater the perceived resolution. A printer with a lower resolution that does a particularly good job of clustering drops of ink together to make each pixel will produce sharper images than one that has a higher resolution but is rather sloppy about the pixel-making process. The best way to tell is to compare pictures printed from the various printers you're looking at.
- **Separate black ink cartridge.** On your monitor, colors are created by adding together red, green, and blue light. Colors on a printer are produced by overprinting three colors of ink: cyan, magenta, and yellow. When all three are printed together, they form black. Some inexpensive inkjet printers use only these three colors, but better printers also add black because the black produced by adding cyan, magenta, and yellow isn't as rich as black from black ink. Ideally, the black should be in a separate cartridge than the colors, because you probably won't use it up as fast (unless you are printing a lot of text). If they're all in the same ink cartridge, you have to replace the whole thing even when you have lots of black left—and since the cartridge is bigger, it costs more. Some of the latest printers use even more colors: six, or even seven. More colors allows for finer gradations of colors on the page. As well, some printers add additional colors specially designed for printing photographs.

Figure 17-2
Ink cartridges.

- **Speed.** Inkjet printers in the $200 to $400 range can typically print in color at a speed of three to five pages per minute. If you need a printer that prints much faster than that, be prepared to either pay more or settle for a lower resolution.
- **Paper size.** Most inkjet printers are limited to paper that's the width of standard letter paper (8½× 11). Larger pages have to be *tiled*, put together like a puzzle from a set of smaller pages, each of which has part of the image on it. (This is usually done in software, not by the printer.) If you need a printer that can print on 11×17 paper, you'll have to pay extra.
- **Interface.** As noted earlier, printers typically use the parallel port, but you can get printers that use the increasingly common, and much faster, USB interface. (USB, or Universal Serial Bus, is a new method of adding peripherals to a computer. The USB interface is able to transfer data faster than the parallel port, which in turn means faster printing.)
- **Software.** Inkjet printers typically come with some form of imaging software. In addition, they typically have software that allows you to change a variety of printer settings—vary the resolution, for instance, or change the way that the printer translates the colors on the monitor into colors on the page (because monitor colors are created with light and printer colors are created with pigments, they're never an exact match; see sidebar). Sometimes, when you can't decide between two equivalent printers, taking a close look at the software instead of the hardware can settle the matter.

How Printers Interpret Screen Colors

No matter how good an inkjet printer you buy, the colors it produces will never exactly match the colors on the screen. The best you can hope for is a close match. Here's why.

- Monitors reproduce colors by adding together three colors: red, green, and blue. These colors are called *additive primaries* because when you add all three together you get white.
- Printers, on the other hand, reproduce colors by overlapping cyan, magenta, and yellow. These are called subtractive primaries because when you add them all together you get black. (Adding pairs of the subtractive primaries together in various combinations gives you red, green, and blue.)
- Because the monitor uses light and the printer uses ink, it's not surprising that the printer can only approximate the colors you see on the monitor. It's up to your imaging and/or printer software to translate monitor colors to the printer as closely as possible. The better the software, the more satisfied you'll be with the printed project. But you'll never match the depth and richness of a monitor image in a print because the monitor image is painted with transmitted light and the printer image with reflected light.

Shopping for a Printer

The best way to compare printers is to compare output. If at all possible, take a digital file of your own to the store and ask to have it printed out on the various printers you're considering. Comparing prints of the same file from different printers will tell you a lot more than the printouts the store itself will have on display.

If you're shopping on-line (for instance, in AOL's Shop Direct), look at three key things: resolution (given in dots per inch), speed (in pages per minute), and any reviews or awards the product has received. Every printer manufacturer posts awards and reviews of their products on their Web site.

Here are a few things to keep in mind as you test-drive printers:

- **Try to view the print under lighting conditions similar to those under which it will usually be viewed.** If you're going to put it in a photo album, where it will normally be viewed under ordinary incandescent room light, viewing it under the fluorescent lights in the store won't accurately reveal how it's going to look in the album. (But do try to view it under light bright enough to show details.)
- **Check details with a magnifying glass or loupe.** This will reveal graininess or blurring in the print that might not be noticeable at first glance.
- **Make sure you use the same kind of paper in each printer.** Don't just use any ol' glossy photographic inkjet paper—use the same kind of glossy photographic inkjet paper. It's the only way to get a fair comparison because papers from different manufacturers can have substantial quality differences.
- **Compare the colors in the print with the colors on the computer monitor.** The closer the colors, the happier you'll ultimately be with the printer.
- **Listen to the printer as it prints your picture.** How noisy is it? Can you live with that much noise? Remember that something that doesn't seem all that noisy in an already noisy computer store may seem annoyingly loud in the confined space of a home office.
- **Time the printer as it prints your picture.** That will give you a better idea of its speed for your typical uses than the figures the manufacturer provides.

Other considerations to keep in mind while looking at printers:

- **What kind of warranty is provided?** Printers are rugged devices, but they do contain parts that can wear out, clog up, or just quit working. You don't want to be stuck with the cost of repair.
- **How much do replacement ink cartridges cost?** If you do a lot of full-color printing, especially at your printer's highest resolution, prepare to be shocked by how quickly the ink disappears. You need to factor in the cost of replacement ink cartridges to the overall cost of the printer. A cheap printer that gobbles expensive ink is no bargain in the long run.
- **Are cartridges readily available?** If you live in a major city, you can probably find cartridges for almost any type of printer. If you live in a smaller city, though, cartridges may only be readily available for some of the more popular brand-name printers. Keep that in mind when making your selection. (Keep in mind too, though, that these days you can order replacement supplies on-line!)
- **Can you print directly from your digital camera to the printer?** This is an increasingly common feature on printers by manufacturers that also make digital cameras. If your printer and camera both support this feature, you can bypass the computer and print images directly from the camera. If this sounds like a feature you want, you may have to buy a printer from the company that makes your camera (or vice versa).
- **What are the critics saying about this printer?** Again, do your homework, preferably *before* you head out to the store. Read all the reviews you can find in computer magazines and on-line. Find out which printers the critics like and why. And if you come across a printer you haven't read about, but like the looks of, don't be pressured into buying it at that moment. Go away, find some reviews about it, and then make up your mind.

A good place to look for information is the CNET Buyer's Guide on AOL (keyword Buyer's Guide). Click on the Printers listing under Hardware (see Figure 17-3).

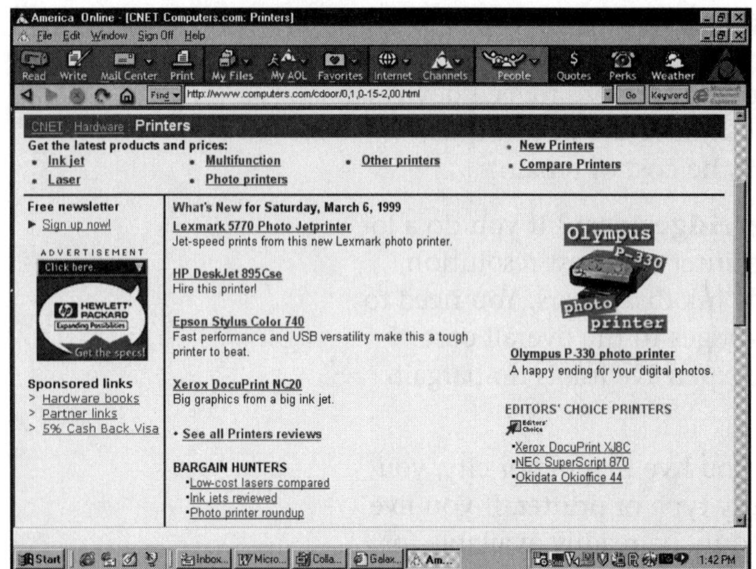

Figure 17-3
Find out more about printers from the CNET Buyer's Guide on AOL

Click See All Printer Reviews to read all the reviews currently posted, and click Compare Printers to conduct a side-by-side comparison of many popular makes.

Figure 17-4 shows a typical printer review.

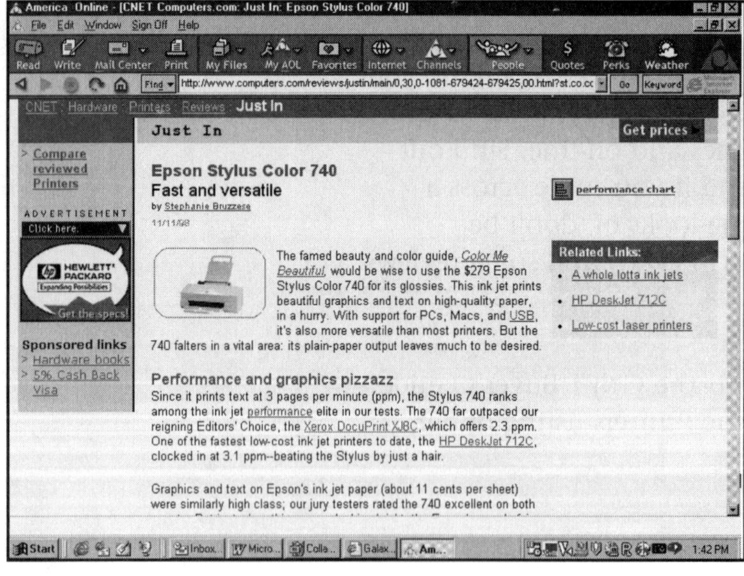

Figure 17-4
Printer reviews even include a photo of the printer, plus complete performance statistics and editorial comments.

To do your digital images justice when they move from the computer screen to the printed page, you need a good printer. But take your time and do your homework, and you'll soon have beautiful copies of your pictures to hold in your hand.

CHAPTER 18

PROJECT: Selecting Data Storage Options

Introduction

You don't have to work with digital images very long to come to one inescapable conclusion: They take up a lot of data storage space.

Oh, a Web-quality JPEG may not be very large, but just try scanning an 8x10 color photograph at 300 dots per inch (dpi)—never mind the interpolated 9600 DPI your scanner may be capable of—and see how many megabytes it munches.

And the thing about digital images is once you delete them, they're gone. You may have a printed version, but that's not the same.

As a result, if you take a lot of high-resolution pictures with your digital camera or do a lot of high-resolution scanning, you're soon going to find that you're running out of storage space on your computer—and your floppy drive won't do you much good because high-resolution images take up far more space than an ordinary floppy has available.

In this chapter you'll look at some possible solutions for that problem, and I'll provide a buyer's checklist you can use when you go shopping for your own personal data storage solution.

First, let's look at each data storage option.

Figure 18-1
A hard drive.

Hard Drives

If you simply need more storage space on your computer and aren't concerned about being able to transport your digital images somewhere else or keep them safely locked up somewhere, the most straightforward solution is simply to buy a larger hard drive.

Hard drives are fast and cheap, and they hold a lot of data: tens of megabytes. But you may find yourself bewildered by the many different types you'll find on the store shelves. Here are some points to consider:

- **What kind of interface does it use?** The fastest hard drives use the SCSI interface, but if you don't already have a SCSI card in your computer, you'll have to add one to use a SCSI drive, which adds $100 or so to the cost of the drive. However, for transferring large graphics files speed is important, so the extra cost might be worth it. EIDE drives are more common and don't require an additional card, but they are slower. IDE drives are the oldest and slowest drive.

- **What rpm does the drive run at?** The most common drive speed is still 5,400 rpm, but you can get drives that run at 7,200 rpm. The faster the drive spins, the faster it can transfer data—again, an important consideration when working with graphics files.
- **What's its transfer rate?** This is the rate at which your drive can deliver data to you, expressed in kilobytes per second. The higher the number, the better.
- **What's its seek time?** Seek time is how long it takes the drive to locate a specific bit of data. Seek time usually ranges between 4 and 12 milliseconds, and in this case, the lower the number, the better.
- **Do I have room for a new drive in my computer?** Make sure you have a bay available to put a new drive in (usually a 3.5-inch bay). Also be aware that opening your case and installing the drive yourself could void your manufacturer's warranty. External hard drives are available if you don't have a bay free or don't want to open the case, but they're more expensive.

Superfloppies

Superfloppies look like oversized floppy disks, but they hold a lot more data, typically from 100 to 250 MB. They're a very popular choice, especially Iomega's Zip drives. In fact, Zip is in danger of becoming a generic term for superfloppies.

Figure 18-2
A Zip drive.

One reason why superfloppies are so popular is that they're the cheapest way to both save a reasonable amount of data and take that data with you. As well, Zip drives, in particular, are available for just about any kind of interface: SCSI, the parallel port, USB, and even notebooks. A different type of superfloppy, which adheres to what's called the LS-120 specification, can also read ordinary floppies. LS-120 superfloppies also tend to be more reliable than Zip disks.

Unfortunately, all superfloppies suffer from fairly slow transfer and seek rates, which can make using them with graphic files annoying. As well, even 250 MB can get eaten up in a hurry.

Still, if you're on a budget and also want to use a type of storage that you can almost always find a reader for, superfloppies should probably be your first choice.

Winchester-Based Drives

If you want removable data storage in larger chunks, you might want to consider a Winchester-based drive, instead. They're more expensive, but in addition to holding more data, they're faster than superfloppies.

The best-known Winchester-based drives are the Jaz drives, manufactured by Iomega, APS Technologies, and LaCie. Jaz drives, unlike

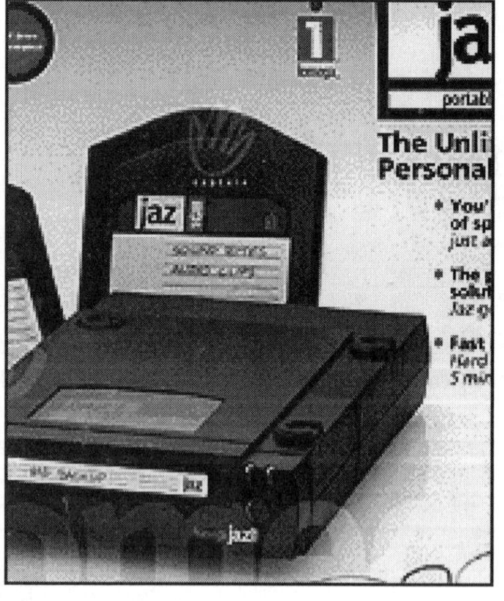

Figure 18-3
A Jaz drive.

superfloppies, are fast enough to run full-motion video, which means they're also very fast at transferring large digital images.

Even though Jaz drives and Jaz disks are more expensive than Zip drives, their larger storage capacity and faster speeds might actually make them more economical in the long run.

If you're really into large digital images, I'd personally recommend a Jaz drive if you want the convenience of removable data storage.

However, you still have additional options!

CD-R and CD-RW Drives

It wasn't all that long ago that devices for writing CDs cost tens of thousands of dollars. Now they're inexpensive enough that, especially if you're interested in long-term storage of your digital data, they may suit your home needs perfectly.

All the other storage devices I've mentioned so far store data by magnetizing areas of a disk. CDs store their data as reflective pits on a disk, which can then be read by a laser.

Figure 18-4
CD-R.

The main difference between CD-R and CD-RW disks is that CD-R disks can only be written to once, while CD-RW disks can be recorded over and over. As well, CD-R disks can be read by older CD-ROM drives, while you need a new Multiread CD-ROM drive to read a CD-RW disk.

Although CD-R and CD-RW writers are fairly expensive, the disks themselves are relatively cheap. Although they don't hold as much data as a Jaz disk—around 493 MB—their low price offsets that disadvantage.

They're great for long-term storage because they take up very little room (you can store them in your regular CD rack!), and they simply last longer than magnetic storage devices. Their biggest disadvantage is that they're quite slow at reading and writing data.

DVD Drives

DVD drives work much the same as CD-RW drives, but a DVD disk holds a lot more storage. Current double-sided DVD disks hold up to 4.7 gigabytes, and in the near future, that could reach as high as 17 GB. The disks are much more expensive than CD-RW disks, but again, that's offset by the higher data storage capability.

Best of all, DVD drives can read all the various types of CD and DVD disks.

Figure 18-5
DVD drive.

Unfortunately, some debate is still going on among manufacturers about standards for DVD drives, so unless you're what the industry calls an *early adapter*—someone who just has to have the latest and greatest technology—I wouldn't recommend jumping into this just yet.

Tape Drives

Just for completeness sake, I want to mention tape drives. You can store more data for less money on a tape than on any of the other storage media I mentioned, but you'd better not want to get to it in a hurry, and you'd better not be in a hurry when you're transferring data to it.

Tape drives take hours to back up large amounts of data, and once the data is on the tape, it takes a long time to find it. That's because tape drives, unlike the other types of drives I've mentioned, aren't a disk that the reading mechanism can skip across at will: They're a long, thin strip that has to be wound and unwound until the portion containing the data you're looking for can be found. In other words, they're just like regular cassette tapes, which you have to rewind or fast-forward to find your favorite song.

Nevertheless, if you're primarily concerned with archiving digital images and don't plan to access them on a regular basis, a tape drive is the cheapest route to your goal.

Need More Information?

If you've read the previous three chapters, you probably know where I'm about to send you for more information on data storage: the CNET Buyer's Guide on AOL (keyword Buyer's Guide). Click on the Removable Storage listing under Hardware (see Figure 18-6).

Click See All Storage Reviews to read all the reviews of storage devices currently posted, and click Compare Storage to conduct a side-by-side comparison of many popular makes of removable storage. Clicking New Storage takes you straight to the reviews of the latest products.

Figure 18-7 shows a typical storage review.

So there you have it! Just because your hard drive is full, there's no need to panic. You can choose from a lot of data storage options out there, and they're not as expensive as you might think.

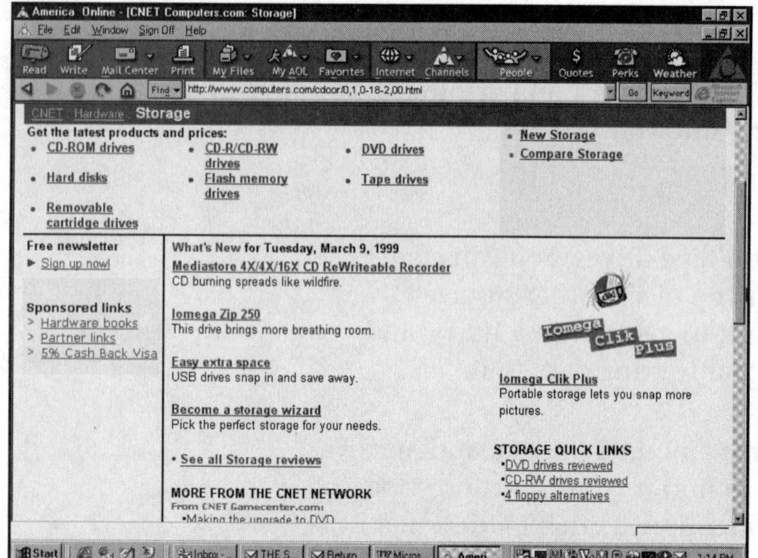

Figure 18-6
The Buyer's Guide on AOL offers you all the latest information on data storage devices.

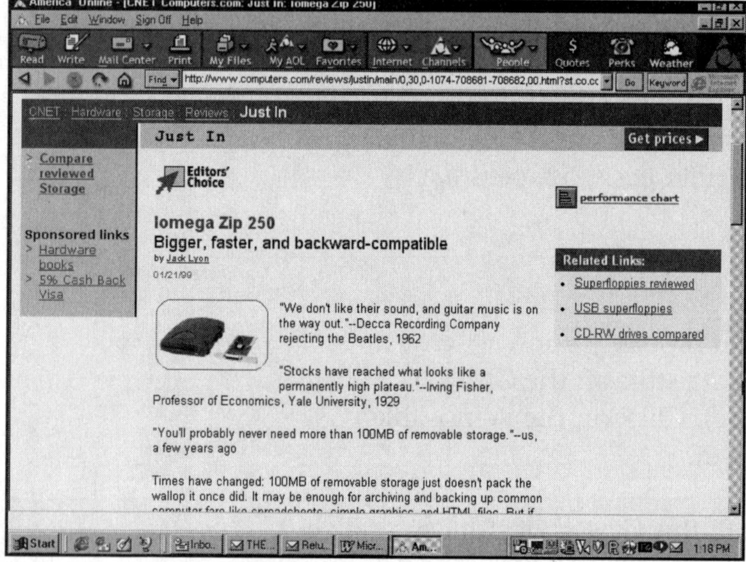

Figure 18-7
Find out everything you need to know about removable storage with the Buyer's Guide.

CHAPTER 19

PROJECT: Understanding Graphics Software Better

Introduction

The CD that comes with this book contains lots of great graphics software, but it's only a small sampling of what's available. In fact, there's such a wide variety of graphics software available, both in stores and on-line from AOL and the World Wide Web, that you may soon find the choices overwhelming.

That's where this chapter comes in. In this chapter, I'll explain in more detail how graphics software works and why it generates so many acronyms (GIF, JPEG, EPS, TWAIN, and PNG—just to name a few!). Then you'll be better able to choose the software that meets your graphics needs.

> **My Favorite Acronym: TWAIN**
>
> The world of graphics software is full of acronyms. Most of them are rather boring: GIF, for instance, stands for Graphics Interchange Format, and EPS stands for Encapsulated PostScript. But my absolute favorite acronym is TWAIN, which stands for Technology Without An Interesting Name.
>
> It may not have an interesting name, but TWAIN is very important to graphics programs of all kinds. Whenever you click Get Picture in PhotoSuite II SE, you'll see, among your choices, Scanner (TWAIN) and Digital Camera (TWAIN).
>
> TWAIN simply allows graphics software to activate graphics hardware, such as a scanner or digital camera. It's invisible to you—it does its job without any fuss or any intervention on your part—but without it, digital projects like those in this book would be impossible.

Choosing Between Drawing and Painting Programs

The two kinds of graphics programs for computers were named after the method they use to create images: vector-based and raster-based. You could also call them drawing programs and painting programs.

Drawing, or Vector-Based, Programs

In vector-based, or drawing, software, images are created essentially as a series of lines, much like the connect-the-dots drawings in children's activity books. Even circles are made up of straight lines—hundreds or thousands of little short lines, each bending away from the previous at a slight angle.

You can create quite complex images using vector graphics by layering many different elements over top of each other. These elements remain separate and can be edited individually. Vector images are often used for original artwork, such as company logos, and special text effects.

Vector-based images have a couple of big advantages. Because the image consists of a series of lines, what is stored by the computer isn't really the image itself, but just the information necessary for the computer to draw the image. This makes for much smaller file sizes than you need for photographs and similar images.

As well, you can change the size of a vector-based image without any loss of resolution: The computer just moves the endpoints of the various lines that make it up further away from one another and draws longer lines between them. A good example of vector-based images you see all the time is TrueType fonts. No matter how big you make these fonts, they always look smooth (see Figure 19-1).

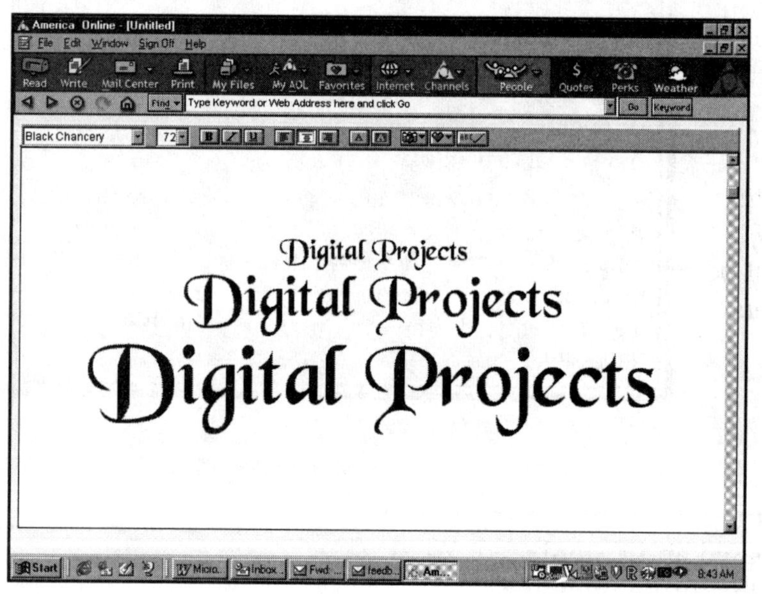

Figure 19-1
No matter how big you make a TrueType font, it always looks sharp. That's because it's a vector-based image.

You've probably used a vector-based drawing program before. Any program that lets you draw circles, squares, or lines is probably vector-based. For example, Microsoft Draw, which is used by Microsoft Office programs to draw simple shapes, is a vector-based program (see Figure 19-2). At the high end of the scale, popular (and expensive) commercial programs such as CorelDRAW, Adobe Illustrator, and Macromedia FreeHand are all vector-based drawing programs.

Vector-based programs are great for creating original artwork, but they can't create a photorealistic image. For that, you need a paint program.

Painting, or Raster-Based, Programs

Raster-based, or paint, programs create images quite differently from vector-based programs. Whereas a vector-based image is made up of a series of lines, raster-based programs are made up of pixels, or picture elements, essentially a collection of dots of different colors which, when viewed together, form the completed image (see Figure 19-3).

Raster-based images, more often called bitmapped images, take up more file space than vector-based images because every single pixel in

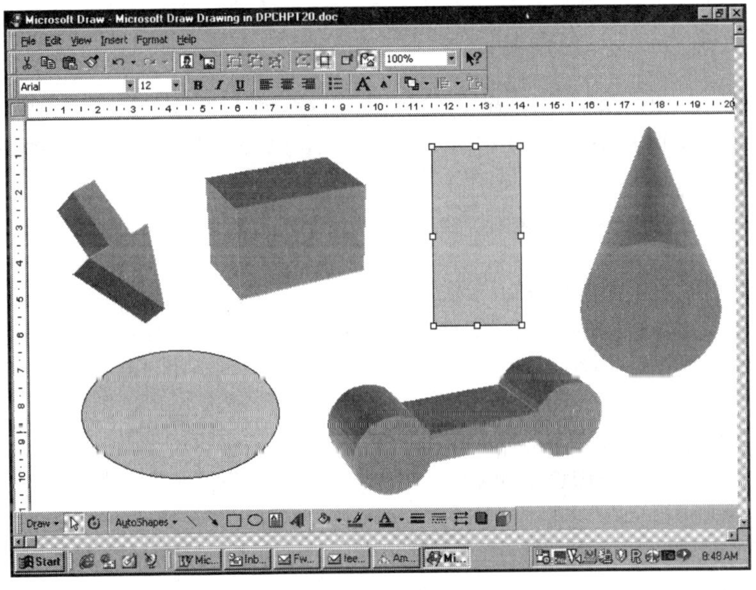

Figure 19-2
Any program that lets you draw shapes like these is probably vector-based.

Figure 19-3
When you zoom in close to a bitmapped image, you can see the individual pixels it's made of.

the image has to have a number assigned to it that tells the computer what color it is. Bitmaps range from very simple black-and-white images in which only one bit of information is used to describe each pixel (on or off), to True Color or 24-bit images, in which 24 bits of information are required to describe each pixel. Obviously this makes the bitmap much larger, but it also allows for many more colors: more than 16 million.

Bitmaps are easy for a computer to edit. Because every pixel in the image has its own number, you can change the image easily by changing the numbers according to some formula—exactly the kind of manipulation of data computers are good at.

For example, changing all the green pixels to red is a simple matter of searching for all the pixels with the number that specifies green and changing them all to the number that specifies red. Special effects, such as those you can apply to photos with PhotoSuite II SE, can be created by passing the data through a filter, which applies preprogrammed changes to all the pixels in image (see Figure 19-4).

On the other hand, vector-based images have the advantage of being built in layers, which makes it easier to reverse changes. If you hide part of an image with a new object in a vector-based program, you can also reverse the change simply by bringing the hidden part of the object to the foreground. In a bitmapped image, hiding a part of an

Figure 19-4
Special effects such as these are created by passing the data that describes a bitmapped image through a filter, which changes the values of the various pixels according to a preset formula.

image involves changing the numbers assigned to the pixels in that area, and once the image is saved, that data is lost forever.

Windows comes with a basic paint program called, appropriately, Paint (see Figure 19-5). Raster-based graphics programs with more features, particularly features designed for manipulating photographs, are called image editors. By this point you should be very familiar with one

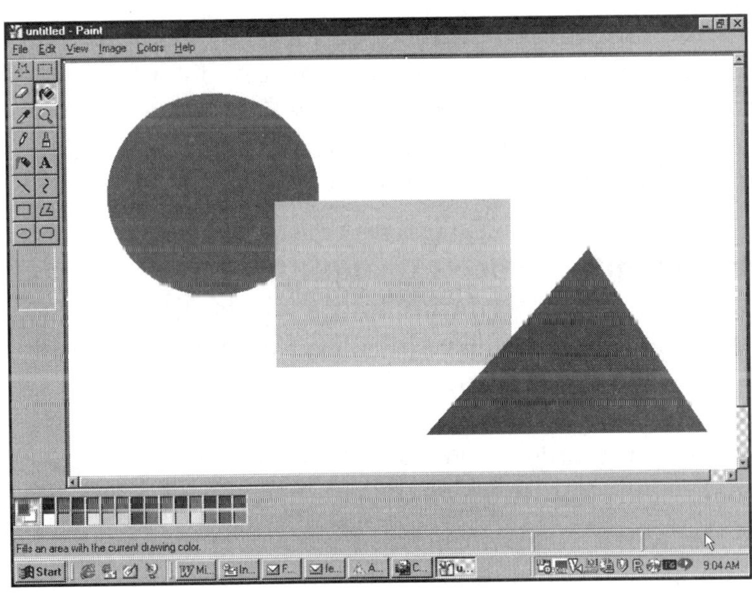

Figure 19-5
Microsoft Paint, which comes with Windows, is a simple raster-based graphics program.

image editor in particular, PhotoSuite II SE; high-end commercial image editors include Adobe Photoshop and Fractal Design Painter.

Most of the graphics editors you can find as shareware on the Web are raster-based. That's because Web browsers can only read bitmapped images without special plug-ins. GIFs and JPEGs, the most common picture formats on the Web, are both raster-based.

Learning the Different Graphic File Formats

You can save digital images in dozens of different ways. Many graphics programs have their own unique method of saving images, which is fine as long as you're editing images within that program. When you want to pass images along to someone else, though, you need to be able to save your image in a format they're likely to be able to read.

Here are some of the most common graphics formats:

- **EPS (Encapsulated PostScript).** PostScript, developed by Adobe, describes pages in terms of point-to-point paths (straight lines, in other words). EPS files, which can be used for vector graphics, bitmaps, type, and even entire pages, contain a PostScript description of the graphic data within them. They can't be read by Web browsers without a plug-in, however.
- **TIFF (Tagged-Image File Format).** TIFF files are uncompressed bitmap files, which tends to make them rather large. They can be read by pretty much all graphics software but not by Web browsers.
- **GIF (Graphics Interchange Format).** Developed by CompuServe (now owned by AOL), this is probably still the most popular format for images on the Web. GIF compresses images, which makes them smaller and faster to load on the Web. GIF images are limited to 256 colors, which makes them best for images with areas of uniform color, such as logos.
- **JPEG (Joint Photographic Experts Group).** This is the other popular Web format, designed specifically for the display of photographic images in full color. Like GIF, JPEG files are compressed; unlike GIF, data is lost when the compression takes place. In other words, if you save a high-resolution TIFF file as a low-resolution JPEG file, you'll lose detail—and, unless you hung on to the original high-resolution file, that data is lost forever.
- **PNG (Portable Network Graphic).** This format is growing in popularity, but only the most recent versions of Web browsers support

it. It has a higher rate of compression than either GIF or JPEG, and unlike JPEG, it doesn't lose data when compression takes place. PNG may well be the graphic file format of choice on the Web in the near future.

Shopping for Graphics Software

You can find graphics software in any good computer store. You can also find it online, both on AOL and on the Internet.

Choosing the Software That's Right for You

Here are some questions that can help you decide which graphics program can best meet your needs:

- **What will I use it for?** Although most graphics programs today contain both drawing (vector-based) and painting (raster-based) tools, they'll lean more one way than the other. In general, you need strong drawing tools if you're planning to create original drawings that can be scaled up or down without a loss of detail. Computer-assisted design (CAD) programs, for example, which can be used for everything from building bridges to designing a deck for your house, are vector-based. If you're planning to create a logo for yourself or someone else, you'll need good vector-based tools, because logos have to be able to be used in many different sizes. If your focus is on photographic or artistic images, however, you'll want to focus more on raster-based programs. Check the program's specifications carefully. If it's not clear from the information on the box, talk to a knowledgeable salesperson.
- **What does the program offer?** For any graphics program, you're looking for the widest variety of useful tools. (Notice I said *useful* tools. I've seen many programs that offer you lots of different tools but include many that I can't for the life of me imagine a use for.) In image-editing programs, look for the greatest variety of special effects. In addition, find out if the program is expandable. Many graphics programs can be enhanced with add-on tools and special effects.
- **Does the program "think" the way I do?** We all have different ways of working and different ways of approaching a problem. There's nothing more annoying than being saddled with a program whose operation seems completely illogical to you, or one that uses strange terms for operations you think should be called something else. The best way to find out if a program and your mental processes are a good match is to try it out. Many software stores will let you test-drive

products before you buy them. (If the store you've been going to won't, I suggest you find another store!) As well, many software programs are available in demo or shareware form on the Web. Download them and give them a try before committing to a long-term relationship.

- **What can I afford?** High-end professional graphics programs can do everything you could possibly want them to do, but they also tend to be expensive. Unless you're a professional designer creating work for paying clients or for your employer, you probably don't need all the capabilities of a program like Adobe Illustrator. Instead, look for products aimed at the home user, such as PhotoSuite II SE. You may find they meet all your needs and still leave you with enough money to pay the rent.

Finding Graphics Programs on AOL

You can find dozens of drawing and painting programs to experiment with right on AOL. Go keyword Download Software to reach the area shown in Figure 19-6. Double-click on the Graphics category under the Shareware tab.

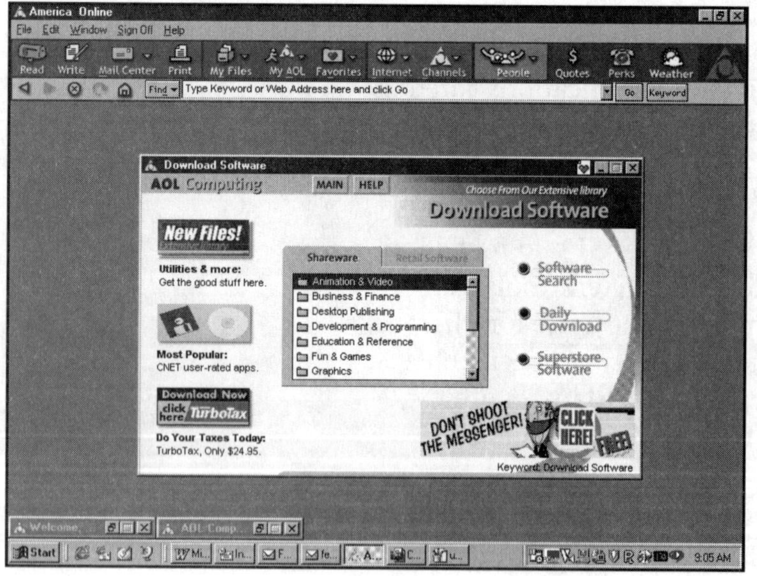

Figure 19-6
AOL's Download Software area is the place to go to find shareware drawing and painting programs.

The next screen asks you to select a category on the left and shows you the available software libraries on the right. Double-click on Graphics Utilities on the left and then double-click on Draw & Paint-Windows on the right. Figure 19-7 shows just some of the drawing and painting programs available for download.

Computers allow you to manipulate images in ways that were unthinkable just a few years ago. But they're still just a tool, and one thing is even more important than a good graphics program when it comes to creating unique and memorable digital projects: a good imagination. Unleash that, and even the sky is no longer the limit.

After all, you can always repaint it.

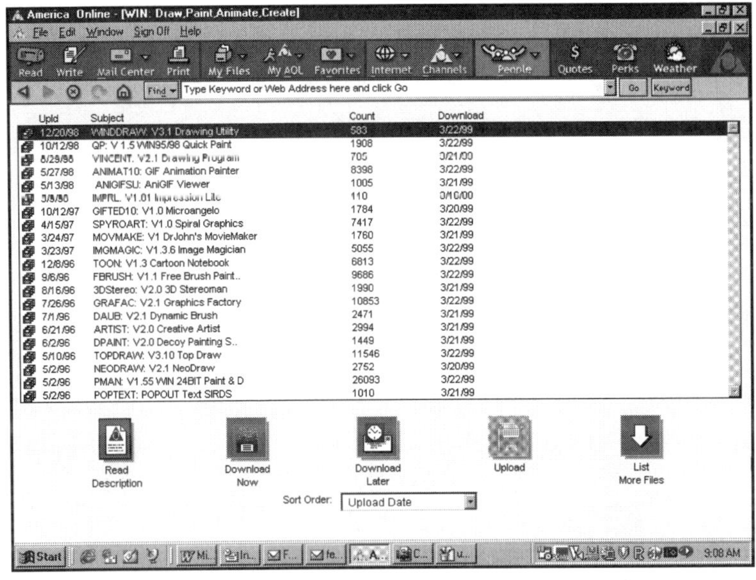

Figure 19-7
You could spend weeks just sampling the many different graphics programs available for downloading on AOL.

APPENDIX A

Sources of More Information

Introduction

Looking for on-line sources of information about digital images and projects? Here are some good places to go:

Pictures

AOL's Pictures is the best place to go for more information on everything from digital photography to editing images to sharing images via e-mail. You can also brush up on your photography skills through links to the Photography Forum and the Popular Photography site. Don't delay, go keyword Pictures today!

Digital Photography

If your digital interest is specifically digital photography, check out Digital Photography (keyword Digital Photo). From here you can enter the Digital Arts Forum to talk to other digitally image-conscious individuals, take part in chats, and visit other resources on AOL and the Web.

Graphics Arts & Animation Forum

Intrigued by the possibilities of digital images that aren't limited to photographs? Visit the Graphics Arts & Animation Forum (keyword Graphics). You'll find lots of resources here covering all aspects of art and animation, including a series of tutorials on everything from creating animated GIFs to creating digital portraits.

AOL Shop Direct Digital Shop

AOL's Shop Direct Digital Shop (keyword Digital Shop) is the place to go if you're searching for great deals on everything related to digital projects, from scanners to digital cameras to data storage to printers.

CNET Buyer's Guide

The CNET Buyer's Guide (keyword Buyer's Guide) can guide you in your shopping for digital hardware with reviews, side-by-side comparisons, and more! (This site is referred to often in the chapters in this book on choose hardware.)

NetFind

Looking for more information about digital images? Conduct a search of the World Wide Web using AOL's NetFind (keyword Net Find). Entering the phrase Digital Images on the day I tried it netted more than 7,000 matches, ranging from corporate sites (Eastman Kodak and Polaroid) to the home pages of individuals who share your interest.

APPENDIX B

Glossary

Animated GIF A series of GIF images that automatically appear one after the other, each replacing the previous one and creating the illusion of movement.

AOL Short for America Online.

ASA/ISO A rating given to photographic film that indicates how sensitive it is to light. The higher the number, the better able the film is to capture images in dim light.

Autofocus camera A camera that uses an infrared sensor or other technology to focus itself without intervention by the operator.

AVI Short for Audio Video Interleaved. A format for playing video files, complete with sound, in Windows.

Bit A binary digit—either a 1 or a 0. The smallest element of information. All computer data is stored as bits. In graphics, the more bits used to store information about the colors in an image, the more life-like the colors will be. See Color depth.

Bit depth See Color depth.

Bitmap A method of representing images digitally in which each bit of information corresponds to some part of the image.

BMP See Bitmap.

Browser A program that lets you navigate and view the World Wide Web.

Byte Eight bits, which can represent any number ranging from zero to 255.

CCD Short for Charge Coupled Device. A form of electronic memory that can be charged by light. The stronger the light source, the higher the charge, which makes CCDs ideal for registering the varying levels of light reflected off of objects. CCDs are the most important component of scanners and digital camera.

CD-ROM Short for Compact Disk-Read Only Memory. A data storage device on which data is stored optically, as reflective pits in a disk that can be read by a laser.

CD-R Short for CD-Recordable. A form of recordable CD-ROM to which data can be written only once.

CD-RW Short for CD-Rewritable. A form of reusable and recordable CD-ROM to which data can be written over and over.

Clipart Artwork available for use in Web pages and other digital projects with few restrictions. Clipart is provided with many graphics programs; collections can also be purchased separately at most computer stores. A great deal of clipart is also available for download from sites all over the World Wide Web.

Collage An image created by combining many other images.

Color depth The number of bits of information used to define a single pixel. The color depth determines how many colors can be displayed at one time. The higher the color depth, the more photorealistic the image.

CompactFlash A popular type of flash memory; memory that holds its content without requiring electrical current.

Contrast The range between the lightest and darkest tones in an image.

Copyright The exclusive right granted by law to an author, artist, or other creator to sell, print, publish, or reproduce his or her work in any way.

Crop To trim an image by adjusting its boundaries.

Digital camera A device much like a regular camera, except it stores images as computer-readable digital images instead of on film.

Digitized image Any image, such as that from a conventional photograph, that has been converted into a computer-readable format.

Download To transfer files electronically from another device (Internet or networked computer, for example) to your computer's hard drive or other data storage device.

dpi Short for dots per inch. The standard measurement of printer resolution.

Drawing program See Vector graphics.

DVD A type of optical disk that can store considerably more information than a CD.

EIDE/IDE IDE stands for Integrated Device Electronics; EIDE stands for Enhanced IDE. A type of interface commonly used to connect data storage devices such as hard drives, tape drives, and CD-ROM drives to a computer.

E-mail Short for electronic mail. Messages sent from computer to computer over a network.

EPS Short for Encapsulated PostScript. A file format used to transfer graphic images among various applications and types of computers.

Fixed-focus camera A camera in which the lens is prefocused at a commonly acceptable point and cannot be changed.

Floppy disk The most common reusable form of magnetic data storage, with limited storage space (typically 1.44 MB).

Font A group of letters, numbers, and symbols in one size or typeface. New Times Roman is a typeface; 12-point New Times Roman Italic is a font.

GIF Short for Graphic Interchange Format. A format for efficiently transmitting images from computer to computer popularized by CompuServe in the 1980s and adopted by the designers of the World Wide Web.

Grayscale A series of shades from white to black. Scanners typically can create grayscale images with anywhere from 2 to 256 shades.

HTML Short for Hypertext Markup Language. The programming language that tells a Web browser what to place on a page and where to place it.

Hue The predominant wavelength of a color. Computer color systems create colors on the basis of their hue, luminance (brightness), and saturation (intensity).

Hypertext A method of organizing data that lets individual elements of the data, especially text, be linked to one another, allowing the user to jump from one place to another without reading everything in between. On the World Wide Web, hypertext typically links to a different Web site entirely.

Imaging software Software that can capture and manipulate digital images.

Inkjet printer A printer that creates images by spraying tiny droplets of ink onto the paper. Inkjet printers, which are relatively inexpensive, are currently the most popular type of printer for home users.

JPEG Short for Joint Photographic Experts Group. A method of compressing graphic files specifically designed for displaying photographs on the Web. JPEG (or JPG) files can display million of colors, while GIF files can only display 256.

Kilobyte One kilobyte equals 1,024 bytes. It's abbreviated as K.

Landscape orientation Orientation of a printed image so that the longest sides of the paper are at the top and bottom.

Laser printer A printer that users a laser to create electrostatically charged areas on a drum onto which toner is applied and then fused to the paper with heat.

LCD Short for Liquid Crystal Display. A technology that uses rod-shaped molecules (liquid crystals) that flow like liquid and bend light. Digital cameras include LCD screens that allow the user to view images taken with the camera.

Luminance The brightness of a computer-displayed color.

Megabyte One million bytes. Also abbreviated MB or meg.

Megapixel Usually used to describe a camera that has a higher resolution than the standard 640x480 pixels.

MIDI Short for Musical Instrument Digital Interface. A method for encoding the pitches, temp, and instrumentation of a musical piece so that computers and synthesizers can re-create it.

Negative The inverted image (black appears as white, white as black, and so on) formed on photographic film from which prints are made.

Painting program See Raster graphics.

Parallel port A socket on a computer used to connect a printer or other device.

Persistence of vision The illusion, caused by the physiology of our eyes, that an image is still visible even after it has actually vanished. Persistence of vision is what makes animation and motion pictures possible.

Personal Publisher 3 AOL's easy-to-use software for creating Web pages.

Pixel Pixel element. One dot of all the dots that make up an image on a computer screen.

Pixellation The appearance of pixels in a bitmapped image. When an image is enlarged too much, the individual pixels become visible, resulting in a blocky, uneven appearance.

PNG Short for Portable Network Graphics. An advanced bitmapped graphics file format endorsed by the World Wide Web Consortium that may eventually replace GIFs.

Portrait orientation Orientation of a printed image so that the shortest sides of the paper are at the top and bottom.

PPM Short for Pages Per Minute. The standard method of measuring the speed of a printer.

Primary colors The three colors from which all other colors can be created. There are two sets of primary colors, additive primaries (the primary colors when an image is created by transmitted light, such as on the computer screen) and subtractive primaries (the primary colors when an image is created by reflected light, such as off of a photograph). The additive primaries are red, blue, and yellow; the subtractive primaries are cyan, magenta, and yellow.

Raster graphics Images created by the computer in bitmapped format. Most painting programs create raster graphics.

Red eye A pink glow in the eyes of people photographed using a flash, caused by the reflection of the flash off the back of the eyeball.

Resolution The degree of sharpness of a displayed or printed character or image. It's usually measured in pixels (for computer monitors) or dots per inch (for printers).

Saturation The intensity of a color.

Scanner A device that captures the reflected light from an image or object and converts it into a digital image that can be manipulated by a computer.

SCSI Short for Small Computer System Interface. Pronounced "scuzzy," SCSI is a hardware interface that allows for the connection of several peripheral devices to a single expansion board that plugs into the computer.

Serial port A socket on a computer used to connect a modem, mouse, scanner, or other device. Data is transferred over the serial port faster than over the parallel port.

Shareware Software distributed on a trial basis. If you use it regularly, you're required to register and pay for it in exchange for technical support, additional documentation, or the next upgrade.

Superfloppy A high capacity floppy disk, such as those used in the popular Zip drives, used for storage.

Thumbnail A small version of a larger image.

TIFF Short for Tagged Image File Format. A widely used bitmapped graphics file format developed by Aldus and Microsoft.

True Color 24-bit color (see also Color depth), which allows the display of 16,777,216 colors.

TrueType A font technology that renders fonts for both the screen and the printer. Because it is vector-based (defined as a series of lines), fonts can be scaled up to any size without losing sharpness.

TWAIN Short for Technology Without An Interesting Name. A programming interface that lets software activate a scanner, digital camera, or other image-capturing device.

Typeface The design of a set of printed characters, such as Arial, Courier, or Times New Roman.

USB Short for Universal Serial Bus. A relatively new hardware interface for peripherals such as the keyboard, mouse, joystick, scanner, printer, and telephony devices. The USB interface is able to transfer data faster than the parallel or serial interfaces.

Vector graphics Graphics that the computer records as a series of lines. Unlike raster graphics, vector graphics can be made larger without losing any resolution. Fonts are a good example of vector-based graphic images.

Wallpaper An image that appears on your computer desktop, underneath the various icons.

WAV The standard Windows format for recording sound.

World Wide Web A collection of electronic documents, accessible through the Internet, that are linked to each other. Each document is called a Web page. Links in one Web page let users jump to other pages, whether those pages are on the same computer or stored on another computer halfway around the world.

Index

Illustrations are in **boldface**.